Praise for *The New Players in Life Science Innovation*

"A wealth of insights and foresights about the global rise of the knowledge-based industry. Drivers and modulators from emerging economies make it necessary to look beyond the usual industry sector horizon. Using *The New Players in Life Science Innovation*'s well researched and comprehensive road map of India and China's approach for becoming future innovative R&D players offers a strong medicine to business leaders who want to build organizations with an understanding on how the future may unfold."

—**Martina Flammer**, Senior Director, Emerging Markets, Pfizer Inc.

"This is a stimulating and original take on the changes in the life sciences industry worldwide."

—**Helen Lawton Smith,** Chair, Management Department, Birkbeck College, University of London

"Really understanding the evolution in science and technology around the world demands numbers and analysis, which can be very difficult to find and combine in a clear manner, but that's just what readers get in *The New Players in Life Science Innovation*."

—**Mike May,** Editorial Director, *Scientific American Worldview*

"*The New Players in Life Science Innovation* is a valuable resource for academics, policy makers, and practitioners alike as it deals in breadth and depth with currently key related issues in the areas of R&D management, policies, and practices and in the context of a world that is increasingly globalizing as well as dividing. Insights from this book will remain relevant for some time and may well provide prophetic as well. I highly recommend it as a key resource for both academic as well as policy and practice contexts."

—**Elias Caryannis,** Professor of Science, Technology, Innovation, and Entrepreneurship, School of Business, George Washington University

"The book documents that science-based business is no longer the exclusive domain of the West. In the future, competitors from emerging economies will be playing increasingly important roles in life science innovation. This trend is gathering momentum and is indeed irreversible."

—**Y. Eugene Pak,** Director of R&D Sector, Seoul National University Advanced Institutes of Convergence Technology

"Emerging partners and emerging markets are now key. Mroczkowski documents finally what we've been seeing individually as practitioners in technology transfer and biotech business development in recent years. These new regional partners and markets are no longer limited to late stage adaptors or me-too manufacturers, but have the technological capacity and financial strength to push novel early-stage biotech discoveries to market."

—**Steven M. Ferguson,** CLP, Chair, Technology Transfer, Foundation for Advanced Education in the Sciences (FAES) Graduate School at NIH

"The good old days of the pharma industry are gone, the old models are over, and new paradigms and new paths for future successes are opening up. But we don't know precisely what they are going to be. We are facing a bunch of weak or strong signals, and it is difficult to segregate. This means that trial and error is the name of this new game. We all know how errors are expensive and can be scary, too. To minimize the risk, we need to get to grips with new/emerging R&D and business drivers. Definitively, this book is a very relevant tool to achieve that."

—**Charles Woler**, CEO, Evotec

The New Players in Life Science Innovation:

Best Practices in R&D from Around the World

Tomasz Mroczkowski

For Raymond and Joanne
with best wishes to find the
right amount of innovation.

Thomas

London 25 June 2015

Vice President, Publisher: Tim Moore
Associate Publisher and Director of Marketing: Amy Neidlinger
Executive Editor: Jeanne Glasser
Editorial Assistant: Pamela Boland
Development Editor: Russ Hall
Senior Marketing Manager: Julie Phifer
Assistant Marketing Manager: Megan Colvin
Cover Designer: Chuti Prasertsith
Managing Editor: Kristy Hart
Project Editor: Anne Goebel
Copy Editor: Krista Hansing Editorial Services, Inc.
Proofreader: Linda Seifert
Senior Indexer: Cheryl Lenser
Compositor: Nonie Ratcliff
Manufacturing Buyer: Dan Uhrig

Publishing as FT Press

Upper Saddle River, New Jersey 07458

FT Press offers excellent discounts on this book when ordered in quantity for bulk purchases
or special sales. For more information, please contact U.S. Corporate and Government Sales,
1-800-382-3419, corpsales@pearsontechgroup.com. For sales outside the U.S., please contact
International Sales at international@pearson.com.

First Printing July 2011

Pearson Education LTD.
Pearson Education Australia PTY, Limited.
Pearson Education Singapore, Pte. Ltd.
Pearson Education Asia, Ltd.
Pearson Education Canada, Ltd.
Pearson Educación de Mexico, S.A. de C.V.
Pearson Education—Japan
Pearson Education Malaysia, Pte. Ltd.

Library of Congress Cataloging-in-Publication Data:

Mroczkowski, Tomasz F.
  The new players in life science innovation : best practices in R&D from around the world /
Tomasz F. Mroczkowski.
      p. cm.
  Includes bibliographical references and index.
  ISBN 978-0-13-211990-0 (hbk. : alk. paper)
1. Biotechnology industries--Developing countries. 2. Life sciences--Research--Developing
countries.
3. Research, Industrial--Developing countries. 4. Technology and state--Developing
countries. 5.
Science and state--Developing countries. 6. Industrial policy--Developing countries. I. Title.
  HD9999.B443D486 2012
  338.4'76606091724--dc22
                          2011015844

ISBN-10: 0-13-211990-0
ISBN-13: 978-0-13-211990-0

To my wife, Joanna, and our children,
Janek, Basak, Magda, and Adrian

Contents

Acknowledgments

This book required extensive research, travel, and fact checking. The chapters took shape often as a result of lively discussions with colleagues in academe and industry in a number of countries. The book would not have been written without the help and generous support of a number of people.

First, I want to thank my family, and especially my wife, for their patience and support during the time I was researching and writing the book.

I extend warm thanks to Roland Kozlowski, Martina Flammer, Pamela Demain, and Richard Scroth, who shared with me their profound knowledge of the biopharmaceutical industry. They also read chapter drafts and provided valuable comments and criticisms. Discussions with Janek Rozycki helped me greatly in understanding better recent developments within genomics and molecular biology and how they impact the life science–based industry. Dr. Eugene Pak and Miroslaw Miller provided me with information and invaluable insights about the emerging innovation clusters they are involved with.

I want to thank colleagues at the Kogod School of Business: Kathy Getz for her unfailing support for the book project, Michel LeGoc and Shyam Chidamber for valuable comments and insights, and Bonnie Auslander for reading and providing editorial comments on several chapters. I wish also to acknowledge the support of The Kogod Global Management Institute for some of the research during the final phase of the project, without which the book would not have been completed on time.

I also want to extend special thanks to my research assistants, who performed a tremendous amount of diligent work on behalf of the book: Shareen Jolly, Camilla Kuo, Ozden Deniz, and Nicole Jawerth. Their patience and dedication was remarkable.

About the Author

Tomasz Mroczkowski has studied innovation, the management of change, and economic transition for most of his career. He is the author of more than 100 published works on these subjects. He combines interests in business history with a fascination about how to think strategically about the future.

Based at the Kogod School of Business, American University, Washington, D.C., where he serves as a professor in the International Business Department, Mroczkowski has also lectured on innovation in emerging economies at universities in France, United Kingdom, Poland, Japan, and India. He has conducted executive development seminars for leading American and European companies and has served as advisor to central and local governments on economic development strategy and technology cluster formation. He serves on editorial boards of several international journals. Mroczkowski is a Fulbright Scholar and a recipient of a number of grants from private and public foundations.

This book is based on several years of research, work experience, and travels in the rapidly developing economies. It grew out of numerous visits, interviews, and informal discussions with entrepreneurs, government policymakers, and company strategists in more than a dozen countries, East and West.

1

Power Shifts in Global R&D and Innovation: What They Mean for Firms in Life Science Businesses

"In the twenty-first century, citizens of the United States and Europe will consider themselves fortunate if they produce maybe one of every four or five major inventions."

—Don Tapscott and Anthony Williams[1]

The New Post-Crisis Economic Game: Emerging Economies Gain Advantage and Speed Up R&D Spending

This book is about the emerging new order of global innovation in the life science business. Just as the global center of gravity in manufacturing has shifted east in the past two decades, a power shift is underway in science, technology, and innovation. For most of the past several centuries, the West has dominated science and technology. We tend to forget, however, that, historically, Asian nations such as China have equaled, if not exceeded, Europe in many areas of invention and application of discoveries. Explorers such as Marco Polo were amazed by what they saw in China. In fact, until the industrial revolution in the West, the Middle Kingdom was technologically ahead of Europe in most fields. During the twenty-first century, we

1

may well be witnessing a swing of the technology pendulum back in favor of China and other rapidly developing economic powers of Asia.

Yet most recently, two bastions of Western advantage have seemed to remain in place: research and development (R&D) and finance. However, the recent global economic crisis has shaken the foundations of Western preeminence in finance. Indeed, it has also shaken the foundations of our beliefs in the model of a capitalist economy based on free markets, a model that leading Asian nations regard as flawed. Similarly, Western science and technology remain strong, but many signs indicate that, in the crucial area of R&D—which ultimately underpins technology and innovation—the beginnings of a major shift away from Western dominance may be underway. The current economic crisis and the period of subdued economic growth in the West that follows may well speed up this development.

What accounts for this transformation? The last decade has seen a significant transformation in the economic and financial power of emerging economies. Most developing countries have run persistent external accounts surpluses, even as the United States has been running a deficit. A remarkable aspect of those surpluses has been a pickup in economic growth and trade. As a result, the emerging economies have become creditors to the United States, thus accumulating claims against the United States while simultaneously gaining an ability to influence markets around the world through the pricing of bonds, company shares, and currency exchange rates. As Mohamed El-Erian puts it, "Developing countries have shifted from operating in debtor regimes to creditor regimes."[2] As El-Erian also observes, history suggests that the current mix in emerging economies of internal macroeconomic stability and high financial cushions acts as a strong catalyst for the development of internal financial markets.[3] Thus, emerging economies will increasingly constitute a consequential and independent driver for growth in the world.

The growth strategies adopted by leading emerging economies have resulted in a rapid increase in their share of world trade; those economies are also increasingly moving to higher value-added goods. Emerging economy governments will have every incentive—as well as the means—to continue to increase spending on education and R&D, to broaden the number of citizens who can benefit from technological progress. This will allow larger groups to benefit from globalization and will enable those groups to reap the benefits of their countries' new technological capabilities and skills.

Experts warn that, in the post-crisis conditions, Western countries face the risk of stagflation, or an extended period of low growth combined with unemployment. Inflation could replace the deflationary pressures of the crisis conditions, as governments are tempted to monetize the huge piles of accumulated debt. As commodity prices move up and low-cost labor becomes less available, inflationary forces may develop at a time when mature Western economies face weak economic growth and weak productivity.

Furthermore, reports by such prestigious consultancies as Boston Consulting Group point out that, in forthcoming years, we can expect emerging Asia—led by fast-growing economies such as China, India, Singapore, and South Korea—to enjoy double the economic growth of the transatlantic West.[4] An August 2009 article in *The Economist* notes that emerging Asia may enjoy annual growth rates of 7%–8% over the next five years, several times the rate of the rich world.[5]

Innovation, which is the commercial application of scientific inventions, will drive today's economies—and especially those of the future. Scientific discovery, in turn, depends on a complex set of factors, including national R&D systems, education, and technological infrastructure (especially information communication technologies, or ICT), as well as intangibles such as freedom of ideas and a strong culture of scientific rationalism. Those are the foundations of what has become known as the knowledge economy. Economists argue that the future wealth of nations will depend increasingly on the excellence of the workforce skills and the strength of institutions that underpin the innovation-based knowledge economy. Building innovation-based knowledge economies, as the experience of leaders such as Finland, Sweden, and South Korea shows, requires careful strategic planning built on a long-term vision; by themselves, markets will not suffice. Until about a decade ago, a challenge to Western R&D seemed very remote: Countries outside the triad of the United States, the European Union, and Japan lacked the resources to spend significantly on R&D. In both relative and absolute terms, their spending was small, and their scientific and innovation systems were not competitive with the West. Emerging economies were advised that it was more efficient for them to import technology than try to develop it themselves. Until recently, the only Asian nation that garnered significant investment in R&D from multinational companies was Japan.

The governments of leading Asian nations have been building plans for the future based on a mix of public and private-sector efforts. Strategies carefully designed by governments partnering with the private sector play a key role. The cited BCG report states that the big emerging economies are committed to investments in innovation: "They realize that innovation is the next battleground and they are aggressively fighting that battle now."[6]

The deep economic reforms undertaken over the past two decades in key emerging economies such as China and India have enabled a take-off toward sustained rapid economic growth. This growth has facilitated steady increases in the portion of gross domestic product (GDP) that can be allocated to science, education, and innovation. By the early twenty-first century, smaller emerging economies such as Taiwan, Singapore, and Korea, which had been pursuing accelerated economic growth strategies longer than India and China, have now matured economically enough that they can afford to spend significant resources on R&D. Today they are not just consumers, but are gradually becoming producers and exporters of technology as well.

Perhaps more important, a broad group of emerging economies—especially in Asia—have been concentrating on making drastic improvements in their innovation capabilities. Leading Asian economies are not leaving the development of their knowledge economies to market forces alone. They have launched sophisticated national catch-up strategies and have implemented many needed reforms in their science and education policies. Malaysia and Thailand are following the example of leaders such as South Korea, Taiwan, and Singapore, which today spend a higher percentage of their GDP on R&D and have better-educated workforces than many Western countries. But the emergence of giants China and India as major players in the global R&D effort will likely have the greatest impact on the West in the longer term. Other Asian nations are sure to follow their lead.

Just a decade ago, in 1999, the combined R&D spending of Asian countries was at about the same level as that of Europe at purchasing power parity (PPP) and well behind that of the United States (see Figure 1-1). Since that time, Western spending has been growing slowly (especially in the United States), yet spending in Asia has been soaring (see Figure 1-2). Already by about the middle of the past decade, Asian spending had surpassed both the European total and the U.S. total. By 2003, Asia's spending on R&D as a share of domestic product (1.92% of its GDP) exceeded that of Europe (1.81% of its GDP).

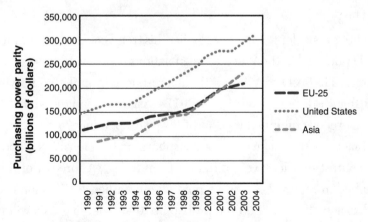

Figure 1-1 Gross expenditures on R&D, by selected region and country, 1990–2004
Source: National Science Foundation; available at www.nsf.gov

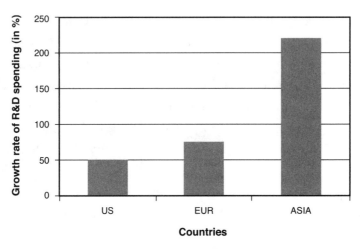

Figure 1-2 Comparison of country growth in R&D spending, 1999–2008
Source: National Science Foundation; available at www.nsf.gov

In the next chapter, we present a "map" of global R&D spending. As of 2008, Asia accounted for more than 40% of global R&D spending (US$494.4 billion at PPP), with the United States in second place, at 30.1% (US$365 billion), and Europe in third place, at 23.9% (US$288 billion). China, Japan, and India account for more than 80% of the Asian effort; China was well ahead of Japan in total R&D spending and India was pulling ahead of its former colonial master, Great Britain.

Let's consider for a moment what this trend could mean for future R&D potential in the West. If Asian nations continue their aggressive increases in R&D spending without a response from the West, within less than a decade—that is, by 2017—Asian expenditures on R&D could exceed combined U.S. and European spending *by a factor of 2.* By that year, the relative size of the spheres in the global R&D spending contest may look very different from today. (A forecast of this is graphed in Figure 1-3.) As we pointed out earlier, the economic crisis has actually increased the probability that emerging Asia will pull ahead of the rich world in spending ability. With vast debt burdens and low economic growth, increasing R&D spending in the leading

Western economies will be difficult. Asian nations are also investing more in the education and training of their huge workforces. Those investments have been showing results in the form of increasing participation in scientific research and patent activity.

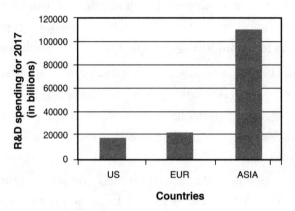

Figure 1-3 Projected R&D spending in 2017, by region
Source: National Science Foundation; available at www.nsf.gov

Asia's Growing Army of Scientists and Engineers Is Increasing Its Share of Scientific Publications and Patent Applications

Asia is the home of more than half the world's population and includes the two most-populated countries. In the past two decades, Asian nations have been expanding and improving their educational systems at a faster rate than most other regions of the world. These facts, together with increasing R&D spending, are affecting the numbers of scientific publications and patent applications coming from the region.

Several Asian nations, including Japan, South Korea, and Taiwan, not only match, but in many ways exceed Western levels of tertiary (university degree) education as measured by the proportion of 24-year-olds who hold first university degrees. Asians tend to study science and engineering (S&E) subjects more often than their U.S. or European counterparts and have been doing so in increasing numbers. Already by 1990, Asian production of bachelor degrees in engineering exceeded that of the United States and the European Union combined, and Asia continues to pull ahead. The United States and Europe are experiencing shortages of scientists and engineers, yet Asia appears to be producing them in increasing abundance.

Asian nations have a smaller overall *stock* of scientists and engineers than the United States and Europe combined. However, in the past decade, Asian nations have surpassed the United States in the total number of scientific and engineering (S&E) graduates and also in the number of doctoral degrees granted in S&E. Meanwhile, the West's advantage in numbers is declining. The rate of growth in the number of scientists and engineers at both the primary and secondary (doctoral) levels is greater in Asia than in both the United States and Europe. A look at the numbers of Ph.D. graduates by country confirms the trend. In 2001, the United States graduated 45.3% of Ph.D.s; India and China contributed just 12.8% and 14.3%, respectively. In just five years, the U.S. share has shrunk to 36.8%; China's has increased to 29.2%, and India's has increased to 14.4%.[7]

This rapidly growing army of scientists and engineers is increasingly contributing to academic output as measured by peer-reviewed publications. In 1999, Asia was well behind both the United States and the European Union in number of refereed publications in science and engineering. Since then, as shown in Figure 1-4, Asian publications have grown by 50%, those from Europe by 24%, and those from the United States by only 9.75%. As a result, Asia is now in second place, behind Europe and ahead of the United States.

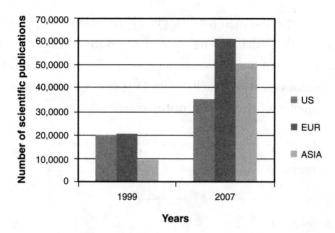

Figure 1-4 Trends in number of scientific publications, by region, 1999–2005

Reproduced by permission from SCImago (2007). SJR: SCImago Journal & Country Rank. Retrieved June 11, 2010, from www.scimagojr.com.

Asians have also been actively maintaining their lead over the United States and Europe in the number of *patent applications* (see Figure 1-5). Of course, large populations partly support these high numbers, but several Asian nations have also demonstrated impressive results in terms of the number of patents *per million of population,* a commonly accepted measure of national innovation performance.[8] In addition to Japan, considered a leader in innovation, Taiwan, South Korea, and Singapore are counted among the top 20 most innovative economies in the world. According to an authoritative report published by the Economist Intelligence Unit, both Taiwan and Singapore are expected to improve their ranking positions in the coming years, displacing several European competitors.[9] The same report places India and China much lower in the innovation performance rankings (because of their enormous populations, neither country scores highly on measures based on per-million inhabitants). However, both

nations are expected to improve their relative positions over the coming years, with China moving up by five positions in terms of both
innovation performance (patents per million of population) and direct
innovation inputs, which include R&D spending, workforce education, and quality of research infrastructure.[10]

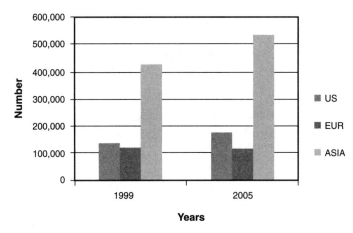

Figure 1-5 Trends in number of patent applications, by region, 1999–2005
Reproduced with permission from WIPO Statistics Database.

Emerging Economies' Catch-up Strategies Target Biotechnology Development

The nineteenth century was the age of steam, the twentieth century was the age of electricity, and the twenty-first century is likely to
become the age of biotechnology. The life sciences have seen some
of the most spectacular growth in recent decades. Life science-based
applications are expected to provide solutions to many of the most
pressing problems modern societies face—specifically, the ever-
growing challenges of healthcare, such as how to provide better and
broader care for aging populations and how to address increasing
concerns over the safety and efficacy of drugs and treatment methods. In addition, emerging economies must greatly expand access to
modern healthcare for their populations. The entire world faces the

problems of environmental degradation and climate change, the need to improve agricultural productivity, and the need to find alternative sources of energy to fossil fuels. Innovation within the life sciences is expected to provide key solutions to these problems. These solutions may come in the form of new drugs and treatments, new medical devices and diagnostic methods, better biofuels, genetically modified crops, and industrial applications of biotechnology (including techniques for providing clean water and fighting pollution), to name but a few examples.

In the next chapter, we explore how leading emerging economies have embraced the idea of the knowledge economy and developed national strategies for catching up with the developed world. Those national strategies target the development of the key technologies of the future. For example, the Chinese 11th five-year plan targets, among others, such future technologies as high-end general-purpose chips and fundamental software, next-generation broadband wireless communication, advanced nuclear power plants, and large aircraft. In addition, several of the designated fields in the plan are related directly to biotechnology, such as transgenic organism cultivation and major new medicines that feature prominently on the list.

So far, the following emerging economies have formulated national biotechnology development strategies: Singapore (2000), South Africa (2001), Thailand (2004), Malaysia (2005), South Korea (2000, updated 2005), India (2007), and Brazil (2007). China has been developing life sciences and biotechnology since the 1980s; its most recent comprehensive biotech industry development strategy was published in 2006. Most of these national strategies list multiple goals, such as creating an innovation-oriented economy, creating a national biotechnology industry, attracting foreign R&D, and developing human resources. A few countries, such as Singapore and Thailand, have more focused strategies with narrower priorities, and Hong Kong lists the goal of creating an export-oriented biotech industry through foreign direct investment or FDI (homegrown biotech is a "secondary concern"). As a component of their national knowledge economy development strategies, most Asian nations have signed the Agreement on Trade-Related Aspects of Intellectual Property Rights (TRIPS), thus committing themselves to international standards of intellectual property (IP) protection (see Table 1-1). This commitment to observing international standards of IP protection has made the countries attractive to R&D investment from abroad and has also helped transform their domestic industries.

Table 1-1 Year of Adoption of Biotech Strategies and TRIPS, by Country[11]

Country	Biotech Strategy	TRIPS
India	2007	2005
China	2006	2001
Singapore	2000	2000
South Korea	2000	1995
Taiwan	2002	2002
Malaysia	2005	1995

Biotechnology and the life sciences feature prominently among the knowledge economy development strategies. The national plans usually entail establishing specialized committees or task forces, or creating an agency that is responsible for coordinating government efforts to support and regulate the biotechnology industry. Several strategies envision substantial public spending on biotech research, to be accompanied by corresponding private spending. Thailand spent the equivalent of more than $599 million on biotech research in 2007, of which $214 million (35%) came from the private sector. Brazil plans to spend 10 billion reais on biotech over the next ten years; the private sector is expected to contribute 40% of that.[12] Other countries do not specify the ratios of public-to-private spending, but are spending substantial sums on research, commercialization, and investment incentives.

On a per-capita basis, countries such as Korea and Singapore are already spending more than the average E.U. nation on biotech research.[13] In 2007, public spending on biotech research of just three Asian emerging economies—China, Korea, and Singapore—easily exceeded 10% of all such spending by all developed economies. Of the approximately 460 international biotech agreements concluded between 2005 and 2008 (involving R&D, technology transfer manufacturing, marketing. distribution, and so on), 46 were with emerging economies; the vast majority were with India[14] and China.[15] Prior to 2005, such deals were rare; they are now expected to accelerate quickly. Add to that expected expenditures by India and recent commitments made by other big emerging economies such as Brazil, and the biotech research spending challenge by emerging economies is likely to become much more substantial in the next five years.[16]

As we detail in Chapter 6, "Accelerating Innovation," the total number of bioparks in operation or under advanced development in such countries as India, China, Thailand, Korea, and Malaysia exceeds 100. Many of these parks variously denominated as technology or science parks offer assorted incentives for firms to locate inside them. The policy objective is to help evolve those parks into biotechnology clusters that will attract collaboration and major investments, especially as multinational biopharma companies increase their offshoring of advanced manufacturing and of R&D.

Any country embarking on a program of bioindustry development should keep in mind that biotech is a long-term game in terms of return on investment. Both the American and European biotechnology industries have been operating at net loss for a long time (global biotech losses were 2.7 billion USD in 2007). Only a few countries, such as Australia and Switzerland, have had profitable biotech sectors. Nevertheless, the Asian governments seem determined to make the necessary investments to create life science industry capabilities. They have embraced a long-term vision of development based on the knowledge economy.

Technological Convergence in the Life Sciences Transforms the Global Pharmaceutical Industry

Today the pharmaceuticals, biotechnology, medical devices, and diagnostics form the backbone of a growing and rapidly integrating *life science industry complex* (LSIC) estimated to be worth a trillion dollars in global sales. Furthermore, the importance of this set of science-based industries will grow significantly in the future. Indeed, a number of prestigious reports estimate the emergence of a bioeconomy by 2020 or 2030. For example, a recent report by the Organization for Economic Cooperation and Development (OECD) predicts that the use of key biotechnologies likely to be commercialized by 2030 will contribute to 35% of chemical output, 80% of pharmaceutical and diagnostic output, and nearly 50% of agricultural output. According to this report, the use of biotechnology will be pervasive, and industrial and agricultural applications are expected to grow even more significantly than the biologics and biopharmaceutical applications that currently dominate biotechnology.[17] The report also predicts that the increase in biotechnology's contribution to the economy will likely be even more significant in the emerging economies than within the OECD. It is not unreasonable to expect that the life science industrial complex may grow to contribute more than 10% of world GDP within a single generation.

The pharmaceutical industry, traditionally based on chemistry, is the largest of the life science-based industries. It developed well before the emergence of biotechnology. Today we see a convergence between the two industries, and the lines between big pharma and biotech continue to blur. Many powerful trends in business and within science itself drive the emergence of the globalized LSIC. Mergers and acquisitions among pharma, biotech, and medical device companies are frequent. In twenty-first-century science, *systems biology* is becoming a key paradigm driving advances in other fields. The complex understanding of biological systems (leading to synthetic biology) is enabled partly by large-scale computing and computational biology, and partly by nanotechnology, with its miniaturization engineering, directed molecular assembly, and novel materials.

The biosciences are becoming a driver of progress and "convergence" in such diverse fields as agriculture, security/defense, ICT/communications, healthcare (monitoring systems and remote diagnostics), and other fields, including even parts of the automotive industry.

As shown in Figure 1-6, the future world of healthcare will be based on a confluence of technologies, such as telemetry and communications (telemedicine), imaging and visualization, IT, genomics/proteomics and use of biomarkers, Electronic Health Records (HER), Evolutionary developmental Biology (Evo devo), and others. With the convergence of biology, chemistry, and semiconductors, for example, researchers have begun to develop biochips that can diagnose blood samples. New types of plastics from the chemical industry and the use of "biomimicry" to emulate the properties of human tissue in the knee and other joints may in the future support the use of synthetic materials in resurfacing bone joints.

Rapid advances in science and its applications, together with changes in market conditions, are forcing a transformation of business models within the life science industries. New market conditions include the emergence of big new markets such as India and China, rapid growth of new R&D capabilities, and new industrial competitors and collaborators from emerging economies. Perhaps the most obvious change in business models is the gradual demise of the large fully integrated pharma company (FIPCO) and its gradual replacement with the virtually integrated one (VIPCO).

Most large Western pharma companies have been in a state of crisis for several years now: New drug approvals are not keeping pace with rising R&D spending, many blockbuster drugs have come off patent (or soon will), and the cost of new drug development keeps climbing. The market capitalization of the top ten large pharma companies has dropped more than $700 billion since 2001.[18] However, the total market cap of biotech companies has increased by more than 50% during this period; even after the recent drops due to the financial crisis, this is close to $300 billion. Observers noted with glee when the worth of Genentech soared in excess of $90 billion just as Pfizer's fell below $90 billion.[19] This symbolizes the emergence of the new biologic drugs, surpassing traditional medicines.

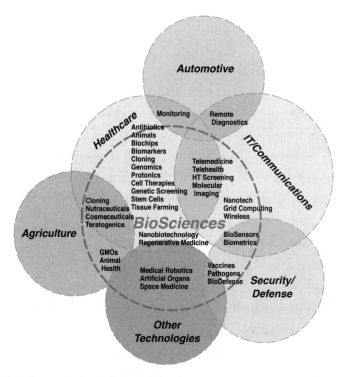

Figure 1-6 Converging technologies of bioscience

Reproduced with permission from Paul J. H. Schoemaker and Joyce A. Schoemaker, *Chips, Clones, and Living Beyond 100*, Pearson Publishing, 2009. This chart appears as Figure 4.1 on page 58. The chart was originally developed by Scott A. Snyder, from Decision Strategies International Inc. (www.decisionstrat.com).

Reacting to those trends, pharma companies have been aggressively acquiring biotech companies. Since 2000, the number and value of biotech therapeutic acquisitions has grown to reach 32 in

2008 worth more than $75 billion.[20] Frost and Sullivan estimate that more than 1,500 alliances between pharma and biotech were formed from 1997 to 2002 and that the contribution of licensed products to total sales is expected to increase from 20% in 2002 to 40% in 2010.[21] These alliances and acquisitions are not just about new revenues from successful biologics drugs: The acquisitions and collaborative agreements also involve learning and mutual transformation. The "biotech-like" model of R&D is seen as a solution to the bureaucracy and lack of accountability in the traditional big pharma R&D strategy. Several big pharma companies, including Pfizer and GSK, have announced strategies of organizing R&D into small discovery units of 100–150 researchers, in an effort to marry the strength of the biotech spirit of entrepreneurship with the resources of big pharma.[22]

As we shall see in Chapter 7, "Company Strategies of Global R&D Collaborations," the new virtually integrated life science company is based on complex systems of partnerships, both with academia and scientific institutions and with contract research, manufacturing, and sales organizations (CRO, CMO, CSO). Until recently, these networks of partnerships have been mostly limited to Western institutions working within a single industry or closely related industries—for example, consider the agreement between Millennium Pharmaceuticals and Abbott Laboratories to develop new diagnostics for obesity and diabetes.[23]

After 2005, and increasingly in the future, partnering is being redirected *in geographic scope* to include not just partners from the West, but also partners from emerging economies, especially in Asia. This new partnering with emerging economy players goes beyond manufacturing, to include different stages of R&D, product code-velopment, design, marketing, and procurement. Partnering and collaboration will also increasingly span more than one industry as combination products become more pervasive—for example, new drugs that are delivered using innovative medical devices that also include diagnostic systems. This perspective has encouraged large traditional companies from outside the biosciences to establish life science business units and to invest in new life science technologies. Examples include 3M, Reliance Group, and Hitachi Chemical Research Center. In Britain, Toumaz Technology and Oracle have a joint venture with the Institute of Biomedical Engineering at Imperial College to develop a market for a pervasive monitoring system that would combine cellphone electrocardiography (EKG) data and medical assessment capabilities for at-risk heart patients. The combined application of new technologies (such as molecular diagnostics, fast computers, specialized software, and genetic databases) and bold research partnerships with emerging R&D centers in Asia may eventually lead to faster, more efficient, and lower-cost drug development.[24] The dream expressed by Ernst and Young of reducing the cost of developing a new drug from a billion dollars to less than $300 million may turn out to be less of a fantasy than it sounds.[25]

Aggressive emerging economies such as South Korea and Taiwan that are eager to increase their participation in high-tech industries expressly base their national strategies of biotechnology development on the notion of *co-joint development with related industries* in which the countries have competitive advantages. The Korean policy points to specialized bioclusters in specific subareas of biotech, such as agrobiotech, but also designates certain bioregions as centers of multiple interrelated industries. Ganwon, for example, is designated the focus of all bioindustries related to environmental protection.

New Markets Constitute New Frontiers for R&D Offshoring

The outsourcing of manufacturing is a well-established practice in business, to such a point that we speak of the "hollowing out" of Western economies, especially those of the United States and the United Kingdom, which have contracted out much of their manufacturing (particularly manufacturing assembly) to cheaper destinations in emerging economies. The offshoring of nonmanufacturing functions came later and has grown rapidly at double-digit rates; today most large U.S. and E.U. companies across a broad range of industries (including automotive, financial services, energy, commercial aircraft, and defense) offshore not just minor but also major business functions, even those traditionally associated with their core competencies. Offshoring today embraces not just IT and business process (back-office) functions, but also marketing, engineering, procurement, product development, design, and R&D, as shown in Figure 1-7. Just as IT outsourcing is showing signs of maturing, the new trend is *global innovation offshoring*, which is growing at double-digit rates and encompasses product development and design, as well as R&D.

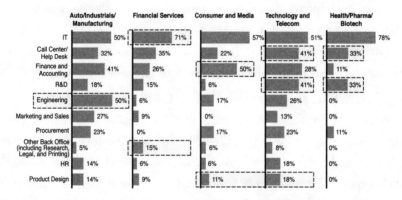

Figure 1-7 Offshored business functions, by industry: percentage of firms offshoring the business function

Reproduced with permission from Booz Allen Hamilton, "Next-Generation Offshoring: The Globalization of Innovation," Duke University, March 2007; and A. Lewin, et. al., "Why Are Companies Offshoring Innovation? The Emerging Global Race for Talent," *Journal of International Business Studies* (40), no. 8: 1,406–1,406.

The software, information technology, and electronic appliance companies first established large R&D facilities in emerging economies. IBM, Intel, AT&T, and Motorola all have high-tech labs in China. GE opened the J. F. Welch Tech Center in Bangalore, India; by 2003, after only three years of operation, the center had filed more than 95 patents. Between 1999 and 2003, the number of employees there had grown by 80% and stood at 21,000 (14,500 are captive and another 6,500 are outsourced). Twenty percent of the center's budget is for long-term projects, such as new-generation washing machines and the key parts of the GE-90 jet engine. Microsoft, which has research facilities in Silicon Valley, San Francisco, and Cambridge, UK, has added Beijing and also opened a large R&D center in India. Industries that are following suit now include pharmaceuticals, biotechnology, and healthcare.[26]

As noted earlier, the huge investments in education, R&D, and regulation reform made by leading Asian nations are extending the landscape of available capabilities beyond the triad of the United States, Europe, and Japan, where the bulk of networked pharmaceutical R&D used to take place. As Asian nations and other emerging economies improve their competencies and accelerate innovation, they are forcing Western pharma companies to rethink what they regard as their core activities and which functions it makes sense to outsource or perform collaboratively in the new destinations.

The global pharmaceutical market is evolving rapidly. As we describe in Chapter 3, "A Reshuffling of Markets and Growth Opportunities," between 2005 and 2015, traditional Western markets will grow considerably, but at a moderate pace; none of these markets will double. The markets in China and India, on the other hand, will triple in a decade. By 2015, China is expected to be the fifth-largest pharma market in the world (after the United States, Japan, France, and Germany). India will be the tenth-largest market, followed by Brazil, Mexico, South Korea, and Turkey. China and India have the second- and third-largest growth opportunity globally.[27]

Indian companies are growing rapidly, as is their international collaboration (which includes licensing, acquisitions, manufacturing outsourcing, joint R&D ventures, and marketing alliances). As a result, many large venture capital and private equity firms have recognized opportunities in India. More than 350 private equity (PE) firms operate in India, and more are coming, with many of them pursuing active healthcare investments. At the same time, Indian companies have been making investments mostly in Europe, focusing on generics and contract manufacturing while creating their own R&D divisions.

As noted, Western pharmaceutical companies face major challenges, including rapidly maturing product portfolios, blockbuster drugs going off patent, and exploding costs of new drug development. In the past eight years (between January 1, 2001, and April 1, 2009), the market capitalization of the top nine pharmaceutical companies has dropped $712 billion. Between 2008 and 2015, drugs worth $300 billion are coming off patent, which means large potential revenue losses for the U.S. and European pharmas. Biotech companies will eventually face some of those same problems: A number of successful biologics drugs will go off patent within a few years.

Western companies face escalating costs of drug discovery and clinical testing just as their revenue streams are coming under pressure. Large emerging markets with improving local capabilities represent potential solutions to those challenges. China and India also offer opportunities for mature product life-cycle extensions based on reformulations, repackaging, and nonpatentable improvements. Collaborative partnerships with Asian companies can be a good way to improve market access for patented drugs through such tactics as comarketing and other joint ventures. Asia also represents a huge outlicensing opportunity. However, U.S. companies apparently have lagged behind their European rivals in key future markets such as India. In particular, U.S. biologics makers such as Genentech and Genzyme have not developed strong direct sales and marketing capabilities in India.

For biotech companies building a biosimilars business, emerging economies may also represent an important opportunity for joint ventures. The production of biologics is much more complex than chemical pharmaceutical generics, so the experience of Western biotech companies could be leveraged to share the cost advantages of emerging economy companies.

As noted earlier, several Asian economies today are viewed as good locations not only for manufacturing, but also for cost-effective innovation. The first step in such a process may be the globalization of clinical trials support. We discuss this process in Chapter 5, "Globalization of Clinical Trials." In 2006, the pharmaceutical industry employed approximately 1.97 million persons (full-time equivalents or FTEs); more than 300,000 of them worked in R&D. Sixty thousand to 65,000 persons worked in clinical support functions, and only about 10% (of related FTEs) are estimated to be "globalized" or "offshored." However, this ratio is likely to reach 30% and could even be as high as two-thirds of FTEs.[28] Different pharma companies have shown different levels of commitment to this process by outsourcing different amounts of chemistry work, data management, biometrics, or discovery. For example, Wyeth is considered a leader in globalizing end-to-end clinical data management. After its 2003 decision to offshore complete data management functions to Accenture, Wyeth transferred 100 full-time jobs to Accenture. This also meant much larger increases in the numbers of globalized jobs engaged in clinical data management for Wyeth. The resulting cost reductions were estimated to exceed 40%.

Of the two R&D production phases, *development* constitutes the lion's share of spending. According to one report, about 70% of the R&D budget goes to development, while the remaining 30% goes to discovery research.[29] In pharmaceuticals, the *development phase* comprises preclinical and toxicology tests, clinical trials Phases I–IV, and also post-clinical research. Some reports estimate that drug-development costs could reach $2 billion per drug in the near future. Since the end of the 1980s, the average cost of a new drug, including failures and clinical trials, has been growing 9% annually. Additional safety data and other trials required by the Food and Drug Administration (FDA) have increased the number of patients needed per new drug application from 3,200 in 1988 to 5,000 in 2004. McKinsey, a leading consultancy, sees the challenge in terms of dramatically rethinking the entire process of drug development based on globalization and eventually resulting in what it calls a "$100 million drug"—an even more ambitious target than the $300 million or so envisioned by Ernst and Young. In such a scenario, discovery and development time would decrease from 12–14 years to 5–6 years, the number of patients needed per approved drug would drop from 5,000 to 2,500, the clinical costs per patient per year would come down from $20,000 to $10,000 and the success rate (discovery to market) would improve from 1 in 5,000 to 1 in 2,500. McKinsey admits that the goal may sound intimidating, but other industries have set and achieved audacious goals, such as low-cost laptops designed for developing countries.[30] Moving toward such a revolutionary objective requires companies to work in powerful consortia of complementary skills and capabilities, open source competition, and a global approach. This would represent breakthrough change because companies would need to be ready to offshore functions associated with their core competencies; until recently, such a move would be regarded as heresy. Today constantly rethinking and updating what constitutes a company's core competencies is becoming standard practice in high-tech industries.

The outsourcing of R&D activities has been going on in the pharmaceutical industry for quite some time, except that this outsourcing used to be strictly limited to Western firms and scientific institutions. Biotech companies, universities, government laboratories, and independent contract researchers have collaborated with the pharmaceutical companies for years. Since the 1970s, the emergence of the biotechnology sector has offered the pharmaceutical industry new opportunities to discover new products at lower risk and cost.[31] Another important development was the Human Genome Project (HGP), which prompted pharmaceutical firms to get involved in genomics research by forming partnerships with companies that had specialized genomics capabilities. The emergence of combinatorial chemistry as an enabling technology that was hard to develop in-house also spurred major pharmas to create research partnerships with providers of combinatorial chemistry expertise. For example, Oxford University partnered with Pfizer. Academic institutions such as Duke, the University of Wisconsin, and Harvard, to name but a few, have partnered with pharma companies in research focused on Alzheimer's disease, diabetes, cardiovascular diseases, and others.

It is worth considering the factors that are pushing pharma and biotech companies to start offshoring more than just manufacturing (for example, India has 75 FDA-approved pharma contract manufacturing plants, while China has 25 and Taiwan has 12) and selected clinical trials. Governments strictly regulate pharmaceuticals development and manufacturing; in the United States, the FDA is responsible for this. As we noted, clinical R&D accounts for 30% of all R&D spending and 23% of all scientific and professional R&D personnel, with Phase III trials by far the most expensive component. These economics have created an entire industry of contract research organizations (CROs), which provide clinical trial services for companies that elect not to conduct those trials in-house. Western-based CROs compete vigorously with ones from Asia, and trials are also conducted in a variety of destinations around the world, including Asia and Central Europe. (See Figure 1-8 for international comparison of labor costs.)

On the push side, three factors are at play: a shortage of talented personnel, competitive pressures to cut costs, and growing company experience with offshoring. The last factor makes companies more confident to extend offshoring to new frontiers and functions. As mentioned earlier, Asia's supply of skilled and relatively inexpensive manpower is growing rapidly just as the West is experiencing relative shortages of science and engineering talent, demographic decline, the retirement of baby boomers, and the new phenomenon of Asian graduates in science and engineering deciding to return home after completing their studies or earning doctoral degrees in the West. Rising healthcare costs, the prospect of comprehensive and regulated healthcare in the United States, and global competition all contribute to an acute need for the drug industry to find ways to drastically cut the costs of drug development.

On the pull side, emerging economies in Asia and elsewhere have not only improved their IP protection systems by signing up to TRIPS. As we have pointed out, these countries have upgraded their scientific, innovation, and educational capabilities as well. They are also becoming increasingly attractive markets for health-related products and are developing local LSIC companies that are becoming competitive partners for JV collaboration, investment, and acquisition. The Asian challenge is indeed formidable, yet crucial areas of weakness will still require time and effort to overcome.

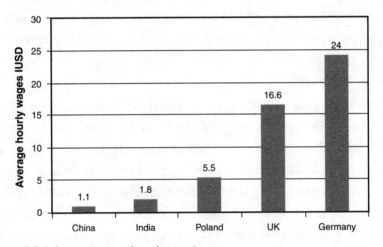

Figure 1-8 Labor cost comparison, by country

Reproduced with permission from Merrill Lynch, KPMG & CII report, March 2008, quoted from Pharma Summit 2008: "India Pharma Inc.—An Emerging Global Pharma Hub."

The Creativity Gap: Asia's Challenge to Achieve Qualitative Parity with the West

Until now, Western economic preeminence has been based on dominance in the science-based high-technology sectors, all of which depend on creativity and innovation. The OECD defines five industrial sectors as high-technology sectors: aerospace, pharmaceuticals, computer and office machinery, communications equipment, and scientific instruments (medical, precision, and optical). In high-tech *manufacturing* in the last decade, the battle for dominance has been between the United States, with a domestic value-add of just more than $500 billion, and Asia, whose share in 2003 was just less than $400 billion. At slightly more than $200 billion, the EU-15 share has not been growing significantly since 1999. During that period, whereas Japan's performance has been static (at around $140 billion), China's share has soared (to nearly $120 billion); South Korea and Taiwan have achieved more modest growth. When we look at high-technology exports, Asia is the world leader, with a global share of 43%; the EU-15 follows, at about 33%, and the United States comes in third, with less than 20%. Asian economies have clearly broken into high-technology manufacturing and have become leading exporters. But a lot of the value-add embodied in those exports still comes from the United States.

In the critical area of exporting high-technology *services,* a different picture emerges. In this field, the United States has pulled ahead of both the EU-15 and Asia. Notwithstanding the Indian success in IT outsourcing, by 2003, India's share of global revenues from high-tech services was barely 1% (despite more than tripling since 1990). Asian nations are still in an early stage in the high-tech services business. In 2003, U.S. revenues in that field were more than $5 billion; those of the EU-15 were $4.5 billion. Asia managed $2.5 billion, with about 60% coming from Japan. In 2003, U.S. receipts from tech licensing (or franchising) transactions—a typical form of trade in IP—with Asia was five times the amount of similar U.S. payments to Asia (again, most of these payments went to Japan).[32]

As noted earlier, Asian S&E publications have grown rapidly, and the Asians have displaced the Europeans in terms of quantitative output. However, when it comes to measures of publication quality, such as citations, Asian progress has been much slower (see Figure 1-9).

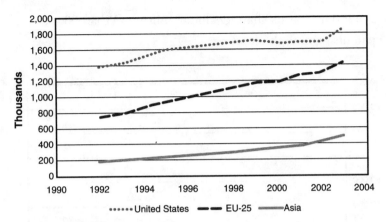

Figure 1-9 Number of citations of science and engineering articles for the United States, the European Union, and Asia, 1992–2003

Source: National Science Foundation; available at www.nsf.gov

In terms of article citations in science and engineering, the United States is still the undisputed leader and the EU-15 is in second place. Articles by Asian authors are less frequently cited than those by U.S. and European authors, and this gap does not appear to be closing. Japan accounts for the bulk of Asian citations, but China, Singapore, South Korea, and Taiwan are making the most rapid progress; India has remained flat, and other Asian nations are making only minor contributions.

Apart from Japan, Asia has a similar quality problem with patents. In the case of U.S. patents granted in 2003, 90,000 of them were granted to U.S. residents and approximately 30,000 were granted to residents of the EU-15. As shown in Figure 1-10, Asian residents took about 45,000 U.S. patents, but about two-thirds of those patents were granted to residents of Japan.

An even more important measure of the value of a patent is seeing it granted simultaneously in the United States, the European Union, and Japan. Such "triadic" patents are the true elite. The United States share of such patents in 2003 stood at about 35%, and that of the EU was about 33%. Asia had slightly less than 30% of these triadic patent families; not only was its share declining, but more than 90% of the triadic patents went to the Japanese.

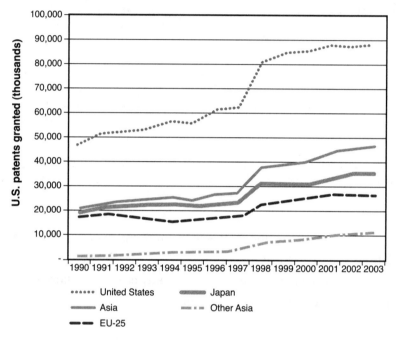

Figure 1-10 Number of U.S. patents granted, by region and country of residence of inventor, 1990–2003

Source: National Science Foundation; available at www.nsf.gov

What about core healthcare innovation skills in leading Asian nations? They have been growing and improving rapidly, but capability gaps in key areas are still a problem. For example, India has significant shortages of principal investigators, experienced biologists, and medical device specialists. This affects the quality of patient recruitment and quality of data in clinical trials and constrains expansion into the biologics and medical device industries. The training of clinical research associates is low, forcing companies to train internally. The country also faces shortages of biostatisticians, epidemiologists, and toxicologists, again constraining the ability of pharma companies to conduct research and increasing some costs.[33] As a result of those deficiencies, companies operating in India have been forced to create education consortia or even establish new universities to improve the supply and quality of talent. Other emerging economies face this problem as well.

Asian education systems have been improving, and, as already stated, the numbers of scientists and engineering graduates are increasing at impressive rates. Yet in terms of the quality of both universities and engineering schools, Asia is still a considerable distance behind the West, as indicated by rankings in Tables 1-2, 1-3, and 1-4.

Table 1-2 Number of World Universities Ranking in Top 100 As of 2008, by Country and Region[34]

Country	Number of Universities in Top 100
United States	58
Europe	34
Asia Pacific (excluding Japan)	8
Japan	4

Table 1-3 Number of Science and Engineering Universities from Japan, the United States, and Europe Among the Top 200 in 2007–2008[35]

Country	Number of Science and Engineering Universities in Top 200
Japan	7
Europe	75
United States	57

Table 1-4 Non-Japanese Asian Polytechnics[36]

1	National University of Singapore (NUS)
2	Tsinghua University, China
3	Nanyang Technological University, Singapore
4	Korea Advanced Institute of Science and Technology

continued

5	Indian Institute of Technology Bombay (IITB)
6	Indian Institute of Technology Delhi (IITD)
7	Seoul National University
8	Shanghai Jiao Tong University, China
9	University of Science and Technology of China
10	National Taiwan University
11	University of Hong Kong
12	Chinese University of Hong Kong
13	Fudan University, China
14	Peking University
15	Nanjing University, China
16	City University of Hong Kong
17	Chulalongkorn University, Thailand
18	Pohang University of Science and Technology, South Korea

Asian and other emerging economy universities will need considerable time to achieve parity with leading Western universities and research centers. Notwithstanding the Chinese achievements in technology, China's educational system, which used to be based on rote learning and respect for authority, has been evolving and has started encouraging individual creativity. Partial evidence from the OECD PISA survey (OECD, Pisa 2009 Database) suggests that Chinese education is indeed improving rapidly. In the 2009 results of the "What Students Know and Can Do" comparative international surveys, Shanghai, China emerged in first place worldwide, well ahead of the OECD average. Chinese students' scores on such dimensions as "integrate and interpret" and "reflect and evaluate" were not only among the highest in the world, but were also higher than in the "access and retrieve" dimension. At least in the Shanghai area, a comprehensive approach has successfully replaced pure rote learning. In terms of Nobel prizes in science, Asia is still far behind the West (see Table 1-5).

Table 1-5 Number of Nobel Prize–Winning Scientists during the Last 20 Years, by Country and Region[37]

Country	Number of Nobel Prize–Winning Scientists During the Last 20 Years
United States	77
Europe	50
Asia Pacific (excluding Japan)	6
Japan	8

Chinese and other Asian governments are aware of the need to foster greater creativity in basic scientific research. For The Chinese Academy of Science, for instance, creating conditions leading to the winning of Nobel prizes in science by Chinese is now a key strategic objective. Singapore and Korea have successfully upgrading the quality of their universities. The West, with its traditions of political freedom, individualism, critical thinking, and tolerance, still has the advantage in this crucial area of blue-sky creativity—but for how long?

Navigating the New World of Global Innovation

The recent trends described in the preceding sections are powerful enough to have transformational impacts on the life science–based industry. Short of some unforeseen world cataclysm, the trends look unstoppable. The new reality of global innovation presents companies with unprecedented opportunities to tap into the comparative advantages of nations, regions, companies, and scientific institutions around the world. In principle, this should allow considerable efficiencies, cost savings, and access to the best talent and to new growing markets. Openness to trade and investment, respect for international IP regulation, and the rapidly improving science and innovation capabilities in key emerging economies mean that we are reaching a new, broader and deeper phase of globalization. More efficient division of labor among countries and regions and the new efficiencies thus gained should result in accelerated scientific discovery and innovation, along with new and better products and processes for the world.

This is a tantalizing vision, but as experience with earlier phases of globalization shows, getting there may not always be a smooth ride. Resistance will come, and both losers and winners will emerge. As R&D resources are relocated to emerging economies, some facilities in Western countries are being closed down or downsized. For example, a number of important pharmaceutical labs in Europe have already closed, and more may follow, as Table 1-6 shows.

Table 1-6 Examples of Pharma Laboratories Shut Down in Europe—Will Europe Become a Cemetery of R&D Labs?[38]

Company	Countries Where Labs Were Closed
Merck	Italy, Spain, and others
AstraZeneca	Spain, Belgium, and Sweden
GlaxoSmithKline	UK
Sanofi Aventis	Ireland, more closures announced

Pharmaceutical companies do not like to announce R&D lab closures, so the real list is longer than what Table 1-6 presents. European governments have seen the danger of Europe becoming a "graveyard of pharma labs," with some major companies relocating to Asia and other competitive destinations. A study commissioned by Leem, the French pharmaceutical industry association, estimates that 32,000 pharmaceutical jobs may be at risk between 2005 and 2015 unless appropriate policy responses are adopted.[39] The danger for the old continent is of gradual dissipation of European capacities to perform certain types of R&D. Depending on their strengths in science and innovation, European countries are exposed differently to the risk: Southern European countries such as Italy are more vulnerable than, say, the United Kingdom which regards itself as a powerhouse in the life sciences area. Some European governments are establishing "countermeasures" against the offshoring trend: For example, France recently announced a strong program of government actions designed to attract international R&D investments. The program includes offering tax incentives, linking French universities into large specialized consortia, and building new competitive campuses and clusters with mixed funding from both the public and private sectors. As the new emerging powers upgrade their R&D capabilities; build science, technology, or knowledge parks; and create special economic zones, Western nations will respond. They cannot match the Asians and others on costs. Instead, they are concentrating on the quality of science and infrastructure—and some are not shy about employing national and regional government subsidies.

This new truly global competition to attract R&D investment provides companies with opportunities to pick and choose, to find the best research groups and the most promising projects, and to spread their risk. To be able to fully take advantage of the range of new opportunities, companies must rethink their strategies and change their structures. We present an overview of how different global pharma companies are reinventing R&D strategies in Chapter 7.

As we indicated earlier, the traditional business model for science-based businesses such as pharmaceuticals relied on the company's own R&D capability to develop new products, which the firm then produced and marketed to generate profits on its own. This model is generally viewed as obsolete. In the age of global R&D, with many new entrants and research centers around the world competing for and contributing to innovations, it no longer makes sense for even a big company to go it alone. Any science-based business, whether in biotechnology, pharmaceuticals, or medical devices, needs to contain costs, enter new emerging markets, and constantly improve R&D productivity. Even the largest companies are using networks of partnerships for a variety of business functions, including research.

Beyond the disruptive changes in the economics of R&D, the life science-based industries are undergoing a period of changes in markets, politics, and the public systems of support and regulation governing food production, energy, and healthcare. Companies face decisions about how quickly they want to change and how to restructure their model of business.

Some companies, such as Lilly and Merck, have moved aggressively; others, such as French pharma giant Sanofi-Aventis, announced major changes only recently. Lilly is quickly transforming itself from a vertically integrated pharmaceutical company into a fully integrated pharmaceutical network that outsources most functions. Merck has chosen to close many of its R&D labs in Europe and relies on a network of collaborative partnerships that include R&D, drug development, and technology licensing. Recent deals include several Indian companies, including Orchid and Ranbaxy, which have been chosen as partners for joint development of novel drugs.

GlaxoSmithKline, Pfizer, and Novartis have used corporate venture capital funds. This approach involves investing in a portfolio of companies in return for a share of the intellectual assets and growth opportunities instead of outsourcing tasks (see www.eba.com.ua). Such venture investments are carefully targeted and may be either specialized in a niche area or diversified to spread risk. The investor company may choose to eventually claim the IP and outlicense it to a third party. Companies also can extend the model much further, to include players from emerging economies; this has already started to happen.

No single business model serves everyone, so companies pursue their own mix of strategic approaches, combining outsourcing with geographic diversification and venturing. One part is certain: The model of the vertically integrated pharmaceutical company is largely gone. Moving to some form of the collaborative network model must include the dimension of truly global thinking. And today, *global* means not just the developed world, but also, increasingly, emerging economies, with their potential role as collaborators in R&D as well as creators of intellectual property.

Of all the forms of business expansion and diversification, *geographical expansion* is the most difficult and most risky. Assumptions, especially those about human behavior, are often proven wrong. Institutions and cultures in other countries work differently, and the economics of operations may be surprisingly different. Therefore, many Western life science–based companies have been cautious about taking full advantage of the many opportunities for collaboration with emerging economies—and not just because of fears of IP dissipation. Lack of knowledge of the quality of the public research institutions and the private companies in high-potential emerging economies has been responsible for the underperformance in many areas of offshoring, including R&D, where the scope for beneficial collaboration is much higher than what exists today. Pioneers or early movers such as Novartis can take advantage of the best opportunities for tapping talent and working with the best research teams in the emerging world. The globalizing companies are also likely to profit from the ability to place more "bets" on discovery targets and take advantage of low costs, tax incentives, and hidden subsidies. In any event, companies should be up-to-date in their ability to assess and understand the present and future innovative potential of emerging economies. This book may help them do just that.

In the following chapters, we take the reader on a tour of the most important future centers of innovation in the key emerging economies that have recently joined the global R&D race. We look at their national and regional policies of support for innovation, including science and education reform and manpower development in Chapter 2, and clusters and bioparks in Chapter 6. In Chapter 3, we evaluate the potential and maturity of the emerging markets for pharmaceuticals and related sectors. In Chapters 4 and 5, we explore Western companies' offshoring of discovery and clinical trials to emerging markets. Chapter 7 reviews the new R&D strategies and recent R&D

investments in emerging economies made by leading international pharma companies.

The two giants of Asia, China and India, feature prominently in our journey. The two countries so far are attracting the majority of Western collaborative and investment projects in the biopharma industry. China currently has the greater potential, but India is in some ways easier for Westerners to work with and may have the greater growth potential in the industry for the long term. Today the "older tigers" of Asia—Singapore, South Korea, and Taiwan—have become advanced economies with significant high-tech capabilities. In terms of cost, Singapore is as expensive as most Western destinations but offers a world-class business and science environment. South Korea and Taiwan have advanced engineering and precision equipment industries and offer sophisticated business environments at lower cost, compared to Singapore. All three countries have ambitious programs for life science industry development. Thailand and Malaysia are less developed but are cheaper and have made rapid progress recently. These two "new tigers" may become destinations of choice in specialized areas such as food-related biotechnology, in the case of Thailand. The newcomer in the Western Hemisphere is Brazil, which not only is a key future market, but also is attracting clinical trials and research collaboration and has vast potential in bio-agriculture and bioenergy.

Looking at R&D and innovation from such a truly global perspective presents myriad choices and opportunities. To take advantage of this enormous potential for successful collaboration, companies must be prepared. They must change their business models, strategies and structures, and cultures and attitudes. This is a complex and challenging process, and this book can help them succeed.

2

The Race for the Best National Innovation System: Who Has the Most Effective Strategy?

"The real in international relations includes not only the state of affairs at the moment of time, but the direction of change as time proceeds."

—Timothy Snyder, *The Reconstruction of Nations* (Yale University Press, 2003), 221

Identifying Future Players in the Global Knowledge Economy

In the previous chapter, we noted that global patterns of research and development (R&D) spending are changing in favor of emerging economies. This raises a question: Who among the new spenders could become a significant new player in the knowledge economy of the future? One way to answer this is to look at long-term economic forecasts, such as the famous Goldman Sachs publication *The World and the BRICs Dream*,[1] to see which nations will gain economic size, say, by 2025. To make meaningful predictions, however, we need a deeper understanding of the factors that will drive economic growth in the twenty-first century. As we ponder this question, we find that leading nations are committing more investments in the innovation-based knowledge economy: research and development (R&D), education, and technological infrastructures. Thus, competition among nations today is largely a race to develop the most effective system of policies that support innovation.

Although many national leaders talk of the importance of the knowledge-based economy, not all nations have developed strong strategies for building innovation systems capable of driving economic growth. In this chapter, we identify a group of key future players in the life science–based industries from among the emerging economies. By looking at their strategies and national resource commitments, we can examine how policies are being used to stimulate the development of new capabilities in innovation.

To make the needed resource commitments, emerging economy leaders first had to acknowledge that deregulation and liberalization alone were not enough—they had to embrace the idea that knowledge has become the key to future economic growth. This is a revolution in thinking about development that has unfolded fully only in the last decade; as we shall see, however, some nations anticipated this trend.

From Capitalist Revolution to Innovation Revolution: Emerging Economies Embrace the Concept of Knowledge Economics

After the collapse of communism in 1989, many countries and regions of the world, starting with Central and Eastern Europe, experienced what we may call capitalist revolutions. The last decade of the twentieth century saw a massive wave of deregulation, liberalization, and privatization spread to the large emerging economies, including China, India, Russia, and Brazil. The subsequent leap to a new level of globalization accelerated international investments, the diffusion of technology, of best management practices—and also greatly increased competition. The turn of the century saw not only developed economies, but also most of the emerging economies accepting the idea that innovation will drive further progress in economic growth. This change in thinking forms much of the basis for justifying public support of R&D spending and establishing policies to promote innovation.

Traditional economics viewed economic growth in terms of investment levels and relationships among the three factors of production: land, capital, and labor. At least since the late 1980s, the economic literature suggests that R&D, innovation, and spillovers are actually *key factors driving self-sustained economic growth* and that these factors are generated from within the economic system by responding to economic incentives.[2] Authors Chen and Dahlman[3] have demonstrated this relationship for *both advanced and emerging economies.* Global competition today is so pervasive that staying internationally competitive even in traditional industries such as wine making or fishing *requires* continuous innovation. For example, without significant programs of innovation, neither the wine industry of Argentina nor the salmon industry of Chile could have achieved successful export growth.

The term *knowledge economy* is widely used to refer to economies characterized by this wealth-generation relationship. A World Bank document describes the shift toward knowledge as a foundation of growth in the following way:

> For countries in the vanguard of the world economy, the balance between knowledge and resources has shifted so far towards the former, that knowledge has become perhaps the most important factor determining the standard of living— more than land, than tools, than labor. Today's most technologically advanced economies are truly knowledge-based.[4]

Some traditional economists view national R&D expenditures as being determined by market forces. The lower a country's level of economic development is, the lower will be the "natural" level of R&D spending measured as a percentage of gross domestic products (GDP). Econo-mists advised developing countries with low levels of GDP per capita to *absorb* foreign technology as efficiently as possible rather than try to replicate the costly acquisition of knowledge and technology by spending scarce national resources on R&D. However, this view has been changing. Even well-functioning market economies do not gen-erate optimal levels of R&D by themselves,[5] and the mere opening up of the economy to trade and foreign direct investment does not itself guarantee the adoption of even current technology.[6] Instead, firms and countries need to *invest* in developing absorptive or "national learning" capacity. Such absorptive capacity, in turn, is a function of R&D spending.[7]

A recent World Bank study focusing on Europe and Central Asia suggests that countries first need to reach a threshold of development in terms of a knowledge economy infrastructure (as measured by a score of 6.5 out of 10 on the Knowledge Economy Index) before a publicly funded innovation support program is justified. Most Central Asian countries do not meet this threshold, but the more advanced emerging economies of Central Europe do.[8]

The Knowledge Economy Index in Figure 2-1 consists of such factors as education, information and communication technologies (ICT) infrastructure, and R&D efforts. It has become a new way of ranking countries' prospects in this century. Some successful emerg-ing economies, such as the four Asian "tigers" (South Korea, Taiwan, Hong Kong, and Singapore), have been supporting and promoting innovation for decades, but since the beginning of the twenty-first century, they have accelerated this support and begun refocusing it on what they perceive as new key areas for the future: bio- and nanotechnology, medical services, and clean energy, among others. Latecomers such as Brazil have urgently begun catch-up programs, but by no means have all nations mustered the determination and resources to join the challenging new race for an innovation-based economy. The laggards include some southern European countries that have failed to reform their university and science establishments and have not managed to increase spending on R&D. Some emerging economies in Central Europe, the Middle East, and Latin America have chosen to remain passive, have not made progress, or have even seen declines in their capabilities to compete in the knowledge-based global industries. As a result, they risk becoming marginalized.

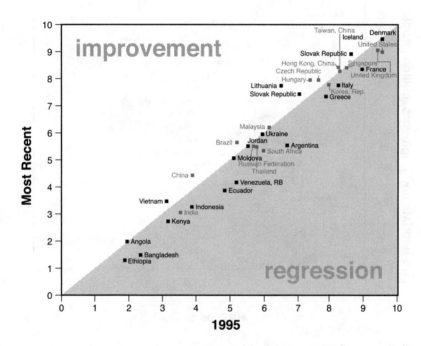

Figure 2-1 Knowledge Economy Index, comparison group: all countries

Reproduced by permission from "Knowledge Economy Index," International Bank for Reconstruction and Development—World Bank, July 2009; available at http://info.worldbank.org/etools/kam2/KAM_page7.asp

The first decade of the twenty-first century is over, and we can begin to discern the likely future players in the innovation economy of the future. These are likely to be nations with sound policies in support of the knowledge economy. Among the lead indicators of future success is R&D spending, which is a good predictor of the ability to obtain international patents, which is regarded as a key indicator of innovation performance. As we saw in the previous chapter, the global R&D spending patterns (see Figure 2-2) for 2010 have been changing rapidly since 2000. The shares of established players such as the United States and especially Europe and Japan are declining, and those of emerging economies, especially in Asia, are increasing.

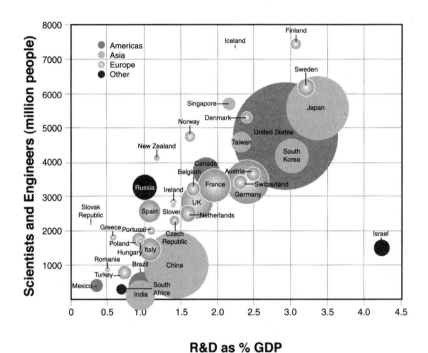

Figure 2-2 Annual R&D spending, by country, 2010

Reproduced by permission from "2010 Global R&D Funding Forecast," *R&D Magazine*, December 2009, 4. Source: Battele, *R&D Magazine*, OECD, IMF, CIA. Size of circle reflects the relative amount of annual R&D spending by the country noted.

China stands out as the leading challenger. Its sheer size, its determined strategy to become an economic superpower, its already huge and growing share (more than 12%) of global R&D spending, and its cultivation of crucial new technologies all make it a key new player in a class of its own. India and South Korea currently are second-tier challengers, with levels of R&D spending that are of similar magnitude to each other today. Although Korea is a more developed country than India, India's size and dynamic growth make it a more important player for the long term, especially given its strengths in pharmaceuticals and biotechnology. As already mentioned, Brazil is a latecomer to the innovation race, but its size and excellent prospects, especially in such areas as biofuels and agro-biotech, place it in the same category of important future challengers as India and South Korea. Below China, India, South Korea, and Brazil, many smaller emerging economies will play significant roles in global innovation. The most prominent of these are Singapore and Taiwan.

Russia is a special case. It has a large population of researchers—five times larger than Brazil on a per-million-inhabitants basis. Unfortunately, Russia's share of scientific articles declined during 1995–2005, as did its global share of researchers. Many of its scientists have taken up posts outside Russia, in the United States, China, and other destinations. Its innovation performance is relatively low. Other than in the areas of defense and security, Russia is not perceived as a future technology leader.[9] However, Russia knows that it needs to reform its science, technology, and innovation systems. If it does, given its size and potential, it could yet emerge as an important player in the global innovation race.

An extensive review of all emerging economies' policies and efforts in promoting innovation lies outside the scope of this book. Instead, we look more closely at the group of key future players. We start with a discussion of the national visions and policies of the two Asian giants: China and India. We then review the new Asian high-tech leader, South Korea, and examine the potential of Brazil. We finish with Singapore, a role model of a highly successful niche player and the most advanced among the newcomers into the new innovation economy. We treat Japan as an established player on par with the West.

In our discussion, we place special emphasis on describing policies that focus on developing biotechnology industries. As the most science-dependent and demanding new industry, biotech is both representative of the life science sector as a whole and a good proxy for other science-intensive sectors. In our discussions, we consider the dilemmas and likely further progress and success of the new players in innovation-based economies in the future.

Exponential China: The "Unstoppable Giant" Shifts Gear to Become an Innovation-Driven Economy by 2020

In 2010, China overtook Japan to become the second-largest economy in the world, as measured by currency exchange rates. A regular visitor to China is often astonished when revisiting a city or a neighborhood after just four or five years: In this time, a whole new city or neighborhood can emerge next to the old one. China's growth seems exponential. The country's expected continued high speed of economic growth likely will enable it to continue its massive programs of support for science and innovation. The Chinese are thoughtful strategists who play a long-term game. They realize that continued economic growth requires the country to switch away from an investment-driven, energy- and labor-intensive model of the economy to one based on technology.

A museum in Macao, a special administrative region of China, compares the emergence of inventions in Europe and China over the ages. The visitor is struck by the demonstration that, apart from rare exceptions such as optics, until the Industrial Revolution, China had been well ahead of Europe in a broad range of inventions and technologies, including gun powder, printing, and paper currency. Contrary to some popular notions, Chinese culture and tradition did not prevent China from being a world leader in invention in the past. Only after the country began isolating itself from the world under the Ming Dynasty did Chinese inventiveness and economic power decline, to reach a trough by the nineteenth century. China sees itself today as rebuilding those great historical traditions of technological leadership.

After the communists took over China in 1949, they largely copied the Soviet model of science and higher education. This was a highly centralized and bureaucratic system that was capable of implementing a few priority government projects but was unsuitable for generating market-driven innovation. The broader agenda of Deng Xiaoping's economic reforms included reforming the science and technology sector. This part of the agenda was called the "third modernization," after agriculture and industry (the fourth was defense). Among the communist countries, China was the first to reform its science establishment. After shaking off the constraints of the orthodox command economy, the Chinese began in the 1980s to develop and perfect their programs of more enlightened government supports for key future industries and sectors—that is, well before China reached its present level of economic development.[10]

Arguably, China has been the most successful when compared to Russia and even the countries of Central and Eastern Europe, which have been able to institute only partial reforms of their science and technology establishments since the collapse of communism in 1989. Today China ranks well ahead of all those countries on "innovation factors" contributing to competitiveness.[11]

By 1988, China had already introduced several reforms to its science and was launching the Torch program, whose goal was to bring science and industry together, to create markets in technology, commercialize inventions, and promote academic entrepreneurship. At the same time, the government was spending money to create innovation support centers for entrepreneurs, especially for returning Chinese expatriates. The government was creating high-technology industrial zones and introducing policies designed to attract investments in technology-based industries. Spin-off companies were created from national research labs. As the system of higher education was reformed, basic research was expanded in the universities, and numerous graduate study programs were created.

China made further progress in the late 1990s after improving corporate governance systems and enacting laws to protect intellectual property rights. It joined the World Trade Organization in 2001). China signed the Agreement on Trade-Related Aspects of Intellectual Property Rights (TRIPS), making the Chinese patent system compatible with international standards. Yet further reforms were needed before a viable national innovation system could emerge. Chief among them were these necessary reforms:

- New allocation mechanisms for public R&D funding
- Transformation of R&D institutions in applied research into business entities and/or technical service organizations, and the incorporation of large R&D institutions into large companies
- Improved functioning of markets for technology
- Reform of human resources management in public research institutions
- Improved enforcement of intellectual property (IP) rights[12]

China has at least partially fulfilled many of these goals by now. Government policy after 2005 emphasized an accelerated investment in science and technology and the construction of a "firm-oriented,"[13] full-fledged, high-performing national innovation system.

The overarching goal is to make China an "innovation-oriented" society by the year 2020 and, over the longer term, one of the world's leading "innovation economies." China's policies emphasize the need to develop capabilities for "indigenous" or "home-grown innovation" instead of importing foreign technology. New tax regulations provide incentives for investments in "nationally supported key high-technology fields." Crucially, *innovation* is seen as replacing exports as a growth engine.[14]

In many ways, China's policies of reform and support for innovation have yielded impressive results to date:[15]

- China's open-door policy has attracted major foreign direct investment (FDI) flows (today China's FDI stock relative to GDP is greater than that of Japan and South Korea and is comparable to that of the United Kingdom) and also is becoming host to an increasing number of foreign R&D labs. Since 2000, the number of new foreign labs has been increasing each year by 10 to 20 new establishments.[16]

- The number of patent applications to the Chinese State Intellectual Property Office increased five-fold between 1995 and 2005 (growing at nearly 40% annually from 1995 to 2005).

- China's R&D expenditures have enjoyed one of the fastest increases in the world (more than 18.7% during 1995–2005) and include not just increased expenditures by higher education institutions, but also rapidly growing expenditures by large and medium-size firms. For example, an estimated 25% of large and medium-size firms have R&D labs, while more than 80% of small firms have some form of science and technology activities.

- Today China is the leading exporter of ICT in the world, ahead of the United States and Japan. The share of high tech in Chinese exports has been growing rapidly since 2000 and now exceeds $30 billion (about 8% of exports).

- In 2003, China had 32,857 firms in science and technology parks, and 27,285 in technology incubators.

- Leading Chinese firms have started to create their own R&D and design labs. For example, Haier has R&D centers in Germany and the United States (Silicon Valley); Huawei has such centers in India, the Netherlands, Sweden, Russia, and the United States; and Foton Motors is located in Taiwan, Germany, and Japan.

While moving along a broad front of innovation improvement, China has designated a few chosen fields for "leapfrogging," including, for example, nanotechnology, biotechnology, and ICT. (Chinese spending on nanotechnology is among the highest in the world, at levels comparable to those of the United States and Japan.)

China's Biotechnology Development Program

China began its biotechnology program in the early 1980s, with multiple sets of goals regarding food security, sustainable agricultural development, the environment, and human health. This raised China's competitive position in international agricultural markets and created a modern, market-responsive, and internationally competitive biotechnology research and development system in the country.[a]

The following table shows major policy measures undertaken in China in biotechnology since the early 1980s.[b]

Key breakthrough science and technology projects	Started in 1982 by the State Development and Planning Commission (SDPC). Updated every 5 years. One of the major components of these projects is biotechnology R&D.
Patent system	Patent law promulgated in 1985.
National biotechnology development policy outline	Prepared by scientists and officials led by the Ministry of Science and Technology (MOST), the SDPC, and others in 1985. The outline defined the research priorities, development plan, and measures for achieving targets.
National Key Laboratories (NKLs) on biotechnology	Thirty National Key Laboratories in biotechnology (15 on agriculture or agriculture related) have been established.
High Technology Research and Development Plan (863 Plan)	Approved in March 1986 with 10 billion RMB for 15 years to promote high-technology R&D in China. Biotechnology is one of seven supporting areas, with a total budget of about 1.5 billion RMB for 1986–2000.
Natural Science Foundation of China	Established in 1986 to support basic science research.
Biosafety regulations	MOST issued the Biosafety Regulations on Genetic Engineering in July 1993.
Agricultural biosafety regulations	The Ministry of Agriculture (MOA) issued the Safety Administration, Implementation, and Regulations on Agricultural Biological Genetic Engineering in July 1996.

973 Plan	Initiated in March 1997 to support basic science and technology research. Life science is one of the key supporting areas.
Agricultural Genetically Modified Organisms (GMO) Biosafety Committee	The ministry-level Agri GMO Biosafety Committee was set up in MOA in 1997. The committee was updated in 2002 to a national level, with its office in MOA.
Special foundation for transgenic plant research and commercialization	A five-year program that MOST launched in 1999 to promote the research and commercialization of transgenic plants in China.
Key science engineering program	Started in the late 1990s under MOST and SDPC to promote basic research, including a biotechnology program.
Foundation for high-tech commercialization	A special program that the SDPC supported to promote the application and commercialization of technologies, starting from 1998.
Seed Regulation and Law	The Regulation on the Protection of New Varieties of Plants was issued in 1999. The first Seed Law was issued in 2000.
Updated and amended agricultural biosafety regulations	MOA issued three regulations on the biosafety management, trade, and labeling of genetically modified (GM) farm products, to take effect after March 20, 2002.
Foreign investment in GMOs	In April 2002, the SDPC, State Economic and Trade Commission, and MOTEC jointly issued a Guideline List of Foreign Investment, which lists GMO as a prohibited area for foreign investment.

In line with its long track record of pursuing development in the biotech sector, the government has incorporated several foreign investment legislations, to encourage multinational companies (especially biotech and pharmaceutical companies) to invest in China.[c]

[a] J. Huang and Q. Wang, "Biotechnology Policy and Regulation in China." IDS Working Paper, 2003.

[b] For more information on China's biotechnology development program, see AgBioForum, *The Journal of Agrobiotechnology Management and Economics*. Available at www.agbioforum.org.

[c] S. Rumpel and John W. Medcof, "A Good Fit for High Tech Workers," *Research Technology Management* 49, no. 5 (2006): 27–35. See also www.ogbioforum.missouri.edu.

Further improvement in Chinese innovation performance, which still lags behind that of world leaders, depends on resolving these difficult challenges:

- Chinese R&D still mainly focuses on technological development, with basic research lagging behind. The basic research effort needs to be balanced with development. China is now expanding the scope of basic research.

- Despite the rapid growth of human resources for science and technology, including university programs, bottlenecks and shortages of specialists may constrain growth. China's answer is to welcome back "sea turtles," Chinese who have studied in the West.

- The Chinese innovation system is still too dependent on top-down policies of "picking winners." The Chinese system needs to evolve in the direction of self-sustaining, market-led innovation. Evidence indicates that private companies, especially joint ventures with Western companies, are expanding their innovation efforts.

- China's financial system is dominated by large state-owned banks that tend to lend to state companies. Insufficient capital is available for financing new ventures. China has not yet developed a modern venture capital system.

- Intellectual property rights regulations are in place and enjoy government support. Yet IP infringements stemming from weak enforcement are still a problem and constitute a barrier to further foreign R&D in China.

China gives no sign of slacking in its government's strategic commitment to developing indigenous innovation capabilities. Evidence also indicates that the country continues to learn from its world experience and is addressing the shortcomings of its innovation system. In fact, Chinese policy toward foreign direct investment is moving away from supporting manufacturing projects and toward developing services, R&D, and technology-intensive projects. Evidence further suggests that international business has been making significant new R&D investments in the country. For many reasons, we can expect China to emerge in time as a significant contributor to global innovation.

India: Leapfrogging into the Knowledge Economy

India is less developed, is less wealthy, and has a less literate population than China. Although the country was never a communist command economy, it had been highly regulated for a long time. Its economic reforms of opening up to the world started later than China's "four modernizations." Still, India has a number of advantages over China, including longer established private firms, a strong democratic tradition, a large English-speaking population, and a greater familiarity with Western institutions.

India went through several stages in evolving its present system of national innovation. Within a few decades of gaining independence, India developed a science and technology capability that placed it as a leader among developing nations. Its achievements included an independent nuclear energy sector, a space sector with strengths in communications infrastructure, and a system of defense research. During that period, India developed national programs of agricultural research and an extension system that improved crop yields and helped increase crop diversity. India also established a system of medical education and research that increased capabilities in several areas of medicine and life sciences, such as vaccines and the production of generic drugs.[17] Indian industry largely relied on technology transfer from more developed economies. Under patent laws that favored national industry, Indian companies became experts at absorbing imported technology and adapting it to Indian conditions, and also at making improvements.

With the founding of the Indian Institutes of Technology (IIT) and other engineering and management training institutions, the Indian government laid the foundations of a modern system of education that would provide the economy with highly skilled graduates. Universities and national labs built science departments. Without these early achievements, India's rapid growth since the wave of reforms in the early 1990s could not have taken place.

The prereform Indian system had some fundamental weaknesses, however. It was based on outmoded ideas of national self-sufficiency and import substitution. As in many countries, the government-supported science and university establishments had weak connections with private business. Academicians were aloof from industry and viewed business as a less prestigious form of activity—hardly an attitude conducive to science-based entrepreneurship.

Economic reforms that the Indian government carried out in the last decade of the twentieth century had a major impact on the policy framework for science, technology, and innovation. The government recognized the idea of opening up to the world economy and abandoned self-reliance as a principle of industrial policy. The global intellectual property rights regime was accepted and approved in 2005. Perhaps most crucially, the private sector, not government science, began to be seen as the key driver of innovation.

The success of the IT sector based on outsourcing in the 1990s, as well as the relatively successful performance in such sectors as biotechnology and pharmaceuticals, has given credibility to the idea that India can leapfrog its way to the global knowledge economy. India's comparative advantages lie in its large base of scientific manpower and wide range of research institutions able to undertake R&D activity at much lower costs compared to developed nations. The new opportunities lie across a range of scientific and technological disciplines and subdisciplines, including engineering, software, clinical trials for new drugs, and pharmaceutical research. The new government policy views private business as best positioned to exploit those advantages.[18]

The question remains whether the policies will, in time, enable India to emerge as an independent player in the knowledge economy of comparable weight with developed nations. The alternative might be playing the role of a cost-competitive outsourcing destination for international companies based in wealthy developed nations. Another important question for the country is whether its science and technology systems will be able to meet the staggering needs of poverty reduction and general development instead of just creating opportunities for the better-educated minorities employed in the cutting-edge sectors of the economy. The question of whether modernization serves the majority of poor citizens will continue to preoccupy public debate in India.

Until recently, India lagged behind China and other wealthier nations in R&D spending as a percentage of GDP (around 1%). Its latest five-year plan (2007–2012) targets moving that share to 2% by the year 2012 and includes a four-fold increase in education spending. According to estimates based on purchasing power parity, India's R&D expenditures are close to those of the United Kingdom, a much smaller economy, As India's economy continues to grow strongly, the country is well positioned to pull ahead of the United Kingdom. Foreign investment can accelerate this process. Foreign companies continue to expand their offshoring to India and spend more than $10 billion on R&D in the country.[19] Indian output of publications saw an increase of 80% from 1998 to 2007. The number of patents filed continues to increase rapidly, with notable successes in such fields as chemistry, agricultural science, and pharmacology, where India's share of world publications is significant and growing.

India's Biotechnology Development Programs

The government of India has recognized biotech as a sunrise sector and has made many efforts to help the country grow as a major global biotech destination. One of the government's most recent policy initiatives was the establishment of the National Biotechnology Development Strategy in 2008. This strategy includes the following initiatives:[a]

- Setting up the National Biotechnology Regulatory Authority
- Establishing an interministerial coordination committee
- Allocating 30% of the Department of Biotechnology's (DBT) budget to public–private partnerships
- Creating a Biotechnology Industry Partnership Programme
- Expanding a Small Business Innovation Research Industry (SBIRI) scheme for supporting SMEs
- Establishing a Biotechnology Industry Research Assistance Council (BIRAC), to nurture R&D and promote tech transfer between academia and industry
- Setting up star colleges in life sciences and focused biotech mini-centers in college departments
- Creating Centers of Excellence in Biotechnology
- Beefing up biotech infrastructure

The government is also promoting sector-specific promotion policies and is establishing infrastructure support in the form of bioparks and special economic zones (SEZs). Through the National Policy on Biofuels approved by the government, a National Biofuel Coordination Committee and a Bio-Fuel Steering Committee have been set up. The government has also approved several Nano Electronic Centres and technology research clusters and centers. The former have been launched in collaboration with the Indian Institute of Science (IISc), Bangalore, and the Indian Institute of Technology, Bombay (IITB), with an investment of $20.54 million.

In terms of infrastructure, the government has proposed the following measures in its 11th five-year plan:

- Biotech incubators and parks (at least 10)
- Repositories of biologicals for agriculturally and therapeutically important organisms, plasmids, and so on
- Good Manufacturing Practice (GMP) regulations scale-up facilities for pilot production
- Large animal houses
- Testing facilities for GMOs and living modified organisms (LMOs)
- Testing of GM crops and GM food
- DNA and stem cell banking facilities
- Gene banks
- Bio safety level III and IV labs
- Molecular and chemical libraries for screening therapeutic leads
- Custom infrastructure and processing for biologicals
- Trade-related testing and certification accredited laboratories

To attract more foreign investment into the sector, the government has proposed the following incentives:[b]

- 100% foreign equity investment allowed in the manufacture of all drugs except recombinant DNA products and cell-targeted therapies
- A single window processing mechanism, provided by the DBT, for all mega biotechnology projects involving FDI of $22 million or more under the Foreign Investment Implementation Authority (FIIA) with its Fast Track Committee (FTC)
- Depreciation allowance on plant and machinery
- Customs duty exemption on goods imported in certain cases

- 150% weighted tax deduction on R&D expenditures
- Three-year excise duty waiver on patented products
- 100% rebate on own R&D expenditure
- 125% rebate if research is contracted to publicly funded R&D institutions
- Customs duty on import of reference standards reduced from 25% to 5%
- Special fiscal benefits for joint R&D projects
- Recently announced tariff and nontariff government measures to further stimulate market development in biotechnology

[a] Department of Biotechnology, *National Biotechnology Development Strategy*, Government in India, 2008. Available at dbtindia.nic.in/biotechstrategy/ National%20Biotechnology%20 Development%20Strategy.pdf.

[b] Indian Industry Overview: Biotechnology, Directories Today. Available at www.directories-today.com/Biotechnology.html. See also www.ice.it.

Despite this progress, the Indian innovation system is still immature, with the government funding 74% of R&D and industry funding only 20% (although note that foreign companies' R&D spending amounts to 40% of the government effort). In the medium term, India will lag behind China across the board. In the longer term, however, it may pose a challenge to China. By 2025, India's population will match that of China, just as China's population will start decreasing. In the meantime, India is expected to become one of the world's technology leaders only in selected disciplines such as ICT and in composite, nanotech, and advanced materials.[20] India also will likely become an important player and challenger in agro-science and biopharmaceuticals, both of which have been targeted as a priority.

South Korea: Midsize Challenger

Within just a generation, South Korea has moved from the status of a developing economy to one of an established member of the

OECD, the club of rich nations. In fact, South Korea has joined the small group of countries vying for leadership of the knowledge-based economy. In terms of gross domestic expenditure on R&D, South Korea (at $42 billion PPP) ranks fifth in the world, behind the United States, Japan, China, and Germany, and just ahead of France. A much smaller country and economy than France, South Korea has 223,000 researchers versus 211,000 in France. South Korea is also among the most aggressive spenders in the world, devoting more than 3% of its GDP to R&D.[21]

South Korea's innovation policies are regarded as among the most effective in the world. They started with the establishment of a Ministry of Science and Technology in the 1960s. A number of government research institutes were created at the time. The country introduced tax incentives for R&D, and training of scientists and engineers accelerated. The government's objectives during this phase were to facilitate the absorption and adaptation of foreign technology in support of industrialization.

As soon as the government accomplished this, it began targeting "core technologies" to "pull" South Korean economic growth. The Ministry of Science and Technology established the first national R&D program in 1982, with the goal of fully engaging the private sector with a wide range of measures such as tax incentives and public procurement. The result was an unprecedented increase in private-sector R&D outlays. Within a decade, private-sector R&D overtook public spending. This was a remarkable result even by world standards, and a sign of how quickly the South Korean innovation system was maturing.

In the aftermath of the Asian financial crisis of the late 1990s, South Korea began diversifying its R&D effort away from the hitherto privileged chaebols, the large industrial conglomerates with close links to the government. The government again greatly increased the volume of R&D spending to build a research capability in *basic science*. Policy emphasized knowledge transfers between universities and industry. The 1990s also saw a number of new national plans for innovation, including the famous Science and Technology "Vision 2025" and the creation of the Office of the Ministry of Science and Innovation. South Korea now also has a Ministry of Knowledge Economy, which oversees many large government research institutes.

South Korea has emerged among the 15 most innovative nations in the world and is also home to several large highly successful multinational firms, including Samsung and LG, which are ranked among the most innovative companies in the world.[22] The country has a world-class IT infrastructure, and its universities, although still relatively weak in basic research, are improving rapidly.

On the downside, South Korea has no natural resources, faces geopolitical threats, has low fertility rates, and has a limited domestic market. Its export industries are crucial to continued prosperity and face growing competition from China. To continue to grow, South Korea has little choice but to persist in building a stronger knowledge economy capacity. It must reduce its heavy reliance on ICT and invest in new high-technology fields such as bio- and nanotechnology, where it will be competing directly with Japan, the United States, and Europe. If one is to believe the Goldman Sachs BRIC forecast, despite challenges, South Korea will be among the winners and will become one of the wealthiest nations in the world (third by 2025 and second by 2050), displacing most European countries in terms of per-capita GDP.[23]

Brazil: The Latecomer with Great Prospects

Among the emerging economic giants entering the innovation economy, Brazil is different in several ways. It developed pro-innovation policies later than its Asian competitors, it is developing its own distinctive philosophy of innovation, and it is likely to concentrate on different areas than China, India, or South Korea.[24]

Until World War II, Brazil had a small cadre of scientists and a weak institutional base for research. Its economy was based on agriculture, with industry in traditional sectors such as mining. Not until the 1960s did graduate programs and full-time faculty positions became common in Brazilian universities. Today the country has 70,000 PhDs.

Similar to other emerging economies, Brazil went through a phase of unsuccessful economic policies based on statist regulation of the economy. It suffered a period of hyperinflation and a military dictatorship. As in India, its program of development through deregulation and liberalization did not begin until the 1990s. Only since 2000, after overcoming inflation and achieving sustainable economic growth, did Brazil begin to base its development strategy on innovation.

The new Brazilian Science and Technology policy has created new institutions such as CNDI (National Council for Industrial Development) and ABDI (Brazilian Agency for Industrial Development). Large increases in both public- and private-sector R&D spending have begun, with plans to increase it from the present 0.91% of GDP to 2.00% by 2013. Brazil defines innovation as encompassing both social and technological aspects, and the country has had some remarkable successes with its poverty-reduction programs. Not only was the country able to reduce the number of people living in poverty by 32% between 2004 and 2006, but it is the only BRIC country to have significantly reduced income inequality (which has been increasing in many other countries, including those in the OECD). A well-targeted R&D program has enabled Brazil to become a leader in renewable energy. The country has achieved energy sufficiency, and 90% of its cars are equipped to use biofuels on a flex system. Brazilian strategic areas for R&D and innovation spending targets are bio- and nanotechnology, biofuels, health biodiversity, and climate change. The largest number of Brazilian biotech companies are in agro-biotechnology, animal health, and the environment.[25] Brazil plans to spend 10 billion reais on biotech over the next ten years; the private sector is expected to contribute 40% of this.[26]

Brazil is not yet in the same league as China, South Korea, or India. It has only about 625 researchers per million of population, and its innovation ranking in terms of patent activity is relatively low, at 48. Indications suggest, however, that Brazil will play an increasingly important role in innovation in the future. Brazil's share in the world's technical publications increased from 0.5% in 1989 to about 2% in 2007. Its share of the world's 7.1 million researchers grew from 1.2% in 2002 to 1.7% in 2007. Brazil has the highest overall impact per scientific paper among the BRICS and is viewed among the top six countries that will be making major technology gains by 2014.[27]

Singapore Story II: The Emergence of a Model "Innovation Nation"

In his famous book *From Third World to First: Singapore Story 1965–2000*, the father of Singapore's economic miracle, Lee Kuan Yew, chronicles the country's amazing progress until the turn of the century.[28] Of the rising-star economies around the Pacific Rim, Singapore has become one of the wealthiest and most advanced (after only Japan). Even according to the harshest critics, the country has one of the most successful long-term programs of government-driven support and promotion of economic restructuring, innovation, and entrepreneurship. In 1960, Singapore's per-capita income was a mere $427; by 2010, it exceeded $45,000.

Although Singapore is sometimes cited as a role model of a nation that has developed a highly effective policy mix, it is worth remembering that it is a small city-state with a population of only 5.2 million. Nevertheless, its achievements in moving from a manufacturing- to a knowledge-based economy are impressive, especially in regard to the life science and biotechnology sectors.

Singapore has relied consistently on the six pillars of economic growth: tight monetary policy, free trade, a business-friendly environment, encouragement of foreign direct investment, high savings, and an activist and efficient government regarded as one of the least corrupt in the world. By 2000, Singapore had become not only a major Asian trade hub, but also a strong manufacturing base for companies in chemicals, precision electronics, and engineering, which exported those goods worldwide.

The rapid ascent of China in many manufacturing exports forced Singapore to rethink its strategy. As one of the country's leaders put it, "We need to move from being an 'efficiency city' to being an innovation nation."[29] Around 2000, Singapore decided to diversify away from its dependence on manufacturing exports and build a new biomedical sciences cluster to become "the biopolis of Asia." The Agency for Science Technology and Research (A*STAR) was charged with building up the country's knowledge base through a series of five-year plans (of which the 2002–2005 third plan was given a budget of $7 billion). The idea was to build on Singapore's existing strengths in infrastructure, IP laws, education, and excellent medical systems.

Singapore's Biotechnology Development Program

Government initiatives for the biomedical sciences sector include:

- Adoption of the Biomedical Sciences Initiative, a national biomedical development strategy, in 2000, with an emphasis on innovation, exports, and FDI.

- Adoption of FDI-oriented economic developmental policy.

- Development of biotech parks and clusters: two "mega infrastructure projects" (the Tuas Biomedical Park and Biopolis). Biopolis was developed as part of a master plan for a 200-hectare development known as One-North.

- Investment in biotech funds and grants: $1 billion in the Biomedical Sciences Investment Fund;[a] and Bio*One Capital, formed as an investment arm under Economic Development Board for new biomedical sciences.

- Development of science and technology and life sciences research institutions: the National Science & Technology Board restructured into the Agency for Science, Technology & Research(A*STAR); and a Biomedical Research Council to oversee R&D activities.

- New educational policies to train labor in life sciences.

- Joint national biomedical grant call, launched by A*STAR's Biomedical Research Council (BMRC) and the Ministry of Health's National Medical Research Council (NMRC).

- Formulation of a strict intellectual property regime and a "bioethics code," to attract foreign investors.

- Liberal immigration policy for researchers, including post-graduate students, in life sciences.

- "Health Products Act," hoped to improve regulatory practice for both medical devices and pharmaceuticals.[b]

- Lower corporate taxes and even full tax exemption.

The government launched the Biomedical Sciences Initiative in June 2000 to develop the biomedical sciences cluster. The major aspects are listed here:[c]

- Steering Committee on Life Sciences, comprising the Ministers for Trade & Industry, Health, and Education, and an Executive Committee, chaired by A*STAR Chairman and the Permanent Secretary for Health

- Promotion of funding and investment activities

- Public research initiatives: Biomedical Research Council (BMRC) of the Agency for Science, Technology and Research (A*STAR)

- Private-sector manufacturing and R&D activities: Economic Development Board's (EDB) Biomedical Sciences Group (BMSG)

- Investment and funding: EDB's Bio*One Capital
- Phase I (2000–2005): establishing the foundation for basic biomedical research, including bioprocessing, chemical synthesis, genomics and proteomics, molecular and cell biology, bioengineering and nanotechnology, and computational biology
- Phase II (2006–2010): translational and clinical research, and technology transfer from laboratories to clinical applications

[a] National University of Singapore report, 2007.

[b] "Singapore Medical Device Market Intelligence Report," Espicom Report, 2006. Available at www.asianhhm.com/Knowledge_bank/industryreports/singapore_medicaldevicemarket.htm.

[c] A*STAR BMS Initiative. Available at www.a-star.edu.sg/biomedical_sciences/166-The-BMS-Initiative.

The government of Singapore has been proactively developing the biomedical sector in the country. The government's initial objective was to position and market the island as a "bulk pharmaceutical manufacturing" destination. Over the last decade, however, it has been following a more ambitious life sciences approach by assigning priority to research and drug discovery. Singapore is judged to be an example of a successful long-term government strategy that promotes high technology and entrepreneurship through a complex range of activities:

- Creating the right legal environment
- Ensuring access to cutting-edge technology and knowledge
- Creating tax incentives
- Training potential entrepreneurs

Although the steps appear simple, they are by no means easy. For instance, ensuring access to cutting-edge knowledge for BioPolis, the biotech cluster, meant luring world-class researchers from MIT, the National Cancer Institute, Kyoto University, and others with generous funding, state-of-the-art facilities, and top salaries.[30]

The government played an active role in developing a reliable life sciences infrastructure to help develop startups and support existing life sciences companies. Skilled labor is the most important asset of the country, so the government is taking several steps to inculcate life sciences education at the university level.

Singapore's biomedical strategy in Figure 2-3 is part of a broader science and technology strategy. The government has stressed developing innovation and R&D capabilities in the country. The National Technology Plan (NTP), started in 1991, was the first comprehensive effort in establishing a framework for effective development of R&D capabilities. Three more Science and Technology (S&T) plans followed, in 2000, 2005, and 2010 (the most current one).

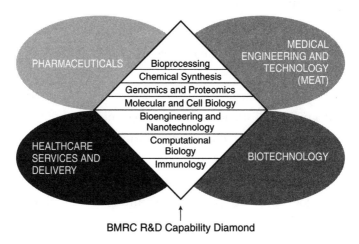

BMRC R&D Capability Diamond

Figure 2-3 Singapore's research strategy

Reproduced by permission from "Sustaining Innovation-Driven Growth: Science and Technology Plan, 2010." Published February 2006, © Ministry of Trade and Industry, Singapore

NTP 1991 dedicated $2 billion in government funding for R&D and technology. S&T Plan 2000 dedicated $4 billion, and S&T Plan 2005 set aside $6 billion, with $4 billion for boosting local R&D capabilities and $2 billion to promote private-sector R&D. The current plan earmarks $13.55 billion to promote R&D.[31] Singapore has become a role model of development for small countries. Its success has also had an impact on its neighbors. Malaysia has been developing its biotech cluster across the water directly opposite Singapore's Biopolis.

Other Players

Aside from the leading challengers profiled earlier, many larger and smaller emerging economies have also been pursuing attempts to switch to innovation-led development. Many have formulated explicit national development strategies based on innovation, with emphasis on the biomedical sector. A complete review would require writing another book, so we mention only a few examples of second-tier players.

Taiwan stands out as a relatively early adopter of TRIPS and successful implementer of innovation policies. Taiwan has been able to create competitive industrial sectors in IT, aerospace, engineering, and medical devices. The Taiwanese government has played a proactive role to ensure that, regardless of its small size, Taiwan emerges as one of the leaders in life sciences in the Asia Pacific region. It declared biotechnology as an industrial development priority in the early 1980s and has consistently strengthened its position in the biomap of the region by following several biotech initiatives, including the development of innovation clusters.

Other nations that have adopted biotechnology or life sciences development strategies include South Africa (2001), Thailand (2004), Malaysia (2005), and Hungary (2004). These national plans usually entail establishing specialized committees, task forces, or agencies responsible for coordinating government efforts to support and regulate the biotechnology industry. Several strategies envision substantial public spending on biotech research, accompanied by corresponding private spending. Some countries do not specify the ratios of public to private spending, but they are spending money on research, commercialization, and investment incentives.

Most of those national strategies list multiple goals, such as creating an innovation-oriented economy, creating a national biotechnology industry, attracting foreign R&D, and developing human resources. A few countries, such as Thailand, have more focused strategies with more narrow priorities. Hong Kong lists the goal of creating an export-oriented biotech industry through FDI; homegrown biotech is a "secondary concern."

In 2007, public spending on biotech research of just three Asian emerging economies—China, South Korea, and Singapore—easily exceeded 10% of all such spending by all developed economies.[32] Additionally, the expected expenditures by India and recent commitments made by other big emerging economies such as Brazil mean that the biotech research spending challenge by emerging economies will likely become much more substantial in the next five years.[33] Of the approximately 460 international biotech agreements concluded between 2005 and 2008 (involving R&D, technology transfer manufacturing, marketing, and distribution), 46 were with emerging economies. The vast majority of these agreements were with India (19) and China (14). Before 2005, such deals were rare, but now they are expected to accelerate quickly, as we will see in later chapters.

To succeed in the race toward highly effective national innovation systems, governments need to learn the lessons from both failed and successful development strategies. Countries must continually improve policies. Innovation policy design is a most challenging task—even more difficult, as one observer remarked, than finding the most effective healthcare system.

The Pitfalls of Public Programs and the Crucial Role of Entrepreneurship

Innovation is a risky and expensive game, especially in novel areas such as nano- or biotechnology. Failure is common, and success can be elusive even when advanced infrastructures are in place and resources are plentiful. Both the American and European biotechnology industries have been operating at a net loss for a long time (global biotech losses were $2.7 billion in 2007, versus $7.4 billion in 2006). The U.S. publicly traded biotech industry in 2007 came close to aggregate profitability and was profitable in 2008. Many smaller private biotech companies fared less well.[34] Any country that embarks on a program of bioindustry development should keep in mind that biotech is a long-term proposition in return on investment. Only a few countries, such as Australia and Switzerland, have had profitable biotech sectors.[35] Other sectors, such as medical devices, are also risky, but developing profitable companies is easier and usually takes less time than in the case of biopharma. That said, biotechnology sectors in many emerging economies are different from the model of pure R&D companies prevalent in developed countries. Many biotechnology companies in emerging economies have viable revenue streams because they sell products and services. Discovery and testing tend to be only a part of their business model.

Despite these dim prospects for quick profitability, the Asian governments seem determined to make the necessary investments to create life sciences industry capabilities. However, a number of authors have expressed concerns about the wisdom of national "catch-up" policies for rapid biotechnology development in countries such as Singapore, Taiwan, Brazil, and South Korea.[36] The common thread of those criticisms is that massive public spending on biotechnology without strong private-sector participation may lead to wasteful failures, as has happened in some European countries.

The emerging economies that are pursuing effective national innovation systems can take advantage of the lessons learned from developed nations and can incorporate international best practices such as tax deductions for R&D, innovation consortia, SME networks, and technology transfer offices in universities, among many others. At the same time, few nations have made the successful journey from developing nation to a successful knowledge-economy nation. In this sense, plenty of uncharted territory lies ahead.

Getting innovation policies right is a huge challenge that requires time, determination, resources, knowledge, and the ability to learn from the best experiences and practices of world leaders. Even when the policies and institutions have been well designed and are in place, they need to be well managed, coordinated, and periodically evaluated for progress.

Typical deficiencies or challenges that can impede progress include these:

- Limited policy coordination among government departments responsible for innovation
- Policies that are mission oriented rather than innovation diffusion oriented
- Weak links between universities and business
- Weak academic entrepreneurship that would lead to commercialization of inventions
- Few highly innovative private-sector companies
- Difficulties for companies, especially small ones, in accessing credit and financing for science-based ventures
- Shortages of key talent and its loss to developed countries
- Limited capabilities to conduct world-class basic research

In his thought-provoking book *Boulevard of Broken Dreams*,[37] Josh Lerner, a professor at Harvard Business School, lists the many ways government programs in support of high technology and entrepreneurship can go wrong, from bad design to mistakes in implementation.[38] Typical design flaws include timing, sizing, and lack of flexibility. Governments of developed nations repeatedly make the mistake of committing to programs that are too short term to succeed. In addition, programs that are too small may not make a difference, and ones that are too large may exclude private funding. The key seems to be flexibility in the willingness of policymakers to learn from mistakes and make needed modifications. Typical mistakes of implementation include lack of evaluation, especially for incentive schemes. Finally, programs should be based on best international practices and should take into account international effects.

The only emerging economy (other than possibly Singapore and, to some degree, South Korea) that has created a truly innovation-based, high-tech economy, virtually from scratch, is Israel. What makes Israel especially successful is something else that is much harder to replicate. Other countries may be larger and have more resources or better infrastructure, but they lack Israel's innovative intellectual culture based on a thousand-year tradition of intellectual curiosity and traditions of adapting to difficult circumstances. This tradition is reinforced by a unique drive toward entrepreneurship that neither South Korea nor Singapore has to the same degree. As Singapore's founding father, Lee Kuan Yew, put it, "We need many new tries, many start-ups."[39] This comment highlights the truth that, without vigorous private sector entrepreneurship, even the best public policies will not succeed. When start-ups succeed and grow, they will gradually create conditions in which the efforts of the private sector can take over the lead role in financing R&D. This outcome needs to be the guiding principle for ambitious emerging economy policymakers, but achieving it is not easy.

Lessons from National Policies in the West: Finding the Exquisite Balance of R&D Funding Among Public, Private, and International Sectors

As economists ponder the growth of technology-based industries, they ask these questions: What are the relative roles of public and private sectors in creating new industries? What kinds of public efforts actually work? What inevitably wastes taxpayers' money?

Of the emerging economies analyzed so far, only South Korea and Singapore have reached the stage of mature innovation support—that is more than 50% of R&D funding comes from private industry. Taiwan is nearing that threshold, but China, India, Brazil, and most other emerging economies still operate with mostly government expenditure. These countries are trying to change the proportions as they learn from the lessons of more developed nations.

The experiences of Europe and America with developing knowledge-based industries differ from each other in some important respects. Japan differs from both. America, the world leader in high technology, is often regarded as *the* country, which achieved that by relying on the private sector. This is not entirely true. Public funding also played a role, as the history of the biotechnology industry shows. The United States has been a clear leader since the emergence of the field, but contrary to many people's notions, this American success was made possible by sustained federal spending on research in basic science. Private-sector spending followed only later and eventually superseded public spending. Only since the 1980s has private industry spending on R&D exceeded federal expenditures related to biotechnology. Currently, private-sector spending constitutes more than 65% of all R&D spending.[40]

Europe has an academic potential similar to that of the United States and has been spending significant public funds trying to develop high-technology industries. The E.U. Lisbon Strategy specifically creates a vision of a high-tech Europe that could compete with the United States. So far, however, Europe has failed to match the United States in terms of innovation and commercialization of inventions.[41] Many other countries outside the E.U. have made similar, repeated attempts to emulate American success in creating high-tech clusters and developing new industries such as biotechnology.

European universities tend to be distant from business, so the transfer of knowledge from academia to industry is difficult. European academics are less entrepreneurial than their European colleagues, and financing for start-ups is difficult to obtain. Universities in emerging economies, often modeled on the European tradition, suffer from similar deficiencies.

Without sufficient venture capital, public funding has been filling in to support technology start-ups in Europe. For example, most biotech ventures in Germany have benefited from public financing. This public support resulted from an attempt to compensate for the much lower levels of risk taking in many E.U. countries and a shortage of start-up entrepreneurship when compared with leaders such as the United States or Israel.

Japan has achieved impressive results by absorbing foreign technology and becoming one of the world's leaders in innovation and design. Japan has secured a top position in innovation performance as measured by patents per million inhabitants. The Japanese system relies on the R&D and innovation capabilities of corporations. Its universities have played a less important role than in the United States or Europe. Government spending on key new technologies of the future has been an important catalyst, but private industry leads the nation's R&D effort, with a share of 77% of R&D spending, the highest ratio in the world. Developing these remarkable capabilities to generate innovation inside companies is an achievement of Japanese management. The Japanese system of corporate-based innovation has, to some degree, been emulated by leading South Korean companies, but it is regarded as deeply rooted in Japanese culture and society. The more open U.S. system, based on individual entrepreneurship, is still the role model for the rest of the world.

To successfully promote innovation, emerging economies need to devise carefully thought-out strategies that will avoid waste and balance the roles of public and private sectors. The challenge for emerging economies to catch up with the United States is, in some ways, harder than the catch-up challenge for Europe, as emerging nations lag behind developed countries in education and science. The leading emerging economies are showing a greater determination than some of the Europeans to muster the needed resources. As we noted in the previous chapter, Asia today spends more on R&D than Europe and will likely be able to spend even more in the future as post-crisis developed economies fall behind the emerging Asian economies in rates of GDP growth. Private investment in R&D by national companies will be important, but that is not the whole story.

The recent rise of global R&D opens up another crucial source of funding for emerging economies through international investments and collaborations. Funding from abroad already plays an important role in the total R&D spending of such developed economies as the United Kingdom (21%), Austria (17%), and Denmark (13%). Emerging economies are taking advantage of this trend, with South Africa financing 23% of its R&D from abroad; Mexico (13%), Hungary (11%), and Poland (7%) are following suit.[42]

As the new players learn from each other and improve their policies, the emerging system of globally interdependent innovation will have an impact on national capabilities. Global R&D investments and partnerships will accelerate needed reforms of science and education and help compensate for national weaknesses. Emerging economies will find many ways to build innovation systems. The expanding world of global R&D offers many different opportunities for business to find profitable niches for partnering or outsourced services and manufacturing.

The future world innovation system should never be viewed as a zero-sum game, but rather as a win–win opportunity for those with international competitive advantages. The size of a country's market can act as an important factor in attracting international investment and R&D collaboration, but market size alone is not sufficient. International companies look for a combination of market potential and innovation capabilities when deciding where to establish a new R&D center or whether to partner with a local company. In the next chapter, we evaluate the new players from this perspective.

3

A Reshuffling of Markets and Growth Opportunities

The Brave New World of the Bioeconomy

In Chapter 1, "Power Shifts in Global R&D and Innovation," we noted that experts see the emergence of biology as the leading field of science in this century. The broad applications of discoveries in the fields that comprise the life sciences, especially in genetics and molecular biology, are creating the potential for a bioeconomy. Such an economy will include pervasive applications of life science discoveries in many industrial processes and commercial markets, from health to food and fuels. Several arguments promote the emergence of the bioeconomy.[1] The affluence of highly developed Western societies with their saturated consumption needs—together with aging populations living longer (half of the population born this decade is expected to live to 100 years)—will lead to an increasing demand for health services, better drugs, and treatments, and for higher-quality food, water, and environmental conditions. Similar trends will affect emerging economies, several of which, such as South Korea and China, are aging. As these nations grow wealthier, consumption of health services and medications will grow beyond the bare essentials, especially as the incidence of so-called life-style diseases increases with economic growth. All these developments will have profound effects on biopharma industries and markets globally.

Human health biotechnologies based on scientific advances must address these growing needs. Human health products likely to reach the market by 2015 include biopharmaceuticals, experimental therapies (such as cell and tissue engineering and gene therapy), small molecule therapeutics, diagnostics, bioinformatics (including gene sequencing and pharmacogenetics), functional foods and nutraceuticals, and various new medical devices.[2] We expect biotech industrial and agricultural applications and biofuels to grow in importance perhaps even more quickly.

The bioeconomy of the future depends on scientific discovery and on our ability to commercialize the resulting inventions. Although long-term forecasts tend to be speculative, the short-term ones are usually more reliable. The Organization for Economic Cooperation and Development (OECD) has made short-term predictions for the next five years; they document important trends and tell a compelling story.[3] The OECD predicts steadily growing usage of biopharmaceuticals. Not only will their share increase to around 15% in all pharmaceutical registrations, but their impact on public health will be even greater because biopharmaceutical drugs offer greater therapeutic value than traditional chemistry-based pharmaceuticals. By 2015, the large majority of small molecule drugs in development will likely depend on the use of biotechnology—for example, in the discovery phase, biotech can help improve target identification or the efficiency of clinical trials. If you add to that experimental therapies—such as cell and tissue engineering, gene therapies, and synthetic biology—the vast importance of biotech as a key technology becomes apparent. Thanks to the rise of bioinformatics, the variety of information stored in large genetic databases will greatly expand—following the declining cost of genome sequencing. After 2015, more widespread use of pharmacogenetics to identify respondent groups in clinical trials will likely occur, changing prescribing practice and creating a shift to personalized medicine. The potential for healthcare improvement is enormous by *preventing* illnesses from occurring instead of just *treating* debilitating diseases.

The impact of these developments on the different life science business systems will be profound and will change both public policy and business practice. One of the reasons this book places so much emphasis on biotechnology is that, although the biotech industry is still relatively small, it will increasingly underpin and drive developments in many of the industries related to health, nutrition, the environment, fuels, and so on. Having a strong biotechnology sector is important to a nation's future if it wants to be a player in the global bioeconomy instead of just a consumer. Twenty-five countries have one or more biopharmaceutical molecular entities in clinical trials. Of those, 18 are OECD economies and 7 are not. The most important emerging economy players include China, South Korea, and Cuba, all of which have received market approval for biopharmaceutical drugs in the past 20 years. Looking forward, among countries with biotech drug candidates in clinical trials, we additionally see Brazil, India, and the Russian Federation, with South Korea and China leading the pack in terms of number of drugs.[4] China claims to have commercialized 30 biotech drugs, with 150 more in the pipeline. By 2012, the country plans to develop 40 new Class 1 innovative biopharmaceuticals.[5]

Pharmaceutical Markets in Turmoil: Crisis and Opportunity

Having acknowledged the crucial role of biotechnology for the future, the chemistry-based pharmaceutical (small molecule) markets still dominate today. Biotechnology, which is currently approximately a $100 billion industry, is smaller than the medical device market. Medical devices account for less than half of the traditional pharmaceuticals market, which is worth more than $700 billion.

In 2005, the U.S. pharmaceuticals market was the largest in the world, at $250 billion, followed by Japan, at $68 billion. France and Germany each had markets worth more than $30 billion, followed by Italy, the United Kingdom, Spain, and Canada, with markets less than $20 billion each. In 2005, China was only the ninth market in the world, at $13 billion, followed by Mexico, Brazil, South Korea, Turkey, and India, with markets of less than $10 billion.[6] This market landscape is changing, however, with a lot of growth occurring in emerging economies. Citing one of the more conservative forecasts, pharmaceuticals markets will look very different by 2015. China will become the third largest in the world and worth at least $40 billion, with India, Brazil, and Mexico advancing to the top ten with markets of approximately $20 billion each.[7] Between 2005 and 2015, the markets in China and India are expected to triple in size and will likely continue to grow rapidly after that. Rapid growth in Asian emerging economies will compensate for modest market growth in developed European economies.[8] In 2009, the pharma market in the United States was estimated to have actually declined slightly, and markets in Europe grew slowly, at only 1%–3%. However, emerging market growth was estimated at 10%–15%, and the China market alone grew at an astonishing rate of more than 20%. More than half of the growth in the entire sector came from the seven so-called "pharmerging" markets.[9]

From the industry's viewpoint, ways of making money by selling drugs have been changing and will continue to change dramatically in the coming years. Market turbulence is affecting both developed and emerging economies, and it's more complex than the cited higher market growth rates in the emerging economies. For several decades, the "big pharma" industry has been very privileged. It was a fast-growing sector generating high margins and favored by financial markets with high valuations. The business model was based on innovation and the development of new, patented "blockbuster" chemical drugs. This business model is under great pressure today and is quickly becoming obsolete. Today the industry is in crisis. Companies are having a difficult time renewing their product portfolios, just when many blockbuster drugs are losing patent protection—enabling generic producers to take away their market share.

In Chapter 4, "Improving R&D Productivity," we discuss the R&D productivity crisis in the drug industry and explore some of its deeper causes. New drug approvals have not kept pace with steeply rising R&D expenditures, and the number of product launches has not seen adequate growth. Customers, many of whom are aging, are pressuring governments to regulate prices, especially in Europe. As patent expiration often comes before product obsolescence, pharmas have been battling a number of related unfavorable trends: a decrease in the time it takes for competition to proliferate and the rapid growth of generics producers. Public agencies are setting higher standards for clinical trials, which increases the time to market, in spite of real improvements in the efficiency of the drug-development process. New products are making lower profit contributions because of increased scrutiny of their value from doctors and healthcare providers. The global pharmaceutical industry is experiencing a downturn in growth, to around 6% a year. These developments have resulted in significant revaluations of the market capitalization of major pharmaceutical companies. As noted earlier, the market cap for top-tier pharmaceutical firms has dropped by more than $700 billion in the past eight years.[10] For example, Pfizer was valued at $287 billion on January 1, 2001, and it dropped to $92 billion eight years later. Merck fell from $213 billion to $56 billion during that period. In the last five years, the top five pharma companies have lost 20% of their market capital, while biotechs have appreciated 18%, even under the recent harsh conditions of financial markets. The leading biotech company, Genentech, was worth $100 billion in 2009—more than Pfizer.[11] The rise of biotech drugs is an opportunity for big pharma, which has been merging with or acquiring biotech companies. Roche's merger with Genentech is a well-known example.

To continue to prosper, the pharmaceutical industry must make many difficult changes in its business models. What makes the challenge unique is that the industry is simultaneously facing changes driven by diverse forces, including new technologies, aging populations, new government policies, capital markets, and market diversification. It is a stupendous challenge that is forcing the industry to rethink market growth priorities.

Among the different ways that businesses can diversify, geographical market diversification is considered among the hardest to perform. In the case of the biopharmaceutical industry, accelerating growth is occurring precisely in the less familiar and culturally distant countries. In 2001, the three top markets of the United States, Europe, and Japan accounted for almost two-thirds of the growth in the world market for drugs; by 2007, that number had slipped to less than half. Emerging markets advanced from 8% to 25%. By 2011, more change will occur. Although the United States and Europe will still be the largest regions in dollar terms (38% and 29% of market share, respectively), the group of top emerging markets will have leap-frogged Japan to third place, with more than 15% of market share, leaving Japan with 10% and the rest of the world with just 5%.[12] By 2020, annual pharmaceutical sales in emerging markets are expected to reach $400 billion—that is nearly the level of current sales in the United States and the top five European markets combined.

The fastest-growing emerging pharmaceutical markets—known as "pharmerging markets" or the "emerging seven"—are China, India, Brazil, Mexico, Russia, Turkey, and South Korea (some observers add Indonesia), which together will account for nearly half of the world population by 2012. This group of markets is expected to grow more than 11.5% and reach revenues of $116 billion by 2012, in contrast to a growth rate of less than 5% for the top seven developed world markets.[13] Although the emerging markets share fast growth, they are also quite different from each other. For example, India, China, Russia, and Indonesia are dominated by generics, which have lower penetration rates in Brazil, Mexico, and Turkey. Fast growth depends on levels of government support, which seems strongest in China and Russia. Based on a variety of forecasts, we can estimate that, until 2015, China will grow at a rate of more than 20%, Russia at 14%–20%, Turkey and India at 8%–14%, Brazil and South Korea at 7%–10%, and Mexico at 4%–7%.[14]

Because of fast economic growth, healthcare systems in leading emerging economies will increasingly be able to afford paying for drugs. With urbanization and changing life-styles, the demand for drugs curing "Western diseases," such as diabetes, will increase. In the medium term, however, the emerging markets will demand "essential medicines" (acute therapies) that the industry regards as "older drugs," which have been losing sales in developed economies to so-called chronic therapies. As the rapidly growing countries change and develop, so will the therapy mix demanded by the market— requiring different approaches to marketing, distribution, and even R&D priorities. Not least among the challenges is pricing. Expanding markets and increasing access to medicines in less wealthy economies mean differential pricing strategies between countries. For example, GlaxoSmithKline (GSK) has already moved in the direction of a dual market among the rich and poor for some categories of medicines. Other companies are following similar approaches.

The Medical Device Markets: Steady Growth

A medical device is a product that is used for medical purposes in patients, such as for diagnosis, therapy, or surgery. The effect of a medical device is physical, as opposed to biochemical effect in the case of drugs. Leading segments of medical devices include cardiovascular, general surgery, imaging, in vitro diagnostics, ophthalmology, orthopedics, neurology, urology, and respiratory applications.

The United States dominates the world medical device market. In 2008, the global medical device industry was estimated at around

$210 billion to $220 billion; of this, the United States accounted for $97.9 billion, Europe for $67.5 billion, and Asia for nearly $40 billion. Africa and the Middle East accounted for $5.5 billion. The United States leads in per-capita expenditure on medical devices and is also the home of some of the leading companies in the business, such as Johnson & Johnson, GE, Medtronic, Thermo Fisher, and Boston Scientific. Seven of the world's top ten device makers are U.S. companies. Global medical device giants outside the United States include Germany's Siemens, Holland's Philips, and Japan's Toshiba. Together those companies have a dominating market position in global markets. The U.S. market for medical devices has seen steady growth of about 6.5% between 2002 and 2007. It has slowed some in 2008–2009 but is expected to continue growing and break the $100 billion barrier by 2012.[15] The E.U. market has also seen solid growth, advancing from $50 billion in 2007 to $59 billion by 2009. In the same period, China grew from $11.2 billion to $14.3 billion, and India doubled its market, from $2 billion to $4 billion.[16]

The medical device industry shares some characteristics with the pharmaceutical industry. It is heavily dependent on expensive research and is highly regulated. It also has seen good financial performance. However, it is regarded as less risky than biotechnology. Although international competition is on the rise, local manufacturers often service national markets. Because many medical devices, such as magnetic resonance or X-ray equipment, are expensive, buyers from emerging economies cannot afford state-of-the-art machinery, so they look for less costly solutions, including used equipment or locally made products. For example, China had more than 12,000 registered manufacturers of medical devices in 2007, and the country has been making efforts to develop a strong medical device industry by investing in a specialized industrial park in Beijing dedicated to medical systems. However, the majority of medical devices used in Chinese hospitals need to be replaced with more modern equipment. Imported products were more than 85% of the Chinese medical device market in 2002. China represents a major market opportunity, with double-digit growth and a device market set to reach $20 billion by 2012.[17] But demand is likely to be concentrated on more affordable products.

Although per-capita expenditures in Brazil are still low, the country has the largest medical device market in Latin America. GE Healthcare has decided to install a manufacturing plant there—the first for the company in South America.

South Korea, Taiwan, and Singapore all have successfully developed significant medical device industry segments, specializing in smaller devices such as powered mobility aids and blood pressure monitors (Taiwan), syringes, hearing aids, and contact lenses (Singapore). In 2006, Singapore's investment in production of medical devices reached approximately $1.5 billion and was mostly destined for export to Asia, the United States, and the European Union.[18] Malaysia has significant production of catheters and surgical gloves, supplying a significant portion of world demand for these products. The country plans to become one of Asia's hubs of medical device manufacturing and development. We discuss some of those smaller countries' growing capabilities later in this chapter.

The Challenges of Market Access— Entering and Staying in Emerging Markets

The new pharmerging markets represent considerable diversity. They have different levels of economic development and urbanization. Rapid urbanization can lead to overcrowding and inadequate hygiene, with significant impact on healthcare and disease profiles of the countries. For example, poor air quality increases the occurrence of respiratory diseases. Demographic and life-style changes can lead to a higher incidence of such illnesses as diabetes. According to the

World Health Organization (WHO), the total number of people with diabetes is expected to increase dramatically and at a much higher rate in India, compared to China, during the coming decades. Diseases that are rare in developed countries, such as tuberculosis, are a real danger in Southeast Asia and Africa, where crowded conditions make infection much more likely.

Profound differences are evident in national healthcare systems. For example, private health expenditure, as a percentage of total health expenditures, reaches a level of 75% or higher in such countries as India, Hong Kong, and Vietnam; reaches 60% in South Korea; and stays below 40% in Thailand and Indonesia.[19] Significant differences in the role of generic medicines also appear. Generics' share of the overall drug market exceeded 50% in China and Thailand, but it was less than 30% in countries such as Indonesia, the Philippines, and Taiwan. Generic drug pricing factors represent an even more complex picture. Generic substitution is mandatory in Taiwan, Indonesia, and India, but optional in Malaysia, Thailand, and South Korea. In the Philippines, generic substitution applies to the public sector only. Levels of generic discounts vary from 10% to 30% or more, depending on the policies of the national pricing agencies in the country.[20]

The profiles of major therapeutic segments also differ greatly. Cardiovascular drugs are more important in more developed countries such as Singapore, South Korea, and Taiwan, and less important in India and Indonesia, where antibiotics have higher shares.

The huge new markets in Asia tend to be dominated by the growth of local generic manufacturers who pursue high volume/low margin strategies. International pharmaceutical companies need to develop their own versions of such strategies, to develop and maintain a strong presence in those markets. Often this means cutting prices for some drugs in developing countries—which Pfizer and Sanofi-Aventis have already done. Multinationals are setting up special units for joint ventures, marketing, and supply chain management in emerging markets. For example, Merck has assigned a senior executive for emerging markets whose responsibilities include prescriptions, vaccines, and biologics drugs, and an emerging markets group that will cover China, Asia Pacific, Latin America, Middle East, Africa, and Eastern Europe, including Russia and Turkey. Pfizer has expanded its presence in the generics market, with a deal to license 75 products from two Indian drug makers. The company has acquired rights to products from Claris Lifesciences and Aurobindo Pharma. Pfizer will commercialize the branded generics according to the specific needs of different regions. China, India, Brazil, Russia, Turkey, and Mexico are seen as key priority markets.[21]

Not all pharmaceutical companies have taken advantage of the new markets. Some companies may be slower than others to introduce new drugs to the emerging markets. IMS Health claims that, of the new chemical entities (NCE), only one-third have reached the seven pharmerging countries.[22] Without strong local adaptability, success is hard to achieve in the emerging markets. To succeed, companies need a sophisticated understanding of the healthcare systems, including pricing and reimbursement systems, in the countries. These systems can be very different, such as in China compared with Latin America or the new E.U. states of Central Europe that are obliged to follow European Union regulations. The regulatory and pricing environment is particularly volatile in Russia, with the government acting to impose new maximum sales prices. The challenges of succeeding in the pharmerging markets are formidable, which we will see in looking at three of the biggest markets—China, India, and South Korea.

China, India, and South Korea—The Three Key Markets in Emerging Asia

Emerging Asia includes the most important group of future biopharma markets. Most prominent are the two giants, China and India. However, Asia is also home to some other populous nations, including a number of quickly growing and relatively big pharmaceutical markets, such as Indonesia, the Philippines, Thailand, and Malaysia. Among the relatively more developed markets are the "Four Asian Tigers" of Taiwan, Hong Kong, South Korea, and Singapore. South Korea stands out not just as a big market, but also as a new, technologically advanced player in the life science business. In this section, we compare China, India, and South Korea as markets and industrial players. Each of these countries is important to the future of the global life science–based industry—but in a different way.

China: The Leading Pharmerging Market

The combination of China representing one-fifth of the human population, being an aging society, and having a rapidly growing economy makes it the most important and attractive of the pharmerging markets. Biao Chen, general manager of Sinopharma Group, a leading Chinese pharmaceutical company, predicts that, within a decade, the country will become the second-largest pharmaceuticals market in the world, after the United States. The most recent ranking of foreign direct investment (FDI) confidence places China as the world's most attractive destination, ahead of the United States.[23] China has dealt remarkably well with the recent global recession and has even increased healthcare spending as part of its economic stimulus package. Continuing rapid growth is expected in spite of the challenges ahead, such as a weak banking system, the large number of inefficient state companies, and lower demand for Chinese exports in the developed world. The growth of the Chinese economy has led to higher living standards and increased purchasing power. Household incomes have tripled since 1992. Awareness of new products, including pharmaceuticals, has greatly increased, as has interest in Western medicine.

China joined the World Trade Organization (WTO) in December 2001, and it has been making progress in meeting its WTO commitments. China's urban population is expected to continue to grow from the present 600 million to more than 800 million by 2025. China's middle class will grow with this expanding level of urbanization. According to some estimates, the number of households with annual disposable income exceeding $100,000 on purchasing power parity basis is expected to reach 100 million people by 2025, with another 100 million becoming "affluent."[24] Regardless of the accuracy of those forecasts, it is reasonable to expect that, by 2025, the majority of Chinese will be urban dwellers, and most of them are expected to join the middle class, with annual household incomes exceeding $20,000. The buying power of this vast population will be enormous, and this prospect is only 15 years away.

Traditional Chinese medicine (TCM) is still very important. In 2007, its sales revenue was $21 billion, representing approximately 40% of the pharmaceutical market.[25] The government regards this sector as a strategic growth opportunity. However, to accomplish this goal, the country needs to modernize the production of traditional medicines in compliance with good manufacturing practice (GMP). The Chinese plan to leverage strengths in traditional medicines and create a new export-driven industry. This objective is important for the country's balance of payments in biopharmaceuticals. Unlike India, China is a net importer of pharmaceuticals. By 2014, the value of pharmaceutical exports from China will reach an expected $4.6 billion, but imports will reach $17.2 billion, each growing at more than 30% in U.S. dollar terms.[26]

The size and structure of the future pharmaceutical market in China will depend upon the country's economic growth, the purchasing power of people in different regions of the country, and the success of the government's efforts to reform healthcare and control prices and costs. China spends about 5% of its gross domestic product (GDP) on healthcare, but the present Chinese market remains fragmented, with only some population segments able to afford world-class healthcare. Healthcare costs have been rising, especially in urban areas, restricting the public's ability to pay. A large segment of the Chinese population does not have easy access to affordable healthcare, particularly in rural areas. While many poor consumers have trouble affording basic healthcare services, the affluent consumers are unhappy with the frequent overcrowding of public hospitals and healthcare facilities. The government has responded by undertaking ambitious plans of reforming its healthcare system. The government wants to increase coverage of medical insurance to more than 90% of the population by 2011. The government will use centralized purchasing and distribution for the national essential drug list. The country will invest more in healthcare centers, to drive primary care patients away from hospitals; more hospitals also will be built in the countryside. Public hospitals are undergoing reform.[27] China has about 2,000 private hospitals, many of which cater to overseas nationals. Although the private hospital sector is growing, it represents less than 5% of the healthcare market.[28] China's one-child policy is now resulting in an aging population. In 2000, only 10% of China's population was classified as elderly; by 2050, this group will make up nearly one-third of the population. Population aging will add to the demand for healthcare and will be another factor in the government's efforts to expand access to healthcare services. The biopharmaceutical industry has to incorporate such trends if it wants to succeed in the Chinese market. It should also have a good understanding of the structure and capability of the Chinese domestic biopharma industry.

China is projected to be among the five largest markets for pharma in 2015, with a market size of approximately $40 billion.[29] Some estimates project a much higher figure. The sector has seen continuous growth in the last decade, with sales increasing by almost four times between 1999 and 2006.

China has approximately 3,500 pharmaceutical manufacturers, most of which are wholly state-owned or joint ventures. The private sector has not been involved enough. A major problem of the industry has been overcapacity of cheap, basic drug production; low profit margins; and, therefore, a low level of reinvestment in the sector. Hospitals account for almost 80% of the market. For the next decade, generics are expected to account for 95% of production and 70% of market value. Weak patent laws result in a vast market of "unauthorized generics."[30] In 2007, the Chinese Food and Drug Administration (CFDA) found 329,613 cases of unlicensed drugs. Unsurprisingly, consumers have concerns about the quality of Chinese pharmaceutical drugs—which presents a market opportunity for Western branded medicines. "Nowadays, Chinese people don't trust Chinese medications," Huang Jianshi, the assistant president of the Chinese Academy of Medical Sciences, told Reuters. "They trust Western brands more, as they have a better reputation."[31]

The Chinese biopharmaceutical industry is composed of medium and small biochemical companies, large-scale microbiological firms, and modern biotechnology-based companies. Products include crude drugs, such as medical plants, and biochemical and biological products. Leading Chinese biopharma companies are capable of producing more than 30 biotechnology drugs, including interferon, monoclonal antibody products, interleukin, recombinant vaccines, enzymatic preparations, and others. More than 100 products are under research and development, and more than half of those have independent intellectual property (IP) rights. Chinese biotech enterprises represent a variety of ownership forms, including state ownership, collective and cooperative ownership, joint stock, and private. Overseas-funded and joint venture enterprises appear to be the most successful, followed by private and joint stock companies.[32] Chinese biotechs compete ferociously with each other. They are also able to take advantage of the accumulated knowledge developed in the West, to buy the most modern biotechnology tools available on the market, and to exploit the low local costs.

The Chinese pharma industry has been actively applying for drug master files with the U.S. Food and Drug Administration in support of active pharmaceutical ingredients (API) manufacturing. However, the overall level of manufacturing practice is still short of meeting GMP standards. Given the rapidly growing market and the ambitions and structure of the Chinese biopharmaceutical industry, opportunities for profitable collaboration with international companies abound and cover the full range of the value chain—from discovery, to product development, to clinical trials, and to manufacturing, marketing, and commercialization. Leading international companies—such as Pfizer, Astra Zeneca, Novartis, Lilly, Roche, and others, including smaller firms—have been expanding their presence in China. This expansion is moving beyond manufacturing, sales, and marketing activities to clinical trials, contract research, and new drug development based on the installment of brand new R&D centers located in leading Chinese bioparks, such as Shanghai's Zhangjiang. As has happened in other sectors, future Chinese success in biopharma depends on productive collaboration with the West, with resulting opportunities for all. Not only cheaply produced generics, but also patented, second-generation biotech products developed in China are among the many exciting prospects. We look at those ventures in more detail in later chapters.

India: A Future Export Powerhouse of Pharmaceutical Products

In 2005, India was a relatively insignificant pharmaceutical market—less than half the size of China, and behind smaller countries such as Mexico, Brazil, South Korea, and Turkey. By 2015, with strong growth of more than 8% a year, India's position will advance to the level of around 20 billion euros (or $26 billion)—the second-most significant pharmerging market and among the top ten national markets in the world.[33]

The healthcare sector, including hospitals and associated sectors, in India is also poised for rapid expansion. Comparable to other emerging economies, such as China, Brazil, and Mexico, the sector has seen a growth rate of 9.3% from 2000 to 2009. However, according to the Yes Bank and ASSOCHAM report, the healthcare industry is projected to grow 23% annually, from the estimated size of $35 billion in 2010 to $77 billion in 2012.[34]

Unlike in China, government involvement in healthcare in India is low. In 2005, the public sector accounted for just 1% of GDP and the private sector contributed an additional 4% of GDP to healthcare.[35] Without greater government involvement, many needs will remain unmet.[36] As a result, diseases that have declined in other developing countries are still common in India. Government spending on healthcare declined from 25% to approximately 20% of the country's total healthcare expenditure by 2007, and the annual per-capita government spending in India is well below the minimum needed for essential healthcare, even for a developing country.[37] The problem is compounded by inequalities in access to healthcare based on region, class, caste, and gender, and by inefficient use of resources, including at public hospitals.[38] The proportion of infants reaching their first birthday who were fully immunized is slightly less than 50%. Today about 70% of Indians depend on traditional Indian medicine, to varying degrees, which is cheaper than Western drugs and easily available.

Healthcare in India serves its population through a number of different service channels. Representing 19% of all healthcare expenditures, the public sector is free to everyone and is frequented by less well-off citizens.[39] A subsidized nongovernmental organization (NGO) sector also exists, which charges copayments and is open to people who at least have some regular income. As the government sector has been shrinking, the private for-profit healthcare sector has been growing, especially in the urban areas. It offers world-class service and facilities to the higher-income population. At the time of independence, this private sector was responsible for only 5%–10% of patient care. By 2005, the private sector represented a majority of all healthcare expenditures, at 81%.[40]

The strong economic growth of India, which is expected to be 6%–7% annually during the next 15 years, means rising household incomes. Such consistent growth will broaden the Indian middle class that is able to afford world-class healthcare. An estimated 60 million middle-class Indians currently can afford Western-produced drugs. That number is projected to rise 12% annually through 2025, according to McKinsey estimates. During a period of ten years, a four-member middle-class family has seen spending on pharmaceuticals grow fourfold, to more than $250 annually.[41] Middle-class Indians increasingly have begun to buy healthcare insurance. All these developments make the Indian market an attractive prospect in the medium and long term.

Until the 1970s, India's market was supplied by large international companies, with the domestic sector composed of state-owned companies without the capabilities needed to produce sophisticated drugs. National policy at the time was aimed at reducing the country's dependence on imports with high tariffs and a patent regime that favored national companies. Indian drug companies copied original medicines developed by foreign firms and were able to make generics using alternative production methods. India thus saved on R&D costs while enabling large and efficient generic producers to emerge. A private-sector national pharmaceutical industry developed, and Indian companies became very competitive as generic producers and exporters. Since the late 1980s, India, unlike China, has been a net exporter of pharmaceuticals. India's domestic pharmaceutical industry, unlike China's, is in the private sector, and it has been growing faster than the global average and gaining strength. It has not only survived, but also profited from the 2005 Patent Amendment Bill and the government's signing of the Trade-Related Aspects of Intellectual Property Rights (TRIPS) agreement. Indian companies are no longer able to simply copy drugs with foreign patents to sell on the domestic market. They have to pay licensing fees, produce under contract for international firms, and start developing their own original drugs. They are also increasingly engaged in contract research and development. All these forces are propelling them to become internationally competitive players.

India's pharmaceutical industry currently includes about 20,000 licensed companies, employing approximately half a million people. With the industry's growth rate approaching 10% a year, some observers expect employment in the sector to reach one million within a few years. India has become a powerhouse of generic drug manufacturing, commanding approximately 20% of the world market, and is expected to grow to approximately 30%.[42] India's pharma sector has become technologically strong and has low costs of production, low R&D costs, plentiful scientific and technical manpower, and an infrastructure of national laboratories and many world-class hospitals. It is also diversifying away from making generics. Today Indian pharmaceutical companies make a broad range of drugs, from complex antibiotics and cardiac compounds to biotech drugs. Overall, India produces more than 70,000 different drugs, which is more than Germany.[43] According to a McKinsey report, the pharma sector's growth in India will make it the "third-largest growth opportunity," after the United States and China, by 2015.[44]

The most important segments of the domestic market are anti-infectives, followed by cardiovascular drugs, cold remedies, and pain killers. Medicines against so-called civilizational diseases and life-style drugs are currently less important. Although some new lifesaving drugs under patent formulations are imported, often by the multinational companies, India is largely self-sufficient for formulations. More than 60% of the bulk drug production is exported. Bulk drug production constitutes slightly less than half of exports, with the balance made up by formulations. The pharmaceutical export sector is an ongoing success story, with the vast majority of the drugs sold to the United States and Europe. During the last decade, the export surplus has increased nearly seven times, and exports continue to grow vigorously.[45]

India has perhaps the strongest biopharmaceutical industry among the developing countries. The country is on track to develop competitive positions in a number of strategic areas beyond generics, such as contract manufacturing and contract research, vaccines, and biogenerics. Today India has the greatest number of U.S. FDA-approved plants outside the United States, and Indian companies are the largest submitters of drug master files (DMF) outside the United States. India has three times as many DMFs as China, seven times as many as Italy, and more than ten times as many as Germany.[46] All these advantages have made the country the preferred destination for outsourced manufacturing of pharmaceuticals.

Building a manufacturing plant in India is about 40% cheaper than in Europe. Sandoz, the generics arm of Novartis, has three plants in India. Total contract production worldwide for pharma is expected to rise to 40 billion euros by 2010.[47]

Indian companies are also able to provide FDA-approved facilities for the complete range of services for drug development. The country has the second-largest number of medical professionals in the world, making it an attractive destination for clinical trials and healthcare tourism.

India is also fast becoming an R&D hub. By 2006, the country accounted for a major share in the world's pharma contract research business. India's share was larger than Italy's and was actually ahead of China's. The market for clinical trials in India by 2006 was estimated at 600 million euros.[48] These numbers are increasing quickly because the leading multinationals are making India their manufacturing hub. By 2010, the market for contract research in India could reach 2 billion euro, and the total world market for contract research is likely to rise from 8 billion euros in 2008 to 20 billion euros by 2020.[49]

Glenmark Pharmaceutical S.A. India

In May 2010, Sanofi-Aventis signed a license agreement with Glenmark Pharmaceuticals S.A. to develop and commercialize novel agents in India for the treatment of chronic pain.

Glenmark is a leading player in the discovery of new molecules, both new chemical entities (NCEs) and new biological entities (NBEs), with eight molecules in various stages of clinical development. The company has a significant presence in branded generics markets across emerging economies, including India. Its subsidiary, Glenmark Generics Limited, has a fast-growing and robust U.S. generics business. The subsidiary also markets APIs to regulated and semiregulated countries. Glenmark employs nearly 6,000 people in more than 80 countries. It has 12 manufacturing facilities in 4 countries and has 5 R&D centers.

Glenmark was chosen as the "Best Pharma Company in the World—SME" and "Best Company Across Emerging Markets" for 2008 by *SCRIP,* the largest selling and most respected pharmaceutical magazine in the world. *Forbes,* another leading international publication, recognized Glenmark as the "Best under a Billion-Dollar Companies in Asia" for 2008.

Glenmark's formulations business is currently organized around four regions—India, Latin America, Central Eastern Europe, and semiregulated markets of Africa/Asia/CIS. The formulations business focuses on therapeutic areas such as dermatology, anti-infectives, respiratory, cardiac, diabetes, gynecology, central nervous system, and oncology. India is the largest market in terms of revenue for the organization. The formulations business has five manufacturing facilities—three in India and two overseas. These facilities are approved by several regulatory bodies. The facility at Baddi, Himachal Pradesh, India, is also approved by the Medicines and Healthcare Products Regulatory Agency (MHRA) and the U.S. FDA for semisolids. The overseas facilities are situated in Brazil and the Czech Republic. The manufacturing facility in Brazil services requirements of the Latin American region, and the Czech facility services requirements of the Central Eastern Europe region. Glenmark has also invested in a dedicated R&D facility for formulations development. This R&D center, located near Nashik, India, is engaged in developing specialty and branded formulations for global markets.

Source: Glenmark website: www.glenmark.com. Sanofi-Aventis half-year 2010 report, 23; available at www.sanofi-aventis.com.

The Indian biotech sector has been gaining investor confidence since 2006. Similar to the Chinese market, the Indian biotechnology market is growing rapidly. The Indian biotechnology industry is expected to grow at a compound annual growth rate (CAGR) of 20%, to achieve a market size of $8 billion by 2015.[50]

The sector has experienced growth rates ranging from 35% to 40% during the last three years.[51] In 2008, biopharma's share of the Indian biotechnology sector rose to 75%, with revenues of around $799 million.[52] The bioagriculture sector grew at a rate of 50% in 2006–2007, the largest globally.[53] Because agriculture contributes 24.1% to the GDP of the country, bioagriculture is set to grow even further, bringing in more revenues.[54]

Biogenerics represent a high-growth sector in India, and the government is helping the industry seize this opportunity by providing tax incentives and streamlining drug application and review procedures. India already produces recombinant insulin, granulocyte colony-stimulating factor (GCSF), interferon alpha erythropoietin, monoclonal antibodies, and recombinant vaccines. Many of these products are close to losing their patent protections. The Indian biotech industry has been investing heavily in world-class facilities. Indian biomanufacturers—including Reliance Life Sciences, Wockhardt, Biocon, and others—have been improving their facilities and are seeking approval from the European Medicines Agency (EMEA) to make biogenerics for export to the European market with attractively priced products.

Indian pharmaceutical companies are increasing their investment abroad and are expanding their operations. Ranbaxy (described in the next sidebar) exports its products to 125 countries and has subsidiaries in 50 countries and production plants in 10 countries. More than 80% of the company's sales are generated abroad. Other examples include Wockhardt, which is operating in Germany and the United Kingdom, and Cadila, which is active in France. In 2006, Dr. Reddy's bought Betapharm, a German generics manufacturer for 500 million euros.[55]

Ranbaxy

Ranbaxy is one of India's leading multinational pharmaceutical companies. It makes generics and APIs, but also performs R&D for original proprietary drugs. Ranbaxy was incorporated in 1961 and went public in 1973. The company has a presence in 23 of the top 25 pharmaceutical markets in the world. It has a global footprint in 46 countries, has world-class manufacturing facilities in 7 countries, and serves customers in more than 125 countries. More than half of its sales come from the United States and Europe. Ranbaxy is considered one of the leaders in the generics business, where it innovates new drug combinations (multiple treatments). Through a growing network of partnerships and acquisitions, Ranbaxy is expanding its business model to include new therapeutic areas and biosimilars. It is also expanding its R&D capabilities to develop original drugs in such areas as infectious diseases, oncology, urology, respiratory, and inflammatory diseases, and it has a number of drug candidates in various stages of testing. The company employs more than 1,400 R&D personnel in path-breaking research.

In June 2008, Ranbaxy entered into an alliance with one of the largest Japanese innovation companies, Daiichi Sankyo Company, Ltd., to create an innovation and generic pharmaceutical powerhouse. The combined entity in 2010 ranks among the top 20 pharmaceutical companies globally. The transformational deal will place Ranbaxy in a higher growth trajectory, and it will emerge stronger in terms of its global reach and its capabilities in drug development and manufacturing.

Ranbaxy has an ongoing partnership with GSK for drug development and preclinical studies, which was enhanced in 2007. It includes a joint team of scientists working together on targets in the respiratory-inflammation area. Ranbaxy performs toxicity, inhibition, and enzyme regulation studies. Ranbaxy has a risk-sharing agreement with Merck for drug development through phase II for antimicrobials, with milestone payments and royalty eligibility for the Indian company.

The company recorded global sales of $1.519 billion in 2009. It has a balanced mix of revenues from emerging and developed markets that contribute 54% and 39% respectively. In 2009, North America, Ranbaxy's largest market, had sales of $397 million, followed by Europe, with $269 million, and Asia, with $441 million.

Ranbaxy has world-class manufacturing facilities in seven countries: Ireland, India, Malaysia, Nigeria, Romania, South Africa, and the United States. Its overseas facilities are designed to cater to the requirements of the local regulatory bodies, and the Indian facilities meet the requirements of all International Regulatory Agencies (IRAs).

Source: www.ranbaxy.com.

China is still expected to remain the number-one pharmaceuticals market in Asia for years to come, thanks to its higher expected sales growth. However, India can become a highly successful global player in the industry if it succeeds in its strategic reorientation away from generics to original drugs and contract R&D.

South Korea: From Manufacturing Base to R&D Partner

South Korea is the 11th-largest global market for pharmaceutical products.[56] The country has one of the most developed pharmaceutical markets in Asia, accounting for about 1.24% of the country's GDP, compared with total healthcare spending of around 7.01% of GDP. In 2009, patented products accounted for $5.18 billion, generics stood at $3.31 billion, and over-the-counter (OTC) was at $1.97 billion.[57]

Because of the government's cost-cutting measures, South Korean market growth is expected to be modest compared with China's, but generic products are expected to gain some market share. Patented drugs are expected to continue posting steady revenue growth, arising from growing demand for chronic disease treatment from an aging population. Overall healthcare spending is therefore expected to expand significantly during the next five years, from $59 billion to $130 billion. Annual per-capita spending is expected to double by 2014, and the level of spending will be close to the OECD averages.[58] South Korea is a net importer of pharmaceuticals, and imports (which presently account for 60% of market share) are expected to grow faster than exports during the next five years. Because government reform has made imported drugs eligible for reimbursement, South Korea has become an attractive market for multinational pharma companies, especially from the United States. South Korean exports of biopharma products are primarily aimed at China and Japan, with the United States and Europe relatively less important.

In terms of healthcare, South Korea is very developed. It has a universal healthcare system with well-equipped hospitals and trained medical staff. The market for medical equipment and supplies in the country was estimated at $2.83 billion in 2008. The country accounts for a 1.4% share of the world market. The sector is growing at 7% annually, making it one of the largest and fastest-growing markets for medical devices and supplies.[59] It is expected to grow to $15 billion by 2010. The sector is clocking an annual growth rate of 10%, whereas the industry average is 6%.[60]

More than 2,000 companies are involved in the manufacture of drugs, quasidrugs, and cosmetics.[61] The government is aiming at strengthen their R&D efforts to reduce the industry's dependence on importing generic drugs. Drug discovery is a major element of this effort. Major international pharmaceutical companies have a strong presence in South Korea, including GSK and Sanofi-Aventis—which are among the top five producers in the country. Pfizer closed its manufacturing operation in Seoul, but the company says it will continue to invest in R&D in the country. Lilly has also closed its plants in the country and, like Merck, supplies the market by importing its drugs.

Since 2005, 12 new drugs have been developed domestically. The number of patents registered in the United States increased by 4.7 times from 1995 to 2005. The number of clinical trials has also increased, partly because several multinational companies chose to contract clinical trials to South Korea, to reduce costs. In the area of new drug development, the life sciences industry is focusing on anti-cancer drugs, stem cells, and cell therapy. This has resulted in several product approvals for new drugs.[62]

Some of the drug innovations during the last decade by South Korean life sciences companies include the following:[63]

- **SK Chemicals (1999)**—Sunpla, a third-generation anticancer drug
- **Daewoong Pharmaceuticals (2001)**—Easyef, treatment for diabetic foot ulcers
- **Choongwae (2001)**—Balofloxacin (Q-roxin), fluoroquinolone antibiotic
- **LG Life Sciences Ltd. (2003)**—Achieved new drug approval from the U.S. FDA for FACTIVE (Gemifloxacin), an antibacterial agent

In 2007, South Korea had 2,000 pharma companies and more than 640 biotech companies (broad definition).[64] The publicly listed biotech company revenue earnings amounted to $920 million.[65] Although small, the bioagri segment now has a huge potential, as medical diagnostics include the manufacture of reagents and gene and protein diagnosis.[66]

The biotech market in South Korea saw rapid growth, at an annual growth rate of 18%. In 2006, industry exports amounted to $ 1.35 billion. The biotech market is expected to grow to $6.5 billion by 2010.[67] The government is projecting that the market for biotech and biotech-related products will eventually increase to $60 billion.[68]

International observers such as Business Monitor International (BMI) predict that South Korea will likely emerge as a leader in bio-similar research and development. In 2009, Samsung announced that it would spend $389 million on biosimilars research during the next five years. The South Korean FDA introduced a biosimilars regulatory pathway in 2009. The country completed several clinical trials of biosimilar products of U.S. companies.[69]

Although South Korea's attractiveness for international pharma manufacturing may be moderating, its growing R&D capabilities are making multinational pharmaceutical companies open R&D facilities or codevelop drugs with South Korean firms. Some are growing in a spectacular way, including Green Cross and Choongwa.

Domestic companies are seeking foreign partnerships in the form of joint research collaboration and licensing agreements.[70] Several multinational corporations (MNCs) have also set up various R&D activities in South Korea; these include Pfizer, Novartis, and Astra Zeneca, which has a virtual drug-development project in the country. Other players include Abbott Labs, Merck, and Bayer, who have drug-discovery projects in Korea.

Emerging Europe: A Conglomerate of Different Potentials

Emerging Europe comprises a number of diverse countries, including Russia, Turkey, the new Central European E.U. members, and non-E.U. countries such as Ukraine. Although only part of Turkey is in Europe, it is often counted as part of emerging Europe because of its close business ties and aspirations to eventually join the European Union. Together this group of 20 countries represented sales of $68 billion in 2009, and a pharmaceutical market that nearly doubled in the past five years. According to some estimates, this market is projected to grow at CAGR of 8.43%, to reach $153.5 billion by 2019, giving the region a 11% share of global sales—not far from expected sales of $167 billion for China.[71]

Russia, Turkey, and Poland are the three biggest markets in emerging Europe.

Russia

Russia is the lead market and is expected to grow the most, from approximately $16 billion today to more than $50 billion in 2019 (although this estimate may be considered to be on the high side). As with many emerging economies, approximately 80% of Russia's current medicine needs are met by imported drugs.[72] The Russian government wants to reach a 50%–50% ratio by 2020 and is attempting to attract multinational drug companies to produce in the country through such pilot projects as Pharmpolis. Sanofi-Aventis has bought a majority stake in a Russian insulin producer and has opened a plant in Russia. Nycomed announced plans to build a plant in Russia by 2013. The Russian Corporation of Nanotechnologies (Rusano) has unveiled a $27 million project to create nano-particle drug delivery systems for medicines.[73] If Russia is successful in creating nano-medicines, it would boost its capability to export drugs to the West. A product launch within the next two years is a possibility, but the FDA and EMEA still need to define rules for nano-medicines.[74]

With its considerable scientific potential and spending on R&D, Russia could be the wild card among the pharmerging markets. If the Russian government succeeds in reforming the bureaucratic science establishment and improving the nation's innovation system, Russia could emerge as one of the new players instead of simply a large consumer of drugs.

Turkey

Turkey shares some similarities with Mexico, the next large pharmerging market. In 2009, the two countries' pharmaceutical markets were of similar size, approximately $10 billion. Both countries are net importers of drugs, and their markets are experiencing rapid expansion. In Turkey, the generics market is well developed, representing nearly 40% of the market, with patented drugs having sales of slightly more than 50%.

Turkey has around 300 local pharmaceutical companies and 53 multinationals. Turkish companies operate 42 manufacturing facilities, and international companies operate 14 facilities. The sector employs 23,000 people. Turkey's pharmaceutical trade deficit is expected to increase to around $10 billion by 2014, in spite of expected growth in exports.[75] Turkey has intellectual property shortcomings and has been placed on the U.S. Trade Representative "watch list" of countries with significant problems with IP legislation.

Poland

Poland, the Czech Republic, and Hungary are the three most significant markets in emerging Europe, after Russia and Turkey. As E.U. members, all three countries have agreed to E.U. standards of drug regulation and approval, as well as to international standards of intellectual property protection. All three countries used to have state-owned pharmaceutical sectors (under previous communist regimes), but they have been restructured, privatized, or taken over by international investors. All three countries have become locations for pharmaceuticals manufacturing and are also trying to attract international

R&D collaboration by developing life science clusters. Given their relative strengths in science and technology, access to E.U. funds and markets, and lower wage rates than in Western Europe, the countries have the potential to move beyond manufacturing and clinical trials and become a destination for outsourced drug discovery research. Hungary stands out as the country with the strongest traditions in pharmaceuticals and the most ambitious plans of developing a bio-technology sector. These countries need to reform their traditional science and higher education systems and create modern, national, innovation support systems. In Chapter 6, "Accelerating Innovation," we detail an interesting story of how the Polish city of Wroclaw is developing a life science cluster from scratch.

With its large population, Poland is expected to remain the third-largest market in emerging Europe during the next decade. However, Romania and Ukraine—with their big populations—will displace the Czech Republic and Hungary as bigger markets by 2019. BMI forecasts that, by 2019, Russia will reach $55 billion, Turkey will reach $26 billion, and Poland will reach nearly $20 billion, with the smaller markets all less than $10 billion.[76]

The Latin American Leaders: Brazil and Mexico

Brazil is the second-most attractive pharmaceutical market among the BRIC countries (Brazil, Russia, India, and China). In 2004, its pharma market was valued at $5.2 billion;[77] in 2008, it was nearly $15 billion, a jump of 23%, contributing around 34% to the Latin American pharma market.[78] The sector is expected to grow at an average annual rate of 7.2%, to reach $18.3 billion by 2012.[79]

Brazil is the largest market for generic drugs in Latin America, with almost 12% of its total pharma sales coming from generic drugs.

Generics are expected to account for around 23% of the total pharma market in the country by 2011.[80] An example of a major global company that has recently expanded into Latin America—and Central and Eastern Europe as well as Asia—is Sanofi-Aventis. Figure 3-1 details the company's traditional collaborations and acquisitions in developed economies (DE) and those more recently forged in emerging economies (EE), including Poland, Russia, Brazil, and China.

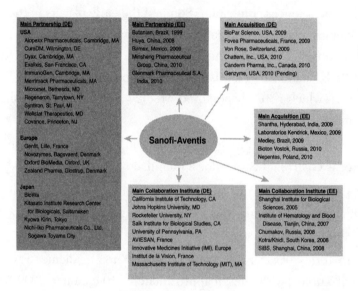

Figure 3-1 Sanofi-Aventis collaborations and mergers and acquisitions with developed and emerging economies[81]

DE = developed economies; EE = emerging economies

In 2001, the biotechnology market was worth $3 billion.[82] Health biotechnology is the largest subsector in the country, accounting for nearly 31% of the total number of life sciences companies in Brazil. The subsector generated revenues of around $212 million and profits of $34 million in 2008.[83] Most companies (about 80%) are small, employing fewer than 20 persons. Only about 10% of the companies employ 50 persons or more.

Brazil has the largest market for medical devices in Latin America.[84] It is a fast-growing sector and is expected to outpace the pharmaceutical market in terms of growth. The market is mostly dominated by consumables and orthopedic and implantable products, with diagnostic imaging apparatus, dental products, and other medical products following close behind.[85]

Brazil is the favored manufacturing and sales destination for many global life sciences companies. Some of the early players in the country include many famous international companies, including Abbott Laboratories, Pfizer, Roche, GSK, Novartis, and Merck.[86] Among the BRIC nations, Brazil is the most important market for Sanofi-Aventis, which recently acquired Medley and increased its share in the market.[87]

An example of a foreign investment in the country's life sciences sector is GE Healthcare (a local manufacturing plant in 2009).[88]

Brazil is a key future market and a strong destination for pharmaceutical manufacturing. However, its status as a destination for R&D investment however still lies in the future.

In terms of size, the Mexican market for medicines resembles that of Turkey, with sales of approximately $10 billion in 2009. Unlike many pharmerging markets, patented drugs account for more than 75% of the market in Mexico; generics are a smaller market, at less than 5%. The market situation in Mexico is complicated by so-called "similares" drugs, which are not regarded as bioequivalent to either the originator drugs or generics. The Mexican market is poorly regulated, and law enforcement and market surveillance are lax—pharmacists are selling prescription drugs as OTC or under-the-counter (UTC).[89]

Mexico's regulatory system has long encouraged local production by requiring a local presence for issuing sanitary certification of manufacturing facilities. Many large multinationals—such as Bayer, BMS, Lilly, GSK, Merck, and Roche—have a direct manufacturing presence. The domestic pharmaceutical industry includes 200 companies and employs 40,000 people, but it is heavily dependent on imported raw materials. The generics market is expected to grow by more than 20% in the next five years.[90] By 2019, the patented drug market, which will continue to dominate, is expected to exceed $20 billion and comprise nearly 75% of the total drug market. Exports are expected to maintain their levels, and Mexico's trade deficit in drugs by 2014 is expected to be moderate, at slightly less than $1 billion.[91]

Mexico has a history of intellectual property shortcomings and has been placed on the U.S. Trade Representative "watch list" of countries with significant problems with IP legislation. However, Mexico has been making progress and stands out among the countries of Latin America where overpricing and unsafe copies of drugs have long been a problem. Enforcement of laws, clarity of regulations, and coordination among regulatory bodies remain a problem. These shortcomings act as a barrier to increased FDI.

Conclusions

This book is about the rise of global R&D and its impacts on international life science–based business. From this perspective, national markets are just one of the factors that multinationals must consider as they ponder expansion. Previously discussed national policies and national industrial competitiveness and scientific capabilities are also important considerations.

As we have seen in this chapter, fast-growing markets can act as a magnet for investments. In many cases, however, these investments are limited to manufacturing. To go to the next level and attract R&D collaboration and investment, a country has to offer more than just a big market. Simply having a large and growing market does not mean that a country will automatically advance and become a player in the industry.

We have seen in the chapter how biopharma, medical device, and healthcare markets are growing dynamically in many emerging economies. Some markets are growing faster than others. However, in some countries, not just the markets themselves are growing. Thanks to aggressive national policies and the activities of the private sector, country competitiveness—which encompasses innovation capabilities, national science, and industrial capabilities—has been growing rapidly but only in some areas.

The matrix in Figure 3-2 compares some of the countries regarded as key future pharma markets on two dimensions: market potential (based on size and growth rate during the next decade on the horizontal axis) and country competitiveness, which largely exemplifies R&D attractiveness (based on the World Economic Forum indicator for 2010 on the vertical axis).

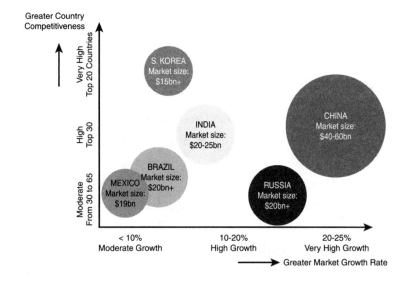

Figure 3-2 Country competitiveness and estimated potential of key pharmerging markets by 2015[96]

Note: Size of sphere reflects estimated market size in 2015.*

Data sources: Vertical axis[92]; horizontal axis[93]; market growth potential as average annual percentage growth[94]; estimated market sizes represented by the size of the spheres[95]

China emerges in a class of its own, with the biggest market and the highest growth rate. It is also an attractive investment destination because of its overall competitiveness, with high R&D spending, low costs, and fast-growing biopharma industry.

Russia, Brazil, Mexico, and Turkey are also fast growing, but their market potential is not as large as China's. Therefore, they are likely destinations for manufacturing rather than R&D investment.

South Korea has a competitive science and industry sector and is an attractive partner for R&D collaboration, although its market potential and growth are more modest compared to those of more populous countries. Although not included in the graph, Central European E.U. member states would occupy an intermediate position. They have promising markets and some potential to become R&D destinations in future.

Finally, although India is a smaller market than China and is less competitive today, it combines a strong science base, an internationally competitive pharma and biotech industry, and good market potential. Therefore, it is an increasingly attractive R&D investment target.

In the next chapters, we look at outsourced R&D (including clinical trials and discovery), the role of high-technology clusters and bioparks in emerging markets, and successful collaborative ventures by multinational pharmas in emerging economies.

4

Improving R&D Productivity: Contract Research and Discovery Collaborations with the New Players As Solutions

"Innovation in the West has simply become unaffordable."

—Kiran Mazumdar-Shaw CEO, Biocon, India, in an interview about the biopharma industry[1]

The Brain Race Goes Global

Human history has always revolved around a race to develop better ways of doing things. Economic history shows a connection between a nation's ability to innovate and its wealth and power. In the sixteenth century, Italy was the wealthiest country in Europe and also the home of amazing innovations in architecture, art, and trade. In the next century, the Netherlands, assumed leadership in wealth development with its inventions in finance, shipping, and civic government. In the nineteenth century, Britain became the banker, trader, and also manufacturer to the world. Britain was soon challenged by Germany, which, after unification, became the largest economy in continental Europe, developed some of the best universities in the world, and became a leader in scientific research. After World Wars I and II, the United States emerged as the wealthiest and most powerful nation of the twentieth century and an undisputed leader in science and innovation. Now China is challenging its leadership position.

For a country to assume and maintain a position of economic leadership, it must be open to the world. China, India, and other emerging powers of Asia have learned that it pays to be open to the world and to continually improve capacities to innovate—and that the two are connected. Both the public and private sectors need to nourish those capacities equally.

Today scientific research is flourishing because of not only spending on R&D, but also increased collaboration among scientific institutions around the world. R&D has also become a global business that offers significant opportunities to make money. Many aggressive private companies from developed as well as emerging economies are determined to profit from this new market. Biocon of India, whose CEO we cited at the beginning of this chapter, is a good example. At a time when many Western companies in the R&D business are reducing head counts or lowering prices for their services, Biocon expects greater than 20% growth.[2] Much of that growth will come from discovery research with international clients, not just clinical trials or outsourced production.

Removing protectionist barriers is difficult enough in the private business sectors. Particularly in emerging economies, most of the educational system, a good deal of infrastructure, and many research institutions are in the public sector and tend to be less open to competitive forces than private companies. However, the global knowledge economy demands that public institutions open up to competition in science, research services, and in higher education. Only in this way will such institutions be able to improve rapidly enough to take advantage of the rising tide of global R&D. The alternative is stagnation behind a wall of protectionism, growing parochialism, and gradual atrophy.

Let's look at how universities are changing in our globalized world. In Western nations, the modern research university developed gradually over decades of change and reform. Emerging economies are trying to design educational reforms that enable them to leapfrog into the twenty-first century without going through all the phases of development that Western scientific and educational institutions underwent. Until the nineteenth century, when the modern research university was born, European universities were preoccupied mainly with teaching and often served more as guardians of orthodox intellectual traditions than as centers of innovation. Useful inventions often resulted from the need to solve practical problems that the country's rulers faced, usually for military or commercial interests. Innovations rarely took place at universities—and if they did, it was because an external sponsor had hired a particularly brilliant scientist to solve a problem. The European university created in the Middle Ages was a place of learning, but the scientific revolution and a basic change in universities' missions were needed to usher in the present age of rapidly advancing knowledge and technology in which the university plays such a central role.

As a result of these developments, the last 200 years have seen exponential growth of scientific knowledge and great discoveries that have given us life-changing technologies such as electricity, penicillin, genome sequencing, and the Internet (illustrated in Figure 4-1).

Genuine science and inquiry have always been international. New ideas and innovations have traveled from country to country, although some secrets (such as the production of silk) were heavily guarded. Competition always existed for talent, with rulers importing experts and advisors to help with new technologies, especially in civil engineering and defense. Today scientific research has become an industry and occurs inside not just within the great research universities, but also in national laboratories and in labs owned by private business. At no other point in human history have so many people worked full time in so many countries on so much research and development. In the twentieth century, most discoveries came from North America and Europe. In the current century, the geographical distribution of discoveries is likely to change.

...and in the last 200 years

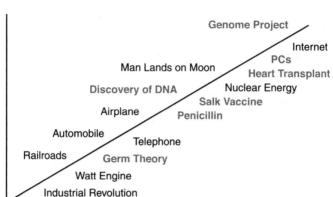

Figure 4-1 Growth in scientific knowledge in the last 200 years

Reproduced with permission from Milken Institute, based on the work of Robert Fogel, University of Chicago. Taken from Burrill & Company, "Biotech 2010 Life Science: Adapting for Success," BIO International Convention, Chicago, 4 May 2010.

As we saw in Chapter 2, "The Race for the Best National Innovation System," the geography of scientific endeavor is changing rapidly, to include new players from emerging economies. Patterns of R&D activity are shifting, and a vast new R&D infrastructure is being built at an astonishing pace outside the traditional centers of science in the United States, Europe, and Japan. The race for discovery and innovation is no longer confined to the club of the wealthiest nations. The race to nurture and attract top intellectual talent has also expanded to a level never before seen.

A recent publication by Ben Wildavsky, a guest scholar at the Brookings Institution, has a telling title, *The Great Brain Race*.[3] The Organization for Economic Cooperation and Development (OECD) estimates that, in 1980, more than a million students were enrolled at universities outside their country of origin. Two decades later, the figure doubled; less than a decade after that, it tripled.[4] Wildavsky documents that, during the last decade, the number of students studying outside their own country has been increasing. The United States hosts more foreign students than any other country, but countries such as

Australia, where foreign students comprise 20% of enrollment, are challenging it. Germany alone, determined to restore its universities to their former glory, attracts nearly 200,000 students from China. Britain also has an impressive record of attracting foreign students to its universities, especially to Oxford and Cambridge.

The Brookings report shows that ambitious emerging economies are upgrading their universities to world standards of excellence. It includes compelling accounts of how relatively unknown universities such as Tsinghua in Beijing and the King Abdullah University of Science and Technology (KAUST) in Saudi Arabia are implementing strategies for an accelerated upgrade to the highest global standards. These universities are not just investing money; they are also employing a new breed of academic "change agents" to manage the process of academic catch-up with the best in the world. The essence of the process is to move as quickly as possible from traditional national modes of learning and academic advancement toward global best practices—which usually means emulating American academic standards, hiring "globally competitive" faculty and staff, and improving physical infrastructure. Typically, rapid improvement is achieved by building strong exchange relationships with world-class universities. Campuses themselves are becoming mobile and opening branches around the world. University exchanges of all types have been growing exponentially in the past decades and increasingly involve academic institutions from emerging markets.

Is it possible, then, with sufficient funds, to create a world-class university in a decade? Critics argue that the "genius loci," the special benefits of location, are impossible to replicate. For all its improvements and success with attracting talent, Singapore universities, for example, may never be able to completely replicate the unique intellectual climates of Oxford or Cambridge, which have evolved over hundreds of years. But perhaps the new up-and-coming universities worry less about replicating famous Western universities and more about creating new institutions, designed in new ways to be highly effective "accelerators of innovation" rather than places of leisurely intellectual debate. Money alone will not do the trick. Innovation in how they better organize science and discovery is even more important.

New centers of research and learning in places such as South Korea are implementing plans for building a new generation of innovative research institutions that will be more productive than the ones in the West—for example, by overcoming discipline-bound "silos" that stifle interdisciplinary research. South Korea's Advanced Institutes of Convergence Technology (AICT), described in more detail in Chapter 6, "Accelerating Innovation," has been designed to educate new generations of interdisciplinary innovators. Students are being trained simultaneously in several converging technologies, for a faster and more efficient innovation process. It is worth noting that a similar process is occurring within some leading pharmaceutical companies that are moving away from "functional silo" structures to interdisciplinary teams. The race for the future among the innovators of the world is increasingly playing out in the new universities and in the public and private laboratories created by the new players. The best of the new institutions as they grow and develop will attract top student and researcher talent from around the world.

In the last two chapters, we documented the rise of the "pharmerging" markets. In this chapter, our focus changes to look at the context of the recent expansion of new global discovery collaborations. We first look at the amazing developments that have been occurring in the past two decades in genomics, a key new field of the biological sciences, and examine the implications of the rise of genomics for the global pharmaceutical business. Revolutionary developments in basic life sciences, such as the sequencing of the human genome, have so far not led to quick drug applications, but they may lead to commercial opportunity in related fields, such as biofuels. We also describe how greater cooperation in science between leading Western institutions such as the American National Institutes of Health (NIH) and public research labs in China, India, and South Korea have paved the way for discovery outsourcing by private-sector companies.

Of Science Paradigm Shifts and Research Plateaus: How Soon Can We See Applications from Genomics?

James Watson and Francis Crick discovered the double helix structure of DNA. Just over a decade ago, in 2000, J. Craig Venter and Francis Collins followed up on Watson's discovery and announced that they had been able to sequence the human genome. This was a major milestone in the history of science and appeared to usher in the "era of biotechnology." The sequencing of DNA was indeed a paradigm shift in biological and medical sciences. After the collapse of the dot-com bubble, BT (biotechnology) seemed to eclipse IT (information technology) as the next new thing in high technology. Predictions arose about new drugs based on genetic targets that were sure to conquer cancer, Alzheimer's, and other diseases.

This has not happened in the way imagined at the time. Disappointments followed as researchers and investors found that much more scientific work must be done before we can move to new therapeutic applications. This does not mean that valuable biologic drugs based on genomics research have not been discovered. For example, the Food and Drug Administration (FDA) is expected to approve a promising drug against lupus, Benlysta, developed by Human Genome Sciences. Amgen's drug for osteoporosis, Prolia, was approved in June, 2010. Oncotype DX, a test by Genomic Health, can identify whether breast cancer is aggressive and, therefore, likely to recur.[5]

Nevertheless, the effort needed to move the field of applications further is simply much greater than anticipated and needs resources and collaborations on a truly international scale. The genome-sequencing project cost $3 billion and was funded largely by public money from the U.S. Department of Energy and the NIH, and by smaller contributions from private international collaborators.[6] The failure to find quick applications to genomics does not diminish the significance or potential of this scientific breakthrough. Ten years after the first sequencing of the genome, backed by $300 million of private venture, we have seen the emergence of synthetic biology: the construction by Dr. Venter of the JCVI-syn1, a living organism built completely from a synthetic genome. This breakthrough is likely the beginning of the age of biological engineering.

The first project of genome sequencing took more than a decade and, as we pointed out, was hugely expensive, costing several billion dollars. Since then, we have witnessed steady and rapid advances of computing power and the development of ultraefficient sequencers. Within several years, we should be able to read a human genome in less than an hour for about $1,000. We are still not quite at this point: Reading a human genome currently takes about a week and costs around $10,000.[7] Even so, progress has been astounding, and the lower cost and the ease of sequencing have enormous implications for science. With this technology, the genomes of humans and other species can be mapped, compared, and analyzed to answer questions fundamental to our understanding of biological organisms and their anatomy, physiology, pathology, and evolution. Detailed genetic information, which is now within reach, will lead to the possibility of engineering animals, plants, and bacteria for useful purposes.

Why is it taking so much longer to reap the fruits of the genomics sequencing achievement? The short explanation is that we need to find out much more before we can develop revolutionary drugs, tests, and therapies based on genomics. No one knows how long this will take or how much it will cost. Our original understanding of how the structure of DNA works in combination with proteins and RNA has turned out to be too simple. The reality is much more complex than the original model of Francis Crick: "one gene equals one RNA messenger molecule which equals one protein."

This sequence used to be known as the fundamental paradigm of modern biology:

DNA → RNA → protein

Only proteins were thought to handle such functions. Another issue, still not fully understood, is the proper *protein folding*, which means the long protein chain has to gain an appropriate three-dimensional architecture. Thus, a more accurate statement might look like Figure 4-2.

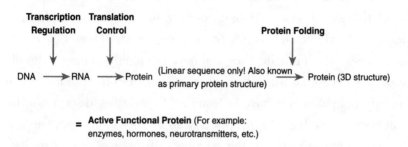

Figure 4-2   Extended molecular biology paradigm

Transcription occurs not just through "RNA-only" genes, but also by a process known as epigenesis, which is a chemical alteration of the DNA. However, the DNA itself, with all its three billion base pairs, a "long-chain" molecule, does not behave in a linear fashion. Instead, it is "folded up" inside the cell nucleus, with bits of the molecule located next to each other and able to interact.

The complexity of this biology is huge and not yet fully understood. Therefore, finding reliable relationships between diseases and genes has turned out to be extraordinarily difficult. Once researchers can find and confirm such links, however, they will be able to develop drugs that will be literally "on target" from the beginning, marking a major improvement over drug candidates that must go through the current long and costly process of trial and error. Until we reach this new point in our knowledge, only vast internationally funded collaborative efforts in basic science will produce breakthroughs.

International efforts will need to be performed on a grand scale. One example is the Cancer Genome Consortium, which involves scientists from 11 countries. Aimed at studying the full DNA sequences of hundreds of patients suffering from different types of cancer, it involves sampling both cancerous and healthy tissues.[8] Pharmaceutical companies tend to avoid such expensive projects and prefer to concentrate research on cancer causes that are much better understood. For example, specific small molecules are known to block the activation of certain cancer-producing enzymes and, therefore, likely will attract money from investors who know that if they are successful eventually, they will have the ability to patent the discovery. Conceptual breakthroughs that remain in the public domain and are not patentable have little appeal to investors; discoveries that can become the basis for proprietary applications have great appeal. To accelerate progress in the conquest of diseases, scientists have even solicited drug companies to cofund basic research to be done in laboratories independent from the government under a consortium model—unfortunately, however, this model has enjoyed little success.[9] Nevertheless, as the case of Enlight Biosciences shows, new interesting instances of precompetitive collaborations on research among big pharma companies and investors are emerging in hopes of funding the development of novel technologies that would enhance drug discovery (such as molecular imaging, drug delivery, and early prediction of safety). Among the backers of this idea are Lilly, Johnson & Johnson, Merck & Co., and Pfizer. Still, this is very much applied research, and although the amounts committed are considerable, they are not enormous—up to a combined $65 million.[10] The burden of basic research still falls on the public sector.

Open-access approaches to gathering genomic data from volunteers in different countries may help the publicly funded basic science effort. Publicly funded "biobanks" may provide an interesting avenue of progress. As the cited recent survey in *The Economist* reported, Britain has already started a project to collect tissue samples from a half million people, to study relationships between genes and health patterns.[11] Ultimately, such research should open up new therapeutic targets and therapies.

The new research capabilities of large emerging economies will become increasingly useful to international consortia attacking highly complex tasks and requiring huge resources and access to large human populations. Many indications show that new players, such as China, will not be satisfied with contributing just supportive roles in basic science. China has ambitions to become a leader in genomics research. Dr. Yang Huanming, the founder of the Beijing Genomics Institute (BGI), wants his institute to lead the first fully global genomic project. He has been building up a state-of-the-art sequencing laboratory in Hong Kong. When completed, this lab will have the greatest sequencing capability in the world. Using American machines, Chinese researchers plan to sample the entire geographical range of humanity, along with key agricultural plants such as rice, animals, and more than a thousand bacteria. The project plans to establish labs in Europe and America to work on the project. In addition to studying diseases such as cancer, BGI plans to study plants and animals that have important business applications (such as lightweight woods and the cloning of pigs). Earlier in 2010, BGI acquired 128 new lllumina HiSeq 2000 systems. In theory, those systems would allow BGI to produce 10,000 whole human genome sequences per year.[12] This capability is more than the entire U.S. sequencing output. Interestingly, the state-owned Chinese banks are helping to fund the research of BGI. However, BGI sees its future also—or primarily—as a world-class contractor for sequencing services.[13]

Nonmedical applications of genomics may actually turn out to be easier and faster to commercialize. These fall in the area of the so-called "green" and "white" biotechnology (agriculture/plants and industry). Genomic engineering possibilities are growing with the number of sequenced species, which include bacteria, animals, plants, and fungi. Genetic engineering may mean making new genomes either from scratch or from the purposeful modifications of existing genes, as in genetically modified plants (which usually have just a single changed gene). For example, by now, most soybean plants grown in the world have been modified, as have much of the cotton and corn that we grow.[14] Yet the long-term impacts of genetically modified (GM) foods on the health of humans and animals are not yet understood and will need to be ascertained.

Beyond agriculture, a whole range of applications of industrial biotechnology seem to be just around the corner. Perhaps most important are biofuels. The World Economic Forum recently released a report predicting that biorefineries will create markets worth around $300 billion by 2020.[15] Energy from plants can be released through a process of fermentation, thus reducing our reliance on fossil fuels. Companies have been working to develop genetic modifications of certain plants known as "energy crops," to increase their energy content. Existing biofuels such as ethanol, whether based on corn or sugarcane, can be improved upon. Researchers are manipulating the metabolic pathways of single-cell algae to improve the rate at which CO_2 can be converted into carbohydrates after photosynthesis and, on that basis, become fuel for cars. Brazil, which is a leader in biofuels today, is likely to emerge as an attractive location where biofuels can be produced. Brazil is especially well suited because it is one of the few countries with large reserves of arable land. In most other nations, new crops have to compete with existing food production.

Energy is just one area of industrial biotechnology where several technologies are advanced enough to be ready for commercialization. Industrial biotechnology can produce bioplastics, biochemicals, and food enzymes. Biological synthesis is often more efficient than chemical synthesis, and gene engineering can lead to a variety of applications that include the production of such products as fragrances and flavorings.[16] Agents that indicate the freshness of perishable food— for example, by changing color from, say, green to red—would be helpful to consumers and have an impact on the food-processing industry. Prospects for industrial biotechnology-based business are good enough for McKinsey to claim global revenues from this industry to be worth as much as 450 billion euros by 2020, a figure that greatly exceeds the present revenues from sales of biologics drugs.[17] Thus, the road to commercial application of plant and animal genomics may be easier and appear sooner than in the case of the much more complex human genomics, where so much more basic research is needed. This is all the more reason to conduct the needed huge international research effort that will accelerate the rise of the global R&D system.

The R&D Productivity Crisis in Pharmaceuticals

Some readers may be surprised the hear that, despite the unprecedented explosion in scientific discoveries, so many of which have been in life sciences, the pharmaceutical industry finds itself in what has become known as an R&D productivity crisis. Accumulation of knowledge does not automatically lead to more inventions that can be readily applied and commercialized. R&D spending by the private sector, which obviously is much more application oriented, tends to follow and take advantage of breakthroughs in basic science. It seems logical to expect that outlays in applied research should lead to more—and more innovative—products. In general, such a relationship holds true, but in the case of pharmaceuticals, the opposite seems to be happening. For a decade now, American-based multinational companies have been increasing their R&D spending, but the number of innovative new medicines introduced and approved has actually been declining as illustrated in Figure 4-3. Pharmaceutical industry R&D spending appears to be suffering from a case of diminishing returns. The causes of this paradox are complex and certainly include increased oversight and regulation; therefore, they are only partly related to the state of science.

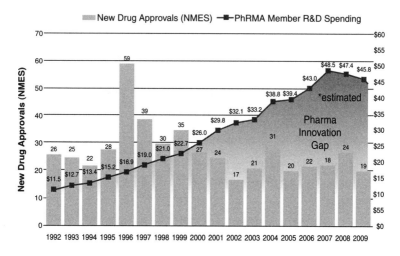

Figure 4-3 Increasing innovation gap: R&D investments versus new drug approvals
Reproduced with permission from Burrill & Company, "Biotech 2010 Life Science: Adapting for Success," BIO International Convention, Chicago, 4 May 2010.

Why does the last decade represent a growing "innovation gap" for the pharmaceutical industry?

In 2006, the U.S. FDA approved 22 new molecular entities (NMEs), with a total R&D budget of about $40 billion; in 1996, the FDA approved more than 50 NMEs, with R&D expenditure less than half the current sum.[18] Those numbers pertain to leading U.S. companies, but the phenomenon goes beyond American companies and appears to have affected Europe as well.

Let's take a look at the shifting geography of drug innovation. Until approximately the turn of the century, Europe was the world leader in the number of innovative medical substances created (new chemical/biological entities), with the United States and Japan vying for second place. As we see in Figure 4-4, after the year 2000, the ranking changed: The United States emerges as number one, while Europe and Japan took over second and third place, respectively. However, the overall numbers *for all three geographical regions declined.* In addition, the contributions of countries outside the

U.S./Europe/Japan triad increased—in other words, the contributions of the new players became noticeable.

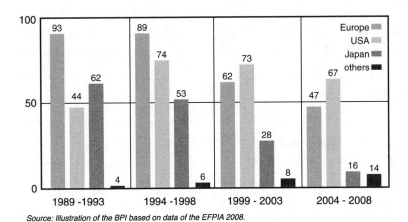

Source: Illustration of the BPI based on data of the EFPIA 2008.

Figure 4-4 Innovative medical substances (new chemicals or biological entities, NCE/NBE), 1989–2008, sorted by invention countries worldwide

Reproduced with permission from BPI Pharma, Data 2009, Bundesverb and der Pharmazeutischen Industrie e.V (BPI), September 2009.

Within Europe, Germany has been losing its position as the traditional "Pharmacy of the World." Overall, the German pharmaceutical industry has continued to succeed in the marketplace, with strong exports and stable and rising employment and revenues. However, in spite of increases in industry R&D spending from 3.4 billion euros in 2002 to 5.2 billion euros in 2008, German pharmaceutical companies are showing signs of declining innovativeness. Patent registration in Germany has seen some decline. For example, an E.U. study showed that, in 2005, only 6 of 140 newly approved pharmaceutical drugs were developed in Germany. When it comes to "enthusiasm for innovation," Germany ranks near the bottom in Europe, especially as compared to European leaders such as Ireland, Sweden, and Belgium. In 2007, only 6% of expenditures in Germany were for innovative pharmaceuticals launched during the previous five years. As a result, Germany spends less on novel pharmaceuticals than most other European countries.[19] (The BPI, the German Pharmaceutical Industry Association, admits to the problem and advocates efforts to make Germany a more hospitable environment to innovation. The German Federal Ministry of Education and Research [Bundesministerium für Bildung und Forschung (BMBF)], with its "Pharmainitiative" and "BioPharma-Competition," has started some initiatives meant to restrengthen Germany as an innovative pharmaceutical location.[20])

The numbers alone do not tell the whole story, however. Critics argue that many of the "new" U.S.-invented drugs are new versions or improvements of existing drugs (new dosage, new indication). Taking this into account, Europe as a whole still comes out ahead of the United States in drug discovery.[21] The controversy is partly a case of transatlantic competition in high technology, in which Europe has been losing ground, and partly a philosophical dispute about drug pricing. Unlike in the IT field, where America is preeminent, pharmaceuticals and commercial aircraft are areas of high-tech in which Europe is still competitive with the United States. In its response to the Grabowski study, a senior vice president of PhRMA, the leading American industry association, talked of a "distorted picture painted by the report" and pointed out that it ignores "the chilling effect of government price controls on such innovation."[22] With new entrants coming from emerging economies, the race for supremacy in drug discovery is just heating up.

Nevertheless, the decline in pharmaceutical R&D effectiveness in the past decade is a fact. The industry is urgently seeking solutions to the problem and must find them if it is to take advantage of the expected doubling of the global pharmaceutical market in the next decade or so. This growth, as we know, is coming mainly from large pharmerging markets, so shifting research resources and activities to where the market growth is occurring makes sense. Western companies are urgently experimenting with new R&D strategies and structures that are being extended into emerging economies.

India and China have begun adding to the intellectual property in the pharmaceutical industry. By 2006, 5.5% of all global pharma patent applications (WIPO PCT application) contained one or more inventors located in India, and 8.4% contained one or more inventors located in China—a fourfold increase from 1995.[23] A number of Indian and Chinese companies are developing their own original drugs targeted for global or regional markets. For example, Table 4-1 shows that leading Indian pharmas such as Zydus, Glenmark, and Ranbaxy have a pipeline of 5–10 new chemical entities, with more than 20 in phases 2 or 3 of development.[24]

Company	Year of commencing discovery research	NCE Pipeline	Key therapeutic areas	R&D facilities	No. of people employed in R&D	Remarks
Sun Pharma	1993	Phase II - 1 NCE, 2 NDDS projects expected to enter trials in the developed/ regulated markets	NA	Two R&D Centers spread over 185,000 sq. ft. A bioequivalence center spread over 25,000 sq. ft.	Over 500 scientists	Research commitment ('06-'07) is 8-10 percent of the turnover. They have put in a total of USD 223 million* for research since 1993
Biocon	1994 - established Syngene (contract research services company) 2002 - forayed into new drug development.	Pre Clinical - 2 NCE, Phase II - 2 NCE, Phase III -1 NCE	Inflammation, Oncology, Diabetes	Syngene's new research facility comprising approximately 20,000 sq mts of floor space is expected to be operational in Q3 of the next fiscal.	NA	In 2008, R&D Revenue Expenditure increased 24 percent to USD 11 million* from USD 9 million*
Cadila	2000	Pre Clinical - 5 NMEs	Diabetes, Dyslipidemia, Obesity, Inflammation.	Zydus Research Centre (ZRC) spread over 360,000 sq. ft. is located in Ahmedabad focuses on NME Research & NDDS	~150 scientists	R&D spending ~7 percent of revenues p.a.
Piramal Healthcare	NA	13 compounds including 4 in clinical trials	Oncology, Inflammation, Infectious diseases, Diabetes/Metabolic Syndrome	NA	NA	Annual Spend on R&D of 5 percent of Sales
Glenmark	NA	13 new molecules under development 8 NCEs and 5 NBEs Discovery- 4 Preclinical- 5, Phase I - 1, Phase IIb - 3	Inflammation, Metabolic Disorders, Dermatology	NCE research facility in Navi Mumbai-India is more than 70,000 sq. ft., NBE Research facility is located in Switzerland	NCE Research - over 300 scientists , NBE Research - 55 scientists	R&D expenditure - 6.09 percent of the total turnover
Ranbaxy	1994	Four to six molecules in preclinical stage, one Molecule in Phase II Clinicals - Anti Malaria.	Infectious diseases, Metabolic diseases, Inflammatory/ Respiratory disease and Oncology	R&D facilities at Gurgaon, India.	1200 scientists	NA
Dr Reddy's	1993	Seven NCEs of which five in clinical development and two in preclinical stages	Metabolic Disorders and Cardiovascular Indications	Research facilities at Atlanta (USA) for target based research and Hyderabad (India) for analog based research	310 researchers	Total R&D expenditure as a percentage of total turnover - 9.85 percent
Suven Lifesciences	NA	Discovery - two NCE, Preclinical - four NCE, Phase I - one NCE	Neurodegenerative Diseases, Inflammatory Disorders, Obesity/ Diabetes	R&D unit located at Hyderabad, India	NA	For FY07 R&D expenditure is estimated at 23.91 percent of the turnover

*Exchange Rate INR/USD = 0.02345/0.02548 (bid/ask)
Source: Company Websites, Presentations and Annual Reports, Press articles

Table 4-1 Examples of Indian Companies Discovery Research

Reproduced with permission from "Pharma Summit 2008: India Pharma, Inc.—An Emerging Global Pharma Hub," KPMG & CII report, September 2008. Available at www.kpmg.com/Global/en/IssuesAndInsights/ArticlesPublications/Documents/Pharma-summit-2008.pdf.

Emerging Powerhouses of Global Life Science Research

The countries that appear to have the most momentum in terms of life science research are South Korea, India, and China. Each country provides a different case of how global R&D is emerging/moving forward. South Korea is at a point where its science is becoming on par with the West. India's strategy is one of developing partnerships and outsourcing relationships with such leaders as the United States. And finally, China is making efforts to identify niches in global science in which it can establish itself as a leader.

South Korea

Ambitious emerging economies such as South Korea have been known to concentrate their resources on applied rather than basic research (which Koreans were happy to leave for the wealthy West to do). But South Korea, as well as other new players in the global R&D game, realizes that, in the long term, it has to develop world-class basic research. South Korea is spending $15 billion to develop an international basic science research park near Seoul.

International studies coordinated by the World Health Organization (WHO) of selected issues such as antimicrobial resistance often involve laboratories from as many as 40 countries. India, China, and South Korea have been active participants in many international research projects coordinated by the WHO. South Korea has 14 institutions participating in ten WHO projects, including research on cancer and TB. China is taking part in three studies and has 76 participating institutions. India is by far the most active. It participates in 8 projects with 300 participating institutions, more than institutes from the United Kingdom, France, and Germany combined.[25]

South Korean has been steadily increasing the amount it spends on R&D. Among the 30 OECD member states, South Korea has the sixth-highest expenditure in R&D. These expenditures constituted 3.37% of South Korea's gross domestic product in 2008, one of the highest ratios in the world. In 2008, 436,228 people in Korea were engaged in R&D activities (researchers, research assistants, other supporting personnel), which represents a 3.5% increase from the previous year. Among the total, the number of researchers was 300,050, showing a 3.8% rise from the previous year. Thus, the number of researchers per 1,000 members of the labor force is 9.7 persons. On the other hand, the number of full-time-equivalent (FTE) researchers was 236,137, a 6.4% increase from the previous year.[26] This increase in South Korean personnel in the R&D field demonstrates that more jobs are being created in this field, so companies clearly are expanding the size of their R&D divisions in South Korea. In terms of the number of researchers per 10,000 of labor force, at 9.7, South Korea has one of the highest ratios in the world, ahead of France, Germany, and the United Kingdom.

India: From Aid Recipient to Strategic Partner with the United States

As we noted earlier, since independence in 1947, India has been a leader in science among the developing nations. The nation has made tremendous strides in improving education and infrastructure, making it today an attractive partner for collaborative basic science research in several areas, but perhaps most in the life sciences. In the late 1950s, Indian and American scientists began collaborating in agricultural research. In the 1960s, those activities were expanded to include the health sector: disease preventions, infectious diseases, and cancer. Over the years, a variety of collaborative agreements were signed between the two countries, and joint commissions on scientific exchange were established. Since India signed the Agreement on Trade-Related Aspects of Intellectual Property Rights (TRIPS) in 2005, collaboration in both applied and basic medical science has increased, with private-sector companies outsourcing more R&D to India. On the American side, the NIH and Centers for Disease Control (CDC) have played lead roles in supporting joint projects, training programs, and exchanges. Nearly all of the 27 institutes and centers comprising the NIH support some form of medical research in India. After American Nobel laureate Fred Robbins visited India in 1984, one of the most successful U.S.–India collaborations programs was launched in the area of vaccines: the Vaccine Action Program (VAP).

Through its grants, the VAP supports lab research, epidemiological studies, and field trials—all key areas that can lead to the development and improvement of vaccines. Through the NIH, Indian institutions collaborate on a broad range of topics with leading centers of research in the United States. Consider a few examples:[27]

- Johns Hopkins University and India MediCity Hospital have collaborated on a study of markers of progression to cervical cancer (National Cancer Institute).
- Duke University Medical Center and the All India Institute of Medical Sciences (AIIMS) in New Delhi have studied therapies for the surgical treatment of ischemic heart failure, comparing the benefits of medical and surgical interventions for patients with coronary disease (National Heart, Lung and Blood Institute).
- New York University and AIIMS have been collaborating on the design of broadly neutralizing anti-HIV antibody responses to develop a better HIV vaccine (National Institute of Allergy and Infectious Diseases).
- The University of Texas Health Science Center and the Indian National Brain Research Center 13 have been studying human brain CYP p450s and psychoactive drug metabolism.

In fact, the range of collaborations between India, the NIH, and the CDC is much more extensive, covering a broad range of diseases and also involving multicountry collaborations.[28]

India is an active player in such projects and continues to contribute to NIH programs. Among the foreign scientists from emerging economies at the NIH, the Chinese were the largest group, followed by Japan, South Korea, and India, and well ahead of such European countries as Italy, Germany, and the United Kingdom.[29] Technology transfer and licensing have been increasing between the United States and India since 2005. For example, the NIH's Office of Technology Transfer (OTT) has more than 50 issued or pending patents in India. In addition, OTT has transferred intellectual property (IP) and biological materials to Indian pharmaceutical and biotech companies, including Nicholas, Ranbaxy, Serum Institute of India (SII), and others. Licensed technologies include vaccines for dengue and for Varicella-Zoster, recombinant proteins for the production of conjugate vaccines against bacterial diseases, human cell line expressing luciferase reporter gene, and others.[30]

Because of its excellence, the SII was selected as the sole producer of the novel meningitis vaccine to combat the disease epidemic in sub-Saharan Africa. Numerous workshops and conferences have further developed U.S.–India technology transfers. It is worth mentioning that, since 2004 and following the Next Steps in Strategic Partnership (NSSP) initiative, collaboration between the two countries is being extended into a number of sensitive areas: high-technology trade, space and missile defense, civil nuclear energy, and clean energy. The U.S.–India High Technology Group (HTCG) promotes public–private sector collaborations in biotechnology, nanotechnology defense, and IT.

Without these high-profile initiatives and the long tradition of U.S.–India scientific collaboration among public-sector institutions, the rapid expansion of private-sector R&D outsourcing to India by U.S. firms would likely have been on a much smaller scale.

Indian Research Institutions in Life Science

India has a number of world-class scientific institutions, including the National Centre for Biological Science (NCBS), Indian Institute of Science (IISC), and Centre of Cellular and Molecular Biology. Outstanding countrywide research institutions also operate in India, listed by region here:

New Delhi

- National Institute of Immunology
- Institute of Genomics & Integrative Biology

(continued)

- Jawaharlal Nehru University
- National Brain Research Centre
- International Centre for Genetic Engineering & Biology

Chandigam

- Institute of Microbial Technology

Lucknow

- Central Drug Research Institute
- Industrial Toxicology Research Centre

Pune

- National Chemical Laboratory

Bangalore

- National Centre for Biological Sciences
- Jawaharlal Nehru Centre for Advanced Scientific Research
- Indian Institute of Science

Hyderabad

- Centre for Cellular & Molecular Biology
- Centre for DNA Fingerprinting & Diagnostics
- Indian Institute of Chemical Technology
- National Institute of Nutrition
- International Crops Research Institute for the Semi-Arid Tropics

Kolkata

- Indian Institute of Chemical Biology

Source: "Indian Life Science Industry—A Presentation at the Forum for International Business 07," ICRA Management Consulting Services Limited, March 2007.

China: Angling for Leadership Niches in Global Science

China offers many of the same advantages of India in terms of low-cost but highly skilled scientists and increasingly competitive world-class research facilities. However, in the past, opportunities for scientific collaboration with Chinese institutions have not been tapped as deeply as those with India, due to both the previous lack of knowledge about Chinese capabilities and language barriers and cultural differences. As we know from Chapter 2, the Chinese scientific establishment has undergone wrenching changes in the past 25 years and is being continually reformed and upgraded. It is also increasingly well funded. With the diverse array of hundreds of state-owned, municipal, military, and private organizations involved in medical and biopharmaceutical research, Western partners have many choices. Good intelligence and contacts are keys to choosing the right partner and to making partnerships work well.

Scientific collaboration between China and the United States started later than with India and dates back to the normalization of relations and the subsequent signing of the U.S.–China Agreement on Cooperation in Science and Technology in 1979 by President Jimmy Carter and Premier Deng Xiaoping. This agreement authorized American federal agencies to negotiate protocols, memoranda of understanding, and agreements with the Chinese government. Cooperation on biomedical and behavioral research was expanded under an amended Memorandum of Understanding (MOU) signed by the directors of the NIH and the Chinese Academy of Science in 2005.[31]

More than just intergovernmental agreements were needed to launch Chinese–Western collaboration in research. The Chinese approach to intellectual property had to change, too. China joined the World Intellectual Property Organization as far back as 1980 and established a Chinese patent office that same year. The Chinese laws on IP protection evolved gradually over time. The 1984 patent law excluded certain products, including drugs, from patent protection. However, an amendment introduced in 1992 extended patent protection to drugs.[32] Chinese regulations grant special protection to Traditional Chinese Medicine (TCM) because the Chinese want to see TCM become a new significant export industry. Enforcement of intellectual property rights (IPR) is a well-known problem of doing business in China. Although the laws today comply with most international standards, differences with U.S. patent laws still exist. Chinese administrators can effectively resolve simple counterfeiting cases. However, the Chinese courts handle more complex IP violations, and convictions are common. Nevertheless, when it comes to enforcing judgments against Chinese companies, authorities may balk at decisions that would cause a Chinese business to go bust. In spite of these problems, China has become such an important market that it has become standard practice for foreign companies to file patent applications with the Chinese Patent Office, and their number has continued to grow rapidly, alongside the much greater numbers of patents filed by the Chinese. The patent-based culture has taken root in China, but prudent IP risk management has to be a part of business strategy in the country.

The Chinese science establishment is vast and complicated. Among the players active in life science research are a variety of lead institutions that include the Chinese Academy of Sciences. With around 60,000 staff, this institution encompasses 5 academic divisions, more than 100 scientific institutes, and more than 200 technology companies, along with other supporting units throughout the country. The country also has specialized Academies of Science dedicated to medicine, agriculture, and the military, and all have significant life science capabilities. The top Chinese universities are improving rapidly and have many talented students and academics. In addition, state-owned scientific institutes and spin-off companies also perform R&D. Finally, the domestic Chinese private sector has becoming increasingly involved in innovation activities, especially companies founded by "sea turtles," or returning Chinese expats. Some state-owned institutes, such as the Beijing Genomics Institute (BGI), mentioned earlier, have achieved world fame for innovative activities.[33]

Life Science in China

The Chinese Academy of Sciences (CAS) was founded on November 1, 1949 and has become a leading academic institution and comprehensive research and development center in natural science, technological science, and high-tech innovation in China. In the field of life science and biotechnology, about 6,000 CAS researchers represent 24 research institutes, 13 research centers, and 26 key state and CAS laboratories. CAS was the first organization in China to carry out such biotechnology research related to monoclonal antibodies, transgenic animals and plants, somatic cell cloning, and stem cell and protein engineering.

In addition to the Medical College, the Chinese Academy of Medical Sciences (CAMS), China's only country-level medical science academic center and comprehensive scientific research organization, has 18 research institutes, 5 branches, 7 clinical hospitals, and 5 institutes.

The Academy of Military Medical Sciences (AMMS) is the highest medical research institution of the Chinese People's Liberation Army (PLA). It includes these branches:

- Institute of Medical Information
- Institute of Radiation Medicine
- Institute of Basic Medical Sciences
- Institute of Hygiene & Environmental Medicine
- Institute of Microbiology & Epidemiology
- Institute of Pharmacology & Toxicology
- Institute of Medical Equipment
- Institute of Bioengineering

AMMS also has 20 cross-disciplinary research centers and key laboratories such as the National Center for Biomedical Analysis, the National Center for New Drug Non-clinical Safety Evaluation (the GUP laboratory), the National Base for Clinical Pharmacology, the

Army Research Center for Preventive Medicine, and the Army Emergency Medical Aid Center for Nuclear Accidents.

The Chinese Academy of Agricultural Sciences (CAAS) is China's national agricultural research organization, which is directly affiliated to the Ministry of Agriculture. CAAS has about 10,000 staff members and 38 research institutes located across 17 different provinces, national municipalities, and autonomous regions.

Universities in China have played an important role in scientific research. Top universities in China (based on Asiaweek.com data in 2005) include these:

- Peking University
- Tsinghua University
- Fudan University
- Tongji University
- Nanjing University
- Tianjin University
- Zhejiang University
- Wuhan University
- Huazhong University of Science & Technology
- Zhonshan University

From 1980, Chinese students came to the United States to start their graduate degrees in life science or biology. The returnees brought back Western education and corporate experience to China and founded a number of successful enterprises, including The Bayhelix Group, South Gene Technology (SGT), and WuXi PharmaTech.

Besides enterprises by overseas returnees, state-owned enterprises are important in life science research. Beijing Genomic Institute (BGI) made China the only developing country to participate in the Human Genome Project. SiBiono GeneTech Co., based in Shenzhen, earned international recognition in 2003 when it developed the first licensed gene therapy medication. Beike Biotechnology

Company, another state-owned enterprise, is one of the leading expert groups in China for separating, purifying, nurturing, and multiplying embryonic, fetal, adult, and, most important, blood cord stem cells.

Source: Steven M. Ferguson, Sally H. Hu, and Uri Reichman, "Biophamaceutical Research Collaboration Between Western and Chinese Life Science Organizations: A Guide to Prospective Partnerships," in *Advances in Biopharmaceutical Technology in China*, ed. Eric S. Langer (Rockville, MD: BioPlan Associates and Society for Industrial Microbiology, 2008), 940–956.

The volume of NIH-supported collaborations with China has grown and covers research grants and contracts to Chinese institutions (valued at about $5 million), as well as subcontracting agreements that are part of domestic NIH awards (valued at more than $7 million in 2004). An example of the latter is epidemiologic studies carried out jointly by Harvard University and Chinese institutions. The visiting program has seen active participation by Chinese citizens (of whom nearly 470 were at the NIH in 2004). The number of guest researchers has also increased to about 60 each year.

As in the case of India, the NIH has transferred valuable knowhow to China—for example, with vaccines used under license in China. The NIH has sponsored programs in natural products and alternative medicine. Many Chinese scientists train in the United States and other Western countries. Although some choose to remain in the West, others return and are instrumental in increasing informal collaborations between individual Chinese and Western scientists. The NIH and institutions in European countries support programs for such collaborations. The total value of NIH-sponsored exchanges is around $30 million.[34] Added to that are sizeable programs of collaborations between China and the American CDC, which cover a broad range of therapeutic areas from anemia, birth defects, and cancer to hepatitis and HIV. Overall, China offers Western partners many advantages and opportunities for scientific collaboration. Some of the drawbacks include overbearing government influence, an opaque regulatory environment, and instances of corruption.

China, India, and South Korea are the most important players of emerging importance in basic science research, but they are not the only ones. Smaller countries, including Taiwan, Singapore, and Malaysia, are making good progress as providers of competitive education and research services. In time, their contributions to science will also grow.

The Private Sector Globalizes Discovery: From Internal Innovation to Global Offshoring

The R&D productivity crisis and the so-called "patent cliff" (expiring patent protection for blockbuster drugs) are putting great pressure on the pharmaceutical industry to find new efficiencies and new models for more efficient discovery and development, as well as better ways to commercialize and sell drugs. The "plateau" in drug development is a subject of debate and controversy among scientists, business executives, and policymakers. Some representatives of the industry argue that fewer drug approvals are simply the result of a much tighter and more rigorous review processes enforced by regulators looking to ensure safety and minimize risks. Some even argue that, under today's standards, some common drugs we know might not have been approved because of their now better-known side effects. Scientists point out that the previous surges in chemistry-based drug approvals in the 1980s and 1990s were simply the result of innovators picking "low-hanging fruit." Science has progressed so much since then that new drug discovery has become more complex than before and requires greater outlays of resources.

One of the principal ways private industry seeks to improve R&D efficiency has been outsourcing. The pharmaceutical industry has practiced R&D outsourcing for some time. Recent pressures on the industry have accelerated this process while also making it more global. The idea of outsourcing is based on the premise that partners with specialized complementary competencies can create more value than would be possible if the same resources were contained within a vertically integrated structure.[35] The principle has been successfully applied to IT and business processes such as accounting and payroll. Outsourcing design and research functions seems to go to the core competencies of companies, yet those functions are also being increasingly outsourced across a number of industries, as we indicated in Chapter 1, "Power Shifts in Global R&D and Innovation."

Proponents of outsourcing say that the experience of the pharmaceutical industry with declining R&D productivity demonstrates the disadvantages of vertically integrated structures that rely on large centralized laboratories for innovation. Large organizations tend to become risk averse and bureaucratic. In the case of pharmaceuticals, where failure of new product ideas is the norm, the natural inclination of decision makers is caution. If they back a particular molecule for development, chances are better than 90% that it will fail in subsequent testing. Thus, strong incentives to stop unpromising projects early are just as important as incentives to invent new molecules.

Internal development may also run into barriers other than high costs. The central lab may simply not have scientists with the right mix of skills to start researching drugs based on novel approaches. Hiring new specialized staff into a central laboratory with all the benefits of full-time employment is much more expensive than using a small, nimble company whose expertise can be "tapped" exactly when you need it and only for the duration of time when it is needed. Small, highly entrepreneurial innovative start-ups, which assume early risks and must be highly competitive on costs, can also assemble a staff with the right mix of skills more quickly. They work hard to come up with proposals that are more attractive and competitive than whatever the central company lab can come up with. Therefore, it is not surprising that the partnerships between biotech start-ups and large pharmaceutical companies continue to proliferate. Sound decision making in pharmaceutical companies requires simultaneously understanding business and medicine. The absence of one of these perspectives among some executives may have contributed to costly failures. It is argued that start-ups with ties to venture capital firms (VCs) better combine the two areas of expertise than big companies do.

Even before the 2008 financial crisis and recession, the biopharmaceutical industry was experiencing steady growth in outsourcing and offshoring. Companies began venturing beyond just cooperation with research institutions and start-ups in the developed West. They started reaching out to companies from emerging economies. The recent financial crisis added even more pressure to improve efficiency. Many Western biotech companies found that financing suddenly became much more difficult, if not entirely impossible, due to the financial crisis. They were forced to become leaner and to rely on cost-cutting outsourcing more than ever.

Emerging economies offered advantages tailor-made for this situation. Competitive advantages that emerging market firms offered went beyond the simple reduction of the costs of, say, chemistry or data management work. Some of the emerging economy companies offered good opportunities to collaborate on discovery; they could also facilitate market access and even help with financing and risk sharing. The highly indebted Western countries will face unprecedented pressures to finance all their government obligations over the coming decades. Present budget cutting so visible in Western Europe, combined with lower growth and aging populations, suggests a future impact on the availability of financing for R&D, grants, seed capital, and so on. New ventures from the West will be on the lookout for financing opportunities and risk-sharing deals, and some of those may come from successful emerging players.

Strategic management of R&D in the biopharma industry today is a quest for the right balance between insourcing, outsourcing, and open innovation systems—all based on a global view of the markets. This is a highly complex process in which each decision is made on a case-by-case basis and both the advantages and disadvantages of outsourcing are carefully weighed. We look more closely at large company strategies in Chapter 7, "Company Strategies of Global R&D Collaborations."

The national debate about R&D outsourcing in the United States seems to be informed mainly by the experience of the IT, automotive, and engineering industries, which started the practice before the biopharmaceutical industry did. Pharma, however, is different: Development costs are much higher, product development duration is much longer, and the pervasiveness of failure is much greater. Given these considerations in biopharma, the decision to move forward with the development of a particular product but not another carries more risk and uncertainty, and implies higher outlays than in most other industries.

Choosing from among promising early-stage assets (such as patented molecules) and moving them as quickly as possible to "critical value inflection points" is the key challenge for product development managers. To illustrate the advantages of outsourced development of a drug candidate, let's look at this process in the way a venture capital firm investing in a biotech would.

Just finding out through the preclinical phase process whether a project is worth pursuing may cost $1 million to $3 million. Nine out of 10 projects fail those preclinical tests. Frequent failures require an ability to regroup quickly and move to the next compound on the priority list. From a pure investment perspective, to get beyond the preclinical stage, "survivors" have to show very high expected returns—perhaps several hundred percent or higher—to move to phase 2 in clinical trials. If all goes well at the conclusion of that phase, an exit becomes possible—for example, with a sale to a big multinational at a price reflecting market potential and the probability of success after phase III trials. To come to this point, the total early-phase investments in a biotech may be $15 million to $20 million.[36] This amount is usually lower than what a large organization would likely spend to arrive at the same phase II, but a large organization faces the additional burden of overhead and the possibility of frequent bureaucratic slowdowns. In the outsourced innovation model, which uses the new asset (NME) as a yardstick, no incentive exists to spend money just to "save" a unit in the organization.

The outsourced model of discovery seeks a more efficient use of capital and human resources. For the industry, it represents a step in the direction of a new generation of innovation process that is strategically integrated, is global in its scope, and assumes many elements of the open innovation model.

We discuss this new model in more detail in Chapter 8, "The Future: The Expanding Universe of Global Innovation." Various companies, including Procter & Gamble, Starbucks, and Lego, have implemented sophisticated open innovation systems that invite customers and suppliers to generate new ideas and even create new products. But designing new toys or coffee mugs is different from inventing a new drug. Because of IP concerns, the pharmaceutical industry has been more cautious than other industries, but it continues to experiment in using open innovation.

Offshoring discovery work internationally certainly carries risk. IP and trade secrets need to be well protected. This requires careful partner screening and selection, as well as astute management of information flows. Building longer-term collaborative relationships based on trust can help. Some core R&D capabilities need to be maintained, along with capabilities to assess and leverage intellectual capital coming from both inside and outside the organization. Well-managed offshoring brings important advantages: It offers more choices about which compounds to develop and where, it enables companies to tap into state-of-the-art expertise without spending internal funds on developing new screening technologies and multiple new scientific specialties, and it helps companies avoid sinking funds into expensive infrastructure (especially if "cluster-hungry" regions will build brand new labs for the company). Perhaps most importantly, offshoring helps tap new creative ideas, all contributing to earning higher returns from limited resources. No single formula finds an optimal balance among internal, outsourced, and open innovation. As we shall see in Chapter 7, companies struggle to develop and refine viable models that work best for them.

Some managers might see improving R&D productivity as a purely technical problem of acquiring the latest equipment (such as advanced sequencing machines). Approaches to improve research efficiency include, for example, high-throughput screening platforms. Companies may not need to purchase those machines if they can efficiently outsource the entire "proof of concept" phase of development. Specialized service providers advertise "lean proof of concept experiments: reaching a go/no-go decision for drug candidates more quickly." For example, the company Flexion Therapeutics promises "proof of concept" for as little as $5 million in less than 24 months.[37]

But Samantha Du, CEO of Hutchison MediPharma Limited, argues that being just "lean" is not enough to increase research productivity. In fact, she critiques the "bare bones" and sometimes fragmented Western biopharma companies, which are so specialized that no *integration of expertise* occurs. She contrasts this model with the "well integrated" companies in China and other emerging economies such as India, where many companies have well integrated capabilities. The Biocon company example shows how integrated capabilities in discovery research, clinical trials, and other functions can be an advantage. Samantha Du argues that the integrated approach can produce more efficient R&D. Taking advantage of these emerging market partner advantages can give Western firms the critical edge to winning the R&D productivity race. Outsourcing to emerging market companies can provide the additional edge beyond just throughput efficiency.[38]

This is an important point in the discussion about whether partnering with emerging economy organizations will bring good enough returns on investments, compared with alternative approaches. Examples of drug discovery in India can be seen in Figure 4-5.

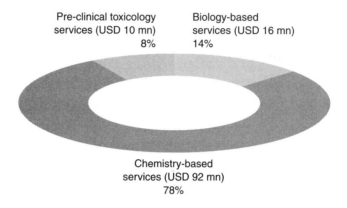

Pre-clinical toxicology
services (USD 10 mn)
8%

Biology-based
services (USD 16 mn)
14%

Chemistry-based
services (USD 92 mn)
78%

*Source: Kotak Institutional Equities Research
January 2008*

Figure 4-5 Drug discovery outsourced to India

Reproduced with permission from "Pharma Summit 2008: India Pharma Inc.—An Emerging Global Pharma Hub," KPMG & CII report, September 2008. Available at www.kpmg.com/Global/en/IssuesAndInsights/ArticlesPublications/Documents/Pharma-summit-2008.pdf.

Outsourcing should be viewed not as a short-term expedient, but as part of strategy. Some companies have developed long-term partnerships with providers. Sanofi-Aventis, the giant French pharmaceutical company, chose to develop a ten-year strategic partnership with Regeneron, giving the latter a steady flow of funding and gaining a steady stream of research output. Companies establishing R&D centers in emerging clusters in China or India are following a similar philosophy.

Early Drug Discovery Investments by Companies: Pursuing Opportunities in Emerging Markets

Although early drug discovery partnerships are less prevalent than clinical trials outsourcing, they are on the rise. R&D outsourcing is moving upstream. The market for outsourced drug discovery (see Figure 4-6) is estimated to be growing by 15%.[39] External developments described earlier have helped create a favorable climate for R&D offshoring by multinational firms. The new climate is based on a greater willingness of countries to respect intellectual property. As we noted, the accumulated experience of international public-sector collaborations in basic science with the emerging economies has also created favorable conditions for private-sector initiatives in the area of discovery.

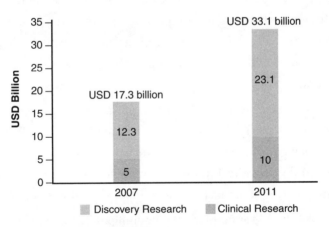

Source: Merrill Lynch, March 2008

Figure 4-6 Global research outsourcing opportunity

Reproduced with permission from "Pharma Summit 2008: India Pharma Inc.—An Emerging Global Pharma Hub," KPMG & CII report, September 2008. Available at www.kpmg.com/Global/en/IssuesAndInsights/ArticlesPublications/Documents/Pharma-summit-2008.pdf.

As Kerry Dolan pointed out in a *Forbes* article entitled "The Drug Research War,"[40] specialized service providers can screen and test compounds against the large numbers of targets available often faster and more efficiently than the largest biopharmaceutical companies. Providers often have at their disposal novel proprietary screening technologies and are specialized in "hot" areas such as antibodies or gene therapy. Some providers who have the latest technology tools and are also located in less costly environments such as India or China emerge as competitive "must have" partners for drug discovery. Here we note a few examples of Western pharmaceutical firms that have been quick to seize the opportunity to start discovery collaborations in China.

As early as 2001, Servier, one of France's leading independent drug companies, founded the Servier (Beijing) Pharmaceutical Research and Development Company as a wholly owned subsidiary. The company collaborates with Chinese universities and research institutes and works on new therapies sourced from the Chinese pharmacopoeia. It has a special interest in developing compounds based on Traditional Chinese Medicine for such areas as diabetes, cancer, and cerebral aging.

An early American investment came in 2003 from Lilly, which opened its research laboratory in the Zhangjiang High-Tech Park outside Shanghai in partnership with a Chinese company, Chem-Explorer. Lilly provides funding and technical support, and the Chinese company implements the research performed by Chinese teams.

In 2004, Roche announced the opening of its first R&D center in China, the first outside Europe and the United States. Working alongside Roche's other global research centers in Basel, Switzerland, and Nutley, New Jersey, the Chinese laboratory specializes in medicinal chemistry and compound screening for antiviral and cancer therapies. This includes development capacities, which span from innovative early exploratory clinical development strategies to efficient late-stage clinical development.[41]

Merck recognized China's excellence in medicinal chemistry even earlier. In 2003, Merck entered a multiyear research collaboration with WuXi Pharma Tech (the company has since been renamed WuXi AppTec after merging with AppTec Lab Services), to speed up drug discovery chemistry. Among other things, WuXi became responsible for new drug discovery libraries to advance lead optimization programs. The program has served Merck well; the Chinese partner contributed not only lower-cost work, but also its own designs for templates.

Novartis is another drug multinational that, in 2006, decided to locate a significant R&D lab in Shanghai's Zhangjiang High-Technology Park. In November 2009, Novartis announced plans to invest $1 billion over the next five years to step up research and development activities in China and significantly expand the existing China Novartis Institutes for BioMedical Research (CNIBR) in Shanghai. CNIBR is expected to become the largest comprehensive research and development center in China, with a staff of about 1,000 people, an increase from 160 people.[42]

In the past four or five years, these types of partnerships and investments by pharmaceutical companies have expanded greatly in scope and geography to include not only China and India, but also several other emerging economies. The idea of globalizing discovery has become part of international best practice in the pharmaceutical and related industries. Chapter 7 discusses more detailed cases of discovery collaborations with emerging economies by the leading big pharmas.

Hutchison MediPharma[a]

Hutchison MediPharma was founded in 2002 a subsidiary of China Meditech Ltd (Chi-Med), which is 72% owned by Hong Kong Hutchison Whampoa.[b] Hutchison Whampoa is an international corporation with diverse holdings, including a number of healthcare firms, such as Hutchison Baiyunshan, Shanghai Hutchison Pharmaceuticals, and Hutchison Healthcare. Hutchison MediPharma has long-term strategic partnerships with companies such as Johnson & Johnson (2008), Lilly (2007),[c] Merck KGaA,[d] and Procter & Gamble (2006)[e] in both oncology and inflammation. In addition, Hutchison MediPharma has formed research and strategic collaborations with renowned universities and institutes worldwide (see below). The company employs more than 200 scientists.[f]

Hutchison MediPharma	
Corporate Partnerships	Johnson & Johnson
	Lilly
	Merck Serono
	Procter & Gamble
Institute Partners	Cambridge University
	University of Maryland
	UCLA
	Cedars-Sinai Medical Center
	Shanghai Institute of Materia Medica
	Institute for Nutritional Sciences
	National Shanghai Center for New Drug Safety Evaluation and Research
	Shanghai Institute of Pharmaceutical Industry
	Shanghai University of TCM
	Peking University School of Pharmaceutical
	Shenyang Pharmaceutical University
Hospital Partners	Chinese PLA General Hospital
	Cancer Institute and Hospital, Chinese Academy of Medical Sciences
	Beijing Cancer Hospital
	Zhongshan Hospital Fudan University
	Shanghai Chest Hospital
	Changhai Hospital of Shanghai
	Mayo Clinic

Hutchison MediPharma's research and development operations are carried out in two R&D facilities in Shanghai's Zhangjiang

High-Tech Park, which totals 75,000 square feet, including a 7,000-square-foot China-certified animal facility. The pharmaceutical research facilities are located in-house and include specialized equipment for most aspects of drug research and development.[g]

Hutchison MediPharma has developed drug discovery technologies, including techniques in the fields of molecular and cell biology, high-throughput screening, genomics, and informatics. Its R&D activities focus on two target therapeutic areas: autoimmune disorders and oncology.[h] The company has several promising anti-inflammatory and anticancer drug candidates in various stages of clinical trials and a pipeline of early stage discovery projects, including HMPL-004 for autoimmune disease and HMPL-011 for inflammation. The portfolio largely focuses on novel synthetic single-chemical entities. Products include a novel oral compound for inflammatory bowel disease that is entering phase III for ulcerative colitis in the United States and Europe, a novel first-in-class IL-10 modulating inflammation compound that completed phase I in Australia, and two other NCEs in oncology at or entering phase I this year in China. More than a dozen NCEs are in preclinical development.[i] The company also has applied for 66 international patents.[j]

Hutchison MediPharma announced a $12.5 million investment from Mitsui & Co., Japan in November 2010, which received convertible Preference Shares that convert into 12.2% of Hutchison MediPharma. The transaction implies a $100 million valuation for the company.[k] In 2009, the company entered into a drug discovery and development partnership with Ortho-McNeil-Janssen Pharmaceuticals, a subsidiary of Johnson & Johnson, to co-develop HMPL-004.[l]

In 2001, its CEO, Dr. Samantha Du, was leading Pfizer's licensing and mergers and acquisitions department in the metabolic diseases area when headhunters lured her to Shanghai to set up Hutchison's pharmaceutical research business. Like Dr. Du, most MediPharma managers have worked at multinational drug companies outside China.[m]

Sources:

a-d, g-j, l. Available at www.hmplglobal.com and www.hutchison-whampoa.com

e, f. "Lilly Works the World," Chemical & *Engineering News*, October 2007. Available at www.pubs.acs.org/cen/business/85/8543bus3.html.

k. "China Biotech Week in Review: VC Investment to Hit New High in 2010," *China Today*, 14 November 2010.

m. See company management team information at www.chi-med.com/eng/management/rnd.htm.

The Future of the Discovery Process in Biopharma

What makes new drug development so frustratingly difficult for investors is the high risk of failure and the long-term payback on invested capital. Can this be changed? Offshoring the discovery and preclinical stages can certainly cut costs and, in some cases, expedite the process. Today a lot of drug discovery still relies on tedious trial and error, often aided by chance. Progress in our basic understanding of diseases should allow for a leaner and more precise design of the drug discovery process and for more accurate targeting and faster and earlier rejection of hypotheses related to the therapeutic impact of a compound under study. According to some optimistic analysts, serious change in the model could come within a decade, although some believe that the process could take longer. Figure 4-7 reproduces a model developed by PricewaterhouseCoopers and cited by S. Burrill.

Moving in the direction of this new version of the discovery process would have great value for the industry and for investors because it would force upstream both the "confidence in mechanism" (CIM) milestone and the "confidence in safety" (CIS) point. Under today's system, both the CIM and CIS milestones happen in the latter part of phase II clinical trials, after a lot of money has been spent.

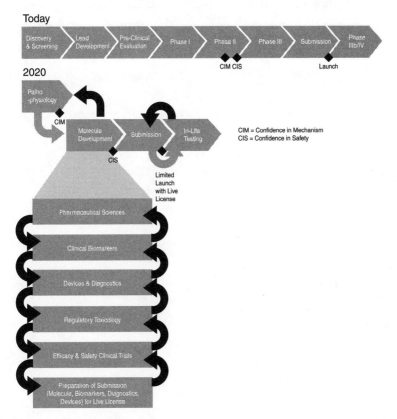

Figure 4-7 Change in discovery process
Reproduced with permission from PricewaterhouseCoopers

The unprecedented global effort to extend the frontiers of basic pathophysiology may usher in some of these new possibilities, with huge impacts on how drugs and therapies will be developed in the future. Nevertheless, it is risky to predict the date when this could actually happen. What we can expect is a process in which research and discovery—both basic and applied—will become increasingly global, with a growing impact coming from the new centers of science in leading emerging economies. But discovery is only one problem. In several of the big pharmaceutical companies, discovery output currently outstrips development capacity. The "bottleneck" is therefore not in discovery, but in development. The latter also poses the greatest financial challenge. Hence, we turn to clinical trials in the next chapter.

5

Globalization of Clinical Trials: It Is Not Just About Slashing Costs

"If we really want to take advantage of global research, we need unified global regulatory requirements that are agnostic to where data is generated. If it is not sufficient for approval in markets that have high commercial value, the opportunity is limited."

—Martina Flammer, MD, MBA, Senior Director, Emerging Markets, Pfizer, Inc.

Clinical Trials Take Up the Lion's Share of Drug Development Costs

In the previous chapter, we saw how scientific research in both the public and private sectors has increasingly become a global enterprise. One of the ways the Western biopharma industry is seeking solutions to its R&D productivity crisis is by more internationalization of outsourcing. Companies have been redesigning models of the discovery process not only to cut costs, but also to improve the speed and efficacy of research. We noted the emergence of a new model of "globally networked discovery." In such a model, companies seek a new balance between internal and external R&D in a system of complex collaborations, alliances, and outsourcing relationships in which organizations from emerging economies play rapidly increasing roles.

Without new inventions, which take place during the research phase of R&D, there is no process of development—which is the path to commercialization. In the pharmaceutical industry, discovery represents only about 30% of the total cost of a new product. The remaining 70% of the costs lie in *development,* especially in the advanced phases of clinical trials (phases III and IV) that involve large groups of human subjects. Therefore, from a strictly economic perspective, improving the efficiency of clinical trials may be the most immediate and pressing condition for reducing overall drug development costs.

Just as discovery is undergoing globalization, so are clinical trials. The task of this chapter is to explain the recent transformation of clinical trials from U.S.-centered to a global system in which emerging economies are increasingly important. We discuss the complex trade-offs and subtle challenges that confront companies that outsource clinical trials overseas, and we explain why cost reduction is only one aspect. In their decisions, companies must also weigh political and regulatory considerations that often determine access to a new market. They must also decide whether to establish their own facilities for the trials or to rely on international or local contract research organizations that have become very competitive players. At the end of the chapter, we make some predictions about how this global system of clinical trials is likely to evolve.

How Clinical Trials Work

Although clinical trials are a substantial and rapidly growing international business, they are not well understood by the general public. They are often seen as obscure and are sometimes surrounded by controversy about the ethical aspects. Our focus in this chapter is primarily on the business side of global clinical trials, but we also briefly discuss some of the ethical and human controversies that have arisen around international trials.

To fully appreciate the advantages brought by the new business models of drug development, we first need to understand how clinical trials work. Until the twentieth century, societies relied on trial and error instead of systematic and rigorous procedures to distinguish successful therapies and medicines from unsuccessful ones. Gradually, more structured experimentation began to take place. Experiments of the British naval doctor James Lind in the mid-eighteenth century were designed to discover the causes of scurvy, a disease that had decimated British naval crews. The experiments relied on comparative groups of men, giving one group vinegar and the other group citrus fruits to treat scurvy. As a result of these experiments, which demonstrated the efficacy of oranges and lemons against scurvy, the Royal Navy began supplying citrus fruits to its ships in 1795.[1] However, it took more than a hundred years from those early experiments for the modern system of drug testing to be born. In the United States, not until 1938 did the U.S. Food Drug and Cosmetic Act subject new drugs to premarket safety evaluation and require Food and Drug Administration (FDA) regulators to review both preclinical and clinical test results.[2] However, even this law did not precisely specify the kinds of tests required for approval, so it gave regulators only limited powers for negotiation with the pharmaceutical industry. Public health disasters caused by poorly tested drugs, such as thalidomide, showed that the system was not adequate to the task. The thalidomide disaster and other, similar ones ultimately prompted the passing of the 1962 Drug Amendments.[3] Those laws explicitly stated that new drug approvals would rely on substantial scientific evidence of a drug's safety and efficacy. Therefore, the FDA was obliged to base its approvals on "adequate and well-controlled studies." The modern clinical trial, based on statistically controlled, evidence-based results, was born and eventually became the requirement for new drug approvals by the FDA. The FDA approval procedure is regarded today as a world standard of the drug industry.

In a double-blind clinical drug study, trials are designed in such a way that neither the patient nor the investigator knows who is receiving the tested drug. Patients are selected according to formalized criteria and then randomly assigned to treatment and control groups; the latter usually is given a placebo or the standard therapy used at the time (active comparator drug). However, before experiments with human subjects can start, preclinical trials must be completed. Under legislation introduced in 1962 and 1963, drug sponsors are required to submit preclinical trial notification and approval to the FDA to show that it is safe to conduct clinical trials. This package of documentation, which must be submitted to the FDA before starting clinical trials, is known by the acronym, IND (investigational new drug). An approved IND constitutes formal permission to launch the actual clinical trials, which involve human subjects. An IND package provides results of animal toxicity testing, indicating that it is reasonably safe to administer the drug to humans. It also describes the chemistry of the drug and describes how the drug is to be manufactured. It details the plan of the initial clinical studies: who will conduct the studies, resources to be used, and the human populations to be studied. An institutional review board must be named responsible for approving the study protocol.

Preclinical studies involve two types of experiments: test tube ones, known as "in vitro," and also experiments carried out with animals or cell cultures, known as "in vivo." The experiments apply different doses of the drug under study to develop acute toxicity and toxicity ranges and to establish a pharmacological profile of the drug. The tests' results inform the decisions related to granting the drug candidate IND status and open the way for further testing of the drug candidate under the actual clinical trials regime.

Actual clinical trials of a new drug typically proceed in three phases. Phase I trials constitute the first stage of testing in human subjects. Usually, a small group of 20–100 healthy volunteers are selected. Phase I includes trials designed to assess the safety profile and initial tolerability, pharmacokinetics, and pharmacodynamics of a drug candidate.

After the safety profile of the drug candidate under investigation has been determined, the next phase of trials is initiated. Phase II is performed on larger groups (100–300) of patients who have the disease the drug aims to treat or prevent, to determine preliminary effectiveness. This outcome is designated as confidence in mechanism (COM). Safety assessments that started in phase I are continued, but in a larger group of volunteers and patients to assess common short-term side effects and risks of the drug candidate. These safety tests should result in reaching a milestone called confidence in safety (CIS). Phase II studies are sometimes divided into phase IIA (related to frequency of dosing) and phase IIB (efficacy at prescribed dosage).

Some trials combine different phases. For example, phases I and II can be blended to test both efficacy and toxicity. Successful completion of phase II becomes a turning point. Establishing confidence in the drug mechanism and its common short-term safety (the CIM/CIS points) opens the way to justifying the very expensive phase III studies. Alternatively, if the drug fails to meet the efficacy and safety profile for phase II, which often happens, the trials are terminated. For investors, phase II provides critical information on whether to support the drug candidate. If the drug candidate meets the criteria in phase II, the chances of success for a new drug are quite strong (approximately 60%). This explains why the possibility of accelerating the process of reaching the CIM/CIS points—such as by using new methods or technologies—is of great interest to investors.

From the perspective of the companies involved, phase III trials expand upon the preliminary data for effectiveness and monitor longer-term safety to determine the overall benefit–risk profile in larger groups of patients. The results form the basis that informs the labeling information, which determines marketing elements of the new drug. Phase III is costly and usually constitutes the "pivotal trials" regulators weigh strongly in their approval or disapproval decision. These studies must meet specific criteria: double-blind design (when this is ethical), randomized, controlled (using placebo or standard therapy as a comparator), and with several hundred to several thousand patients across many clinical study centers in different countries. Phase III is meant to provide definitive answers about the drug's performance for the proposed indication(s). Success in phase III leads to the submission of a new drug application (NDA) to the FDA or equivalent regulatory agencies, such as the European Medicines Agency (EMEA) in Europe or the Pharmaceuticals and Medical Devices Agency (PMDA) in Japan. Documentation required in an NDA is supposed to tell the drug's whole story, including what happened during the clinical tests, the drug's ingredients, the results of the animal studies, how the drug behaves in the body, and how it is manufactured, processed, and packaged.[4] If the drug is approved, it is launched commercially in markets with regulatory approval. Phase IV trials are conducted at the initiative of either the regulator or the company after the drug has been on the market. Phase IV trials involve refining the efficacy or safety profile, determining the optimal use of the drug—such as in patients with comorbidities—ensuring consistent product reliability and quality, and providing technical support of a drug after it receives permission to be sold.

This elaborate sequence of testing requirements (illustrated in Figure 5-1), and the inherent uncertainty of results with very frequent failures make new drug research an expensive and, from an investment perspective, risky undertaking. In the discovery phase, as many as 10,000 molecules may be screened before a drug candidate is chosen for a patent application. About 1,000 potential drug candidates may be further tested at the preclinical phase—before even one reaches the point of actually being tested in a clinical trial. For example, a new cancer drug undergoes an average of six years of preclinical research before it even makes it to clinical trials. Delays and complications are common. On average, about eight years pass from the time a cancer drug enters clinical trials until it receives approval from regulatory agencies for sale to the public.[5]

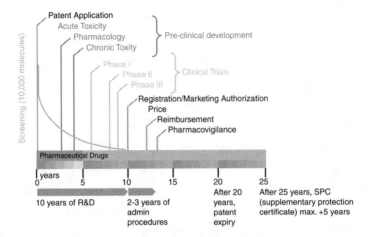

Figure 5-1 Phases of pharmaceutical drug research and development process in the E.U.
Reproduced with permission from The Pharmaceutical Industry in Figures, (Brussels: European Federation of Pharmaceutical Industries and Associations, 2010), 7.

Who Does Clinical Trials? From Academic Centers to Global CROs

The United States used to be the home of more than 60% of all clinical trials carried out in the world. Research institutes, hospitals, and medical schools initiated and carried out clinical trials. This practice has been changing because the global pharmaceutical industry operations are changing. From 1960 until 1980, prescription drug sales used to be flat as a percentage of American GDP; in the next 20 years, however, that number increased several times. Several legislative decisions have enabled this boom. The 1980 University and Small Business Patent Procedures Act (also known as the Bayh–Dole Act) granted universities and small firms the power to patent discoveries from research sponsored by the National Institutes of Health and subsequently to grant licensing rights to the pharma industry. The act encouraged collaboration between academic research and corporations and helped grow the biotechnology industry.[6] These developments ushered in the era of rapidly expanding clinical trials for new drugs sponsored by pharmaceutical companies and eventually also by biotechnology companies. From the mid-1980s onward, companies began outsourcing trial execution to contain costs and improve research efficiency. Today the majority of clinical trials are performed by specialized for-profit companies. The huge increases in private industry spending on new drug research and development that occurred in the 1980s transformed the clinical trials industry and gave birth to the rapid expansion of contract research organizations (CROs), which became specialized in preclinical and clinical trials work. By the 1990s, clinical research largely migrated from academic and research centers to CROs—many of which became highly successful international companies that have gone public.[7]

The sponsoring company hires the CRO, provides the drug substance, develops the protocol together with subject matter experts, and ensures medical oversight. Companies can hire CROs to perform all phases of clinical trials, and some CROs also perform preclinical work and the earlier phases of discovery work, as illustrated in Figure 5-2. Phase IV studies are growing rapidly, as regulatory agencies in the United States, Europe, and Japan require more post-marketing studies as a requirement at the time of approval. The CRO performs all the administrative work related to the trials and collects study data.

Pharmaceutical companies are the largest customer group for CRO services, but biotechnology companies, many of which are on very tight budgets, are increasingly significant and currently account for about one-third of the CRO clients. For biotechnology startups, CROs can be a lifesaver. Although small biotech companies have struggled to maintain solubility in the recession, CROs have been thriving, primarily because they streamline the first massive expense a biotech company must face: clinical trials. A phase I trial may cost as much as $5 million, with phase II trials running at $20 million, and phase III studies often costing $80 million to $100 million. Such costs make or break a new venture.

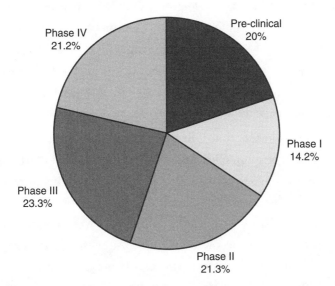

Figure 5-2 Revenue share percentage by phase (world), 2008

Reproduced with permission from "Outsourcing Clinical Trials: Growth Continues," Frost & Sullivan Industry Analyst, PharmTech.com, 1 May 2009.

Consider the example of Rexahn, a U.S. company located on the East Coast. Similar to many small biopharmas, it outsources the entire clinical trial "package" of recruiting and transporting patients, lining up investigators, and covering other testing and administrative costs. Rexahn is saving money and time by using an Indian CRO and running the trials in India, which has plenty of patients; many English-speaking, Western-educated physicians; and a new FDA field station. "If we just did [the trial] in the U.S., it would have taken three years," says one of the company's managers. "Shifting to India cuts the time to 12 to 18 months and saves up to 50% in expenses."[8] Easier recruitment and retention of patients, large heterogeneous patient population, an abundance of treatment-naïve patients, and lower costs of operations make these savings possible.

The recent recession and its shortage of financing for biotechs have fueled the expansion of CROs. CROs have seen their revenues expand as a result of pharmaceutical companies outsourcing more of their clinical trials. Consider the example of Covance, a leading CRO based in Princeton, New Jersey. The company reported second-quarter revenues of $489 million, up from $461 million for the same quarter in 2008. Other major CROs, including Parexel of Boston, Kendle of Cincinnati, and Charles River of Wilmington, Massachusetts, have also experienced strong revenue results.[9]

Evidence suggests that CROs perform clinical trials more cost-effectively than academic institutions. The CRO market today is estimated to be well in excess of $20 billion, with an annual growth rate of 14%–16%. The reason for the rapid expansion of CROs is cost and time efficiency: CRO-conducted clinical trials were completed 30% more quickly than those conducted in-house by sponsors. Therefore, it is hardly surprising that spending on contract clinical services is growing faster than development spending. Headcount among major CROs between 2001 and 2004 grew 6% annually, while sponsor headcounts remained flat or faced declines. Demand for CRO services is expected to grow by 16% annually for the next five years. The CRO industry will benefit from more numerous and complex clinical trials and the globalization of service offerings. High development costs and relatively brief market exclusivity are among the factors that force companies to drive efficiency and launch new drugs on a global scale. Global drug launches and sales prompt the globalization of clinical trials.[10]

According to a Lehman Brothers survey in 2007, the top three CROs were Quintiles, ICON, and Covance. Quintiles, the market leader, "clearly benefited from its global capabilities," and ICON was singled out for "being vigilant in terms of keeping studies on track."[11] Size of the CRO and its market position was seen as contributing to competitiveness. Covance, with a more modest market position, was praised for its strong investment in the business. PPD was fourth in overall quality, followed by Parexel, Kendle, PharmaNet, PRA International, and i3.[12] The survey was addressed to large drug companies and some biotechnology companies, which rated the clinical research services of the CROs in terms of overall quality. Project management and startup speed were areas in which CRO performance had improved, and meeting project timelines was the most frequently cited area for improvement. A majority of respondents anticipated the volume of clinical trials outsourcing to keep growing on account of such factors as lack of internal capacity and cost considerations. The therapeutic and scientific expertise of CROs was cited as very important by about one-third of responding companies. A majority of respondents also identified "access to international sites" by CROs as important.[13] CRO services are estimated to witness double-digit growth, and at least 60% of FDA-regulated clinical trials are estimated to be conducted offshore (outside the United States) by 2012. Consolidation among CROs is also a major trend and is an indicator of the rising demand for large, globalized clinical trials.[14] In the future, competition among CROs is likely to increase as new players based in emerging economies globalize their operations. This chapter profiles several of these companies.

The Economic Geography of Clinical Trials: Cost and Other Considerations

Figure 5-3 illustrates 2005 comparative costs of clinical trials in different countries, and the data is still cited in such authoritative reports as Steve Burrill's "State of the World 2010" presentation. The figure shows that performing clinical trials in Russia, for example, can be four times cheaper than in Germany. The United States is not cheap, but it is on par with South Africa and cheaper than in the United Kingdom, Ireland, and even Singapore. India, China, Central Europe, and South America all appear to be highly competitive destinations.

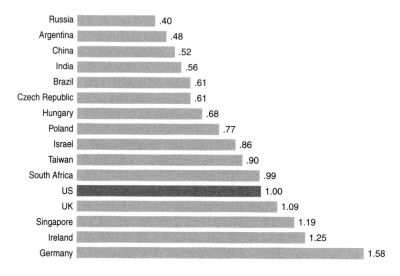

Source: SalaryExpert.com; WDI Database; Economist Intelligence Unit; CBRE Global Markets Rent 2005; A.T. Kearney analysis, Aug 2005; Clinical Trial Offshoring

Figure 5-3 Overall clinical trial costs
Reproduced with permission from Burrill & Company, "Biotech 2010 Life Science: Adapting for Success," BIO International Convention, Chicago, 4 May 2010.

What is the geography of clinical trials today? How deep is the shift to the cheaper destinations located in the emerging markets? Burrill & Company created a world map of clinical trials based on National Institutes of Health data as of March 2010 (see Figure 5-4). The map shows the dramatic increase in the total number of clinical trials in the world in recent years.

In 2006, the overall number of clinical trials in the world was estimated at 20,000.[15] The most recent data suggests that the number of trials has increased almost fivefold since 2006. Also, the share of trials conducted in the United States has shrunk to less than 50%. Clinical trials have indeed become a global business. Of the approximately 96,000 trials conducted around the world, 45,637 were done in the

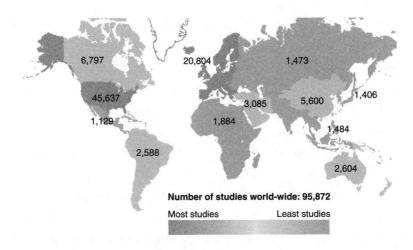

Number of studies world-wide: 95,872

Most studies   Least studies

Figure 5-4 Clinical trials around the world, March 2010

Reproduced with permission from National Institutes of Health, "Clinical Trials Around the World, March 2010," quoted from Burrill & Company, "Biotech 2010 Life Science: Adapting for Success," BIO International Convention: Chicago, 4 May 2010.

United States, 20,804 in Europe (including Central Europe and the new EU member states, such as Poland), and 5,600 in China (less than the 6,797 done in Canada). Latin America had just less than 2,600 trials. India had relatively few trials (1,381), which is less than Australia (2,604) or Africa (1,884).[16] However revealing, these numbers do not tell us much about what kinds of trials are being conducted in particular regions. They say nothing about which countries and continents specialize in what areas and how they perform in terms of quality and reliability. These numbers do show that, in March 2010, the majority of trials were still being done in developed Western countries, although alternative destinations were growing fast.

In 1991, only 10% of trials were carried out in emerging markets; by 2005, according to some observers, that share had increased to 40%.[17] In 1990, 96% of clinical trial principal investigators were based in the United States. By 2007, the figure stood at 57% and has decreased further since.[18]

The extent to which pharmaceutical companies decide to offshore trials varies considerably. U.S.- and UK-based firms appear to be moving in this direction more aggressively than firms located in Germany or Switzerland, for example. According to numbers published in Adriana Petryna's book,[19] GlaxoSmithKline ran 29% of its trials outside the United States and Western Europe in 2004; by 2007, that figure had grown to 50%. Wyeth Pharmaceuticals conducted half of its trials outside the United States in 2004, and that share rose to 70% in 2006. Merck conducted half its clinical trials overseas in 2004—an increase of 45% since 1999. What about patients enrolled at the sites? Central-Eastern Europe had the highest volume of patients (6.27) enrolled per investigative site, followed by Asia Pacific (5.78), South-Central America (4.56), Western Europe (3.08), and the United States (1.92).[20]

Between 1995 and 2006, the highest annual growth in active investigators occurred in Russia, Argentina, India, Poland, Brazil, and China. Of these, Russia had the highest number of investigators listed by the FDA (623), followed by India (464), Argentina (462), Poland (322), China (307), and Brazil (292). Growth in numbers of investigators was strongest in India, China, and Russia between 2001 and 2006.[21]

Rachel Yang from Oracle Health Sciences Global Business Unit cites interesting and up-to-date data on the shift in the geographical distribution of clinical trials from 2006 to 2010.[22] Figure 5.5 shows a decline in the share of clinical trials carried out in Western Europe and the United States, from 55% to 38%, and shows significant increases in Eastern Europe, China, India, and especially in the Middle East and Africa.[23]

However, experts warn that we need to be careful with numbers related to trials. Until there is a worldwide registry of clinical trials by country, phase, target therapy, and so on—as some in the World Health Organization (WHO) have proposed—no one will really know exactly how many trials are indeed taking place and where.

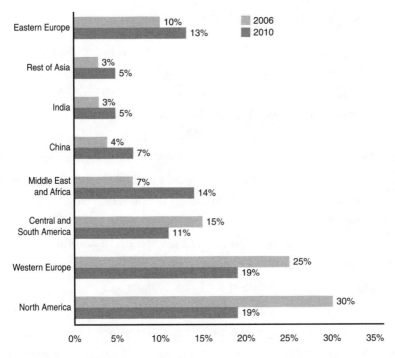

Adapted from McDonnell & Mooraj, AMR Research.[1]

Figure 5.5 Geographical distribution of clinical trials, 2006–2010

Reproduced with permission from Rachel Yang, "New Challenges Call for Innovative Approaches," Eclinical Visions, Touch Briefings: Oracle Health Sciences, 2008, 4. Adapted from W. McDonnell and H. Mooraj, "Clinical Trials Are Moving Out," 13 May 2008. Available at www.amrresearch.com.

The Unique Management Challenges of Global Clinical Trials

Globalizing clinical trials brings with it a number of complex issues, including quality and reliability of the trials and accessing the human populations. The outsourcing and offshoring of clinical trials has been growing rapidly and brings substantial benefits to the sponsors. However, there are still complex ethical and political issues to which solutions need to be found.

Access, Quality, and Reliability

If clinical trials take about half of the ten years of R&D that the drug development process requires, then timely progress with tests is a crucial issue. However, it is estimated that 80% of clinical trials fail to recruit patients on time. In Western countries, clinical trial sponsors compete for a limited pool of investigators and patients. In the United States, the number of repeat investigators continues to decline, and the number of first-time investigators is increasing; many of those are not retained. In emerging economies, patient pools are vast—especially so-called "treatment-naïve" patients—and the pools of qualified investigators are increasing rapidly. In addition to costs, this is one of the causes of clinical trials becoming globalized.

The advantages of global trials are clear; less clear are the complex management challenges that global trials pose. Within just a few years, CROs have had to learn how to move from a situation of conducting trials in the United States, the United Kingdom, and Canada, for example, to projects involving trials in more than 25 different countries. The sheer amount of communications and coordination problems can be extraordinary, with corresponding overhead costs exploding. Data management has to occur in an environment that must ensure data security and protection of intellectual property while at the same time enabling rapid decision making.

The answers have come in the form of standardized, secure, and robust IT systems in which all employees share the same software. Such systems have evolved into so-called clinical trial management systems (CTMS), an industry standard today that can combine electronic data capture (EDC) and interactive voice response (IVR) systems, along with near real-time data visibility into study progress and other features. All of this makes clinical trials more efficient and timely. For example, Dell hardware, Microsoft platforms, and Oracle databases, are employed with the infrastructure based on Cisco Networks. Such technologies enable the use of adaptive trials designs.

Using accumulating data, adaptive design decides how to modify aspects of the ongoing trials to answer the right development questions without the risk of undermining the validity and integrity of the trial.[24] Adaptive trials are still an idea for the future but will likely become a necessity as appropriate CTMS and clinical data management systems (CDMS) solutions emerge.

Such IT-based systems are about improving the speed and accuracy of decision making, ultimately leading to time savings and enhancing the progress of drug development. However, for a global clinical trials management system to succeed, more is needed than just the right CTMS and CDMS systems. Country teams must understand where they fit in the overall business system and how their work affects others. Local environments differ in terms of infrastructures, regulation, economics, and cultural values. Without a deep understanding of these differences, productive global collaboration and innovative solutions will not take place. Productivity improvements need to be specific to the location in question and take all these considerations into account. For example, will it be helpful to ask patients to provide feedback using mobile technology? The answer depends on local conditions, which vary across countries and need to be understood in depth.

Outsourcing and Offshoring Clinical Trials

Although CROs have become market leaders in the clinical trials business, they are not the only option open to sponsors. As we previously mentioned, some pharmaceutical companies may choose to keep the entire chain of research and development for some categories of drugs in-house, under one roof. Sponsors who decide to offshore or outsource need to choose from among several models.

Preclinical research business models might include so-called "utility outsourcing" and "strategic outsourcing." In utility outsourcing, sponsors provide a fee for service, and efficiency is paramount.

In the case of strategic outsourcing, flexibility and speed are important, but so is accessing new knowledge or technology in an environment that is changing and developing quickly and may, for example, reveal new targets or new approaches to therapy. The sponsor and the service provider might pool their expertise and become partners in developing a new product. An example might be a Western multinational working with a Chinese research institute to develop natural compounds and herb-based treatments.

In the case of clinical trials, the two alternative philosophies of entering into a partnership also apply, except that the actual models and relationships tend to be more complicated. The model of complete outsourcing means contracting a CRO, such as Quintiles, for example, with broad capabilities, a central laboratory, and access to many international trial sites. Alternatively, the sponsor company may decide to set up its own R&D unit (with equity investment) dedicated to clinical operations. Such a facility may include a central laboratory to process trial results coming from different destinations. Another approach is to use a mix of providers (known as functional service providers) based on core competencies. Such a mix may include, for example, a local medical department to perform clinical trials while outsourcing specialized services to local companies (such as monitoring and source data verification; obtaining local regulatory permission, test license, and ethics committee approvals; setting up local study logistics; storing and distributing the drugs; and entering clinical data).[25]

To compete with local contract research organizations, the large international CROs keep moving up the value chain to encompass such services as quality assurance and audits, pharmacovigilance support, discrepancy management, and query resolution in data management, statistical analysis, and medical writing. Many pharmaceutical companies use the model of a preferred full-service provider with whom they sign master service agreements.

Another model sometimes used in markets such as India is the contract-staffing model, in which the sponsor hires contract staff through the service provider. The full-time equivalents (FTEs) can be located either at the sponsor's office or at the service provider's office. The sponsor provides functional training and technical support, and the service provider handles the salary and administration requirements. This model offers several important advantages. It enables the sponsor to retain control over the project without the need to entirely outsource it, which would happen in the full-service provider model. It enables effective quality and cost control and reduces time spent on training staff, without the need to recruit staff on permanent head count. It enables timely replacement of staff after attrition—a common problem in environments in which demand outstrips supply.[26]

In biopharma contract manufacturing, outsourcing can reduce overall costs by 30%–35%. The impact on net earnings and cash flow is direct. In the case of clinical trials, the financial argument is more complicated. The downside of using CROs for small firms is loss of control. In practice, companies have to make decisions about which parts of the process they want to retain full control over. CEO Richard Garr of Neuralstem in Rockville, Maryland, says that his company does use outsourcing, "but not in the way a lot of companies do."[27] Instead of outsourcing research, Neuralstem outsources only the processing of "paperwork" through Quinteles, such as electronic filings and quality control forms; Neuralstem maintains control on regulatory matters.[28]

But outsourcing does not come without its costs, as the experience of the IT industry shows. AMR, a market research firm, concludes that although the benefits of offshoring IT research and development are too significant to ignore, the implementation of three projects are needed before a firm will benefit from any cost savings.[29] Effective outsourcing requires investment and can initially add to costs. The cost of selecting a vendor can reach 2%; transitioning work to an offshore partner can cost 2%–3%; layoff, severance, and retention payments can cost 3%–5%; and the so-called "cultural costs," which include achieving ongoing communications and understanding with the vendor, can cost 2%–3%.[30] Then there are the costs of managing an offshore contract, at 6%–10%.[31] In a survey of 101 companies, *CIO* magazine calculated—using the total costs of outsourcing (TCO) formula—that, even in the best-case scenario, a firm that spends $16.2 million on offshore outsourcing contracts will actually spend 15.2% more (a TCO of $18.7 million) in a best-case scenario; in a worst-case scenario, a firm could spend as much as 57% more (a TCO of $25.4 million).[32] In addition, firms can experience real and inherent costs related to high turnover rates. Morale problems can also result within an American workforce of engineers and scientists who are critical of offshore outsourcing. According to the National Association of Software and Service Companies, annual employee turnover in India can reach as high as 35%.[33] The potential loss of core proprietary knowledge and intellectual property (IP) must be considered when calculating the risk of offshore outsourcing of R&D.[34]

Although the peculiarities of IT research may be different from clinical trials, similar key principles apply. Selecting and developing partners requires investment in resources and management time, and IP considerations must be considered. Although working with a reputable international CRO removes many of the headaches of outsourcing, it may not be the best decision from the point of view of building strategic partnerships designed to lead to long-term competitive advantage in a key emerging market. Loss of internal core competencies must be part of the equation of strategic outsourcing decisions.

In reality, international biotechnology and pharmaceutical companies pursue multipronged strategies: They use CROs for some of the clinical testing, they may invest in a facility of their own in a key new emerging market, and they may outsource preclinical and clinical functions to a mix of local or specialized international providers. For example, a company may develop a molecule in-house, use a Russian company for its chemistry work, and then hire a Chinese company to do the clinical trials and continue with contract manufacturing if the compound is approved. In a system of global R&D, selection, development, and management of partnerships becomes a condition of success for biopharma companies.

The Ethics and Politics of International Clinical Trials

Conducting clinical trials has important ethical, cultural, and political dimensions. As clinical trials go global, these dimensions become more complex and challenging. An outsourcing manager needs to have a keen understanding of the sensitivities and issues prevailing in the countries that host the trials.

The notorious cases of criminal abuse may catch the most attention—such as the story of clinical trial investigators representing a multinational pharma allegedly allowing children to die in Nigeria during a 1996 epidemic. This case, reported in the international press, inspired the book by John Le Carré and the related film *The Constant Gardner*.[35]

In her provocative book *When Experiments Travel*,[36] Adriana Petryna offers a critical view of the ethics of international clinical trials, based on extensive interviews with doctors, administrators, and industry experts. She analyzed outsourced clinical trials in Poland and Brazil and found many similarities between these two distant countries. Both are now among the favorite new destinations for trials. Petryna showed how the combination of weak healthcare systems, resource-strapped administrators and researchers, underpaid physicians, and patients desperate for treatment creates a situation that leads to vulnerability of subjects and an imbalance of power between the international trial sponsors and the local patients.

A situation in which it is easy to recruit willing patients and well-qualified physicians at a fraction of the cost they would incur in the United States, for example, is attractive to pharmaceutical companies. The companies argue that, by launching international trials, they are providing valuable treatments at their own expense to patients who otherwise would not get them. Petryna argues that patient vulnerability and opportunism of many physicians, combined with often superficial oversight, creates damaging side effects to global clinical trials. She makes a good case for more scrutiny of trials, at both the national and international levels. Some of this is happening already. For example, the FDA in the United States has established offices in India and other emerging economies.

Poland and Brazil are both middle-income countries. Poland has a high literacy rate and a healthcare system that covers the vast majority of citizens. The risks of negative side effects of trials become much greater in countries that combine low income levels with high levels of illiteracy, and where large segments of the population have no or almost no healthcare coverage.

Let's look at the case of India. According to GlaxoSmithKline CEO Jean-Pierre Garnier's article in the May 2008 *Harvard Business Review*, it costs about $2,000 to track the progress of a single Indian patient in a clinical trial.[37] It costs ten times more in the United States. The United States has one doctor for every 384 Americans, but India has 1,667 patients for each Indian doctor.[38] Whatever the faults of the American healthcare system, the average American patient consumes almost 200 times more money in medical care each year than the average Indian. The vast majority of Americans can read, but 39% of Indians are illiterate.

Patients are especially vulnerable to manipulation by unscrupulous physicians when suffering from serious diseases, such as malignant tumors for which they might not have access to a cure. Therefore, it's hardly surprising that it is "very easy" to recruit and retain patients for clinical trials in India. (Not even half of study volunteers in industrialized nations complete trials. Completion rates in developing countries are frequently close to 90%.) Concerns arise over whether participants in trials conducted in developing countries feel free to quit, based on several reasons related to access to health-care and culture.

A February 2004 survey of nearly 700 researchers reported in the *Journal of Medical Ethics* found that fewer than 60% of trial protocols in developing countries get reviewed by an ethics committee. Only one in ten Chinese trial protocols received an ethics review, according to an April 24, 2008, article in the journal *Trials*. Four in five of those protocols failed to adequately discuss informed consent.[39]

The problems lie not in a lack of international standards governing clinical research. For example, the World Medical Association's Declaration of Helsinki, first adopted in 1964, states that potential research subjects must be adequately informed of risks and benefits and of the right to refuse to participate and to quit the study.[40] The FDA requires that pharmaceutical companies seeking approval in the United States abide by guidelines formulated by the International Conference on Harmonization—a collaboration among industry groups and regulatory agencies in Europe, Japan, and the United States.[41] The document contains language regarding informed consent stating that "neither the investigator, nor the trial staff, should coerce or unduly influence a subject to participate or continue to participate in a trial."[42] Instead, the problems lie in the fact that neither the FDA nor the national regulatory authorities in the countries hosting the trials have sufficient resources to monitor the trials comprehensively.

Developing country governments have to walk a fine line when crafting regulations related to drug approvals and clinical trials. Governments want to protect their populations from abuse and also ensure that only safe drugs enter their markets. However, they realize that they must keep their countries competitive and attractive for international companies to outsource R&D and invest in related infrastructure. Making local clinical trials mandatory before a drug can be approved for sale in the country is one way to regulate market access. For example, China has a relatively more complex process of regulation, compared with India. In India, the phase I business was limited by government regulation that did not allow human volunteers to be exposed for the first time to new drugs. Therefore, molecules developed outside India could not be used to conduct trials. However, this regulation has been changed recently and has opened the door to more phase I trials in the country. As we will see in the next section, conditions in countries vary considerably in terms of regulations, infrastructure, and expertise. In addition to the patient pool size and costs, these factors drive the competitiveness of clinical trials destinations.

The New Players As Clinical Trials Destinations

Traditionally, clinical trials are performed in Western countries as well as in Central Europe. More recently, the attractiveness of India, China, and Latin America has been increasing. Due to their large populations of treatment-naïve patients as well as low costs, these nations are becoming important and highly competitive destinations for clinical trials. We can expect, for a variety of reasons, the importance and attractiveness of these and other new destinations to increase in the future.

What Makes Countries Attractive?

In spite of the serious problems with outsourced clinical trials, emerging economies such as India and others feel that the economic benefits outweigh the disadvantages. Emerging markets are competing to make themselves attractive destinations in what has become a battleground for the international clinical trials business. India, in particular, is pursuing a strategy to make clinical trials an important new industry.

Let's look at several key emerging destinations for clinical trials— including India, China, and Latin America—and compare them with Eastern Europe. A.T. Kearney has developed an overall ranking of country attractiveness for clinical trials based on five criteria: patient availability, cost efficiency, relevant expertise, regulatory conditions, and national infrastructure (see Figure 5-6). Each country is scored on a scale of 1–10. The resulting ranking differs considerably from the ranking based solely on clinical trial costs.

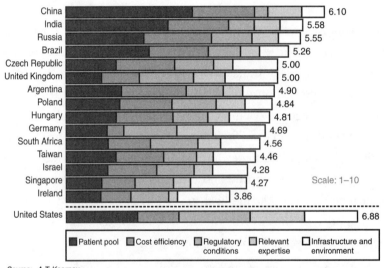

Source: A.T. Kearney
Notes: Higher scores indicate higher levels of attractiveness. The 15 countries analyzed were selected based on size, diversity, and geographical distribution. The Index is not meant to be comprehensive across all potential offshore locations.

Figure 5-6 Clinical trials: overall country attractiveness index
Reproduced with permission from Wynn Bailey, Carol Cruickshank, and Nikhil Sharma, "Make Your Move: Taking Clinical Trials to the Best Location," A. T. Kearney, 2006.

In spite of higher costs, the United States leads the ranking, with an overall score of 6.88. It is closely followed by China, with a score of 6.1. India, Russia, and Brazil, all countries with large populations, follow. In spite of their good infrastructures and expertise, small, developed countries such as Israel, Singapore, and Ireland score relatively lower. In the middle, we have a mix of West and Central European countries. Among Central European countries, the Czech Republic stands out as an attractive destination in spite of its small size.[43] It is important to note that the pharmerging markets we discussed in Chapter 3, "A Reshuffling of Markets and Growth Opportunities," are also being perceived as highly attractive destinations for clinical trials.

India and China

Just a decade ago, the CRO industry hardly existed in India. The country had a shortage of trained investigators, and most doctors and pharmacists had little interest in pursuing careers in clinical trials. Today clinical trials in India are booming. India is making every effort to become a powerhouse of global clinical trials and to turn its competitive advantages into a multibillion-dollar business. India has more than 600,000 physicians, 700,000 nurses, 400,000 pharmacists, and 3 million bioscience graduates and postgraduates. Its universities turn out between 50,000 and 60,000 graduates in different areas of science, including 17,000 medical graduates and 20,000 pharmacists. The majority of these professionals speak English, and many have degrees from reputable Western institutions.[44]

With the support of investors, global CROs such as Quintiles, Covance, PPD, ICON, and Pharmanet have decided to establish themselves in the country—sometimes reducing their operations in traditional Western markets. Leading global pharmaceutical companies—including Pfizer, Novartis, AstraZeneca, Lilly, GlaxoSmithKline (GSK), Roche, Amgen, and others—are expanding clinical trials investment and infrastructure in the country.[45]

India makes a compelling case in spelling out the major advantages (listed in order of importance) of conducting trials in the country:

1. Speed of recruitment
2. Costs that are 30%–50% less than in the United States or Europe

3. Huge patient pool

4. English-speaking investigators

5. Evolving regulatory environment

Between 2002 and 2010, the number of good clinical practices (GCP) studies in India is estimated to have increased at least tenfold, the number of GCP trained investigators also increased more than tenfold, and GCP-compliant sites increased more than 20 times. The number of clinical research professionals has also been increasing at similar rates of growth. Both Indian and international organizations have expended huge resources on training and upgrading the skills of clinical research professionals. The number of investigators in India has also grown and is estimated to be more than 600, representing a broad cross-section of therapeutic areas. Without this effort, the success of the clinical research industry in India would not have been possible.[46]

More than 61% of clinical trials in India were phase III trials, and only 5% were phase I—the rest were phase II and phase IV trials. This ratio reflects India's competitive advantage in terms of its ability to recruit large numbers of patients who have not undergone treatment.[47] The most important therapeutic areas for the trials were infectious diseases, oncology, and endocrinology.

India has made huge strides in improving the quality of its clinical trials, which was previously a problem. Many global companies still manage their quality assurance, pharmacovigilance, medical writing, and regulatory affairs from central offices outside India. Some global pharmaceutical companies have not set up their centralized lab facilities in India and continue using their existing facilities in the United States and Europe. Some Indian labs, such as Specialty Ranbaxy and Metropolis, have seized this opportunity to set up their own central labs to cover global studies. It is expected that as India's clinical trials business continues to expand, more value-added functions will be transferred to the country, including central lab services (see Table 5-1). Utilizing India's competitive advantages in IT, Indian software companies have been expanding their medical data management business. For example, the cost of data entry in India is estimated to be one-sixth to one-eighth that of Western costs.

Table 5-1 Clinical Research Players in India[48]

Organizational Types/ Clinical Area	Players
Contract research organizations	Quintiles, Chiltern, PPD, Covance, Pharmanet, Parexel, ICON, Kendle, Pharm Olam, IGate, PRA International, SIRO, Synchron, ClinInvent, I3, Clingene, ClinWorld, ClinRx, Clintec, PharmaIntel, ACT/Suven, Reliance, Apothecaries, Clinquest, Indigene, RxMD, Helix, KARD Scientific, INC GVK, Medpace, Trident
Bioequivalence and bioanalytic trials	Synchron, Lambda Therapeutics, Lotus Lab, Vimta Lab, Wellquest, Jubilant, LG Lifescience, Phoenix, Oxygen, Therapeutic Drug Monitoring, ClinSearch, Ace Biomed, Bioassay, Reliance, PERD Centre, Medlar
Site-management organizations	Neeman Medical, Odessey Research, Accunova, Metropolis, Quintiles
Patient recruitment organizations	ICRI Synexus
Data management and Information Technology Enabled Services (ITES) business	Quintiles, Chiltern, Synchron, Cognizant, SIRO, Accenture, DnO, CinInvent, TCS, IBM, HCL, Infosys, Persistent, Technologies, Sristek
Central laboratories services	Specialty Ranbaxy, Clinigene International, Metropolis Health Services, Max Healthcare, Dr. Lal's Pathlab, Pathnet, Thyrocare, Lambda Therapeutics, Quest
Centralized electrocardiograms (ECG) services	Quintiles, SIRO–Spacelabs
Clinical research training institutes	Academy of Clinical Excellence, Catalyst Clinical Services, Institute of Clinical Research INDIA, Kundnani College of Pharmacy, SIES College of Management, Kriger, Bioinformatics Institute, PEXA, CRI, Reliance, Bilcare

India has developed a number of successful CROs, such as Matrix Laboratories, Sino Clinpharma, and Jubilant. Some of them are fast becoming not only regional, but also global players. A profile of Jubilant is presented in the sidebar.

Jubilant Life Sciences Limited

Jubilant Life Sciences Limited (formerly Jubilant Organosys, Ltd.) is an integrated pharma and life sciences company. It is the largest custom research and manufacturing services (CRAMS) company and a leading drug discovery and development solutions provider based in India. The company provides life sciences products and services across the value chain, serving its customers worldwide and leveraging the global scale of its operations. The company's success so far is an outcome of its strategic focus on the pharma and life sciences industry, moving up the value chain for products and services across geographies, constantly investing in various growth platforms, and promoting a culture of innovation.

Over the years, Jubilant Life Sciences Limited has extended its footprint beyond India to the United States, Canada, Europe, and other countries across the globe. It expanded its business by building capabilities internally, through strategic build-outs and acquisitions, resulting in a network of 7 world-class manufacturing facilities in India and 3 in North America, and a team of 5,500 people across the globe with 1,400 in North America.[a]

Key R&D activities include the following areas:

• Product development of advance intermediates, fine chemicals, active pharmaceutical ingredients, and generic dosage forms

• Continuous process improvement for cost reduction to provide long-term sustainability to various businesses

• Collaborative drug discovery research that involves discovery informatics, functional chemistry, and crystallography

• Contract research on projects and FTE basis to support customers' preclinical and clinical development programs

As of March 31, 2010, Jubilant Life Sciences Limited had 1,130 employees involved in R&D activities. The company has R&D centers in India at Noida, Gajraula, Nanjangud, Ambernath, and Samlaya. It has 415 R&D employees, including 82 doctorates and additional post-graduates and graduates. R&D supports the activities of various businesses through new product and process development, process optimization, absorption of technology, and technology established on a commercial scale. R&D is a focal point for continuous improvements in the existing processes throughout the life cycle of the product.[b]

AstraZeneca and CrystalGenomics have entered into a research collaboration to discover and develop a novel anti-infective for use as a potential antibacterial agent in 2010.[c] Under the terms of this agreement, Korea-based CrystalGenomics will receive research funding from AstraZeneca for two years. This is the first such infection research collaboration AstraZeneca has entered into with a Korean-based company and further demonstrates its commitment to Asia.

Sources:

a. Jubilant Company website, www.jubl.com/corporate-strategy.html
b. Jubilant Company Annual Report, available at www.jubl.com/pdfs/annual-report-2009-10.pdf.
c. Available at AstraZeneca website, www.astrazeneca.com/partnering/recent-collaborations.

China conducts several times more clinical trials than India and offers a much bigger pharmaceutical market. It also offers many of the same advantages as India: low costs (30%–50% of costs in the West), access to a vast pool of human and animal resources, evolving modern medical facilities and professional staff, rapid recruitment of patients, and a U.S. FDA office in the country. As the A.T. Kearney ranking indicates, China's regulatory regime is more cumbersome than India's. For example, the Chinese State Food and Drug Administration (SFDA) can take from 9 to 12 months to approve trials, and every shipment of drugs into the country requires an import license.[49]

In addition, the language and cultural barriers of doing business in China are significantly higher than in India. Both countries compete vigorously for international CRO business and have successfully attracted major Western firms, many of which have set up shop in both countries.

AstraZeneca opened a Clinical Research Unit–East Asia in Shanghai in 2002 and has conducted tests on 50,000 patients. The decision showed the company's determination to localize not just manufacturing, sales, and marketing, but progressively R&D functions as well. AstraZeneca China has been expanding its clinical research capabilities and collaborations with Chinese CROs such as WuXi for compound collection synthesis and a collaboration with Shanghai Jiao Tong University for research on the genetics of schizophrenia. The company is setting up an Innovation Center in China focused on translational science. In 2008, AstraZeneca announced a further investment totaling $220 million that included a $50 million enhancement of the WuXi site for global formulation and the establishment of the Regional Packing Centre and the High-Tech Receiving Centre.[50] Following in the footsteps of AstraZeneca, Pfizer was the second multinational to set up a clinical trials center in China, which it opened in Shanghai in 2005. It encompasses study design, data management, statistical analysis of global phase I–IV clinical trials, as well as training facilities for Chinese employees and for scientists and medical professionals from Chinese partner institutions. The center will also be engaged in drug development. Pfizer and Peking University's Health Science Center formed the Peking University–Pfizer Pharmacometrics Education Center to support capacity building and fund training of Chinese scientists. Pfizer has ambitious plans to introduce 20 new medications to China.[51] Also in 2005, Quintiles Asia announced that it was changing its agreement with Peking Union Medical College Hospital to enhance central lab services in China. Most leading international CROs have also established a base in China. We provide many more details of the activities of these companies in a later chapter.

Like India, China is growing its own CROs with considerable capabilities in preclinical research and clinical trials that are sometimes combined with discovery or outsourced manufacturing capabilities, data management, and so on. Several of these diversified companies have been founded by "sea turtles," Chinese nationals returning home after work experience in the West. Other companies have found international investors that have helped them become international players.

Beijing-based Bridge Pharmaceuticals provides preclinical services, including animal testing for international clients according to U.S. regulatory standards. In 2005, the company received FDA clearance for clinical studies of drug candidates based on preclinical data generated entirely in China. Starvax, Inc., provides toxicology, pharmacology, and animal studies for drug companies. Other notable Chinese CROs include Shanghai BioExplorer and Vivo Development. The Gaoyao Kangda Animal Research Center is known as a leading primate research center for biologics or drug testing.

A major force among Chinese CROs is WuXi PharmaTech, which offers diverse outsourcing services in combinatorial, medicinal, and synthetic chemistry, as well as manufacturing. A profile of this interesting new player is presented in the sidebar.

WuXi PharmaTech

WuXi PharmaTech is a leading global contract research outsourcing provider, serving the worldwide pharmaceutical, biotech, and medical device industries. The company is headquartered in Shanghai and has operations in both China and the United States. It provides a broad and integrated portfolio of laboratory and manufacturing services throughout the R&D process. The parent company is known as WuXi PharmaTech, and its operating divisions are known as WuXi AppTec.

WuXi PharmaTech is the result of a merger in early 2008 of WuXi PharmaTech, Inc., a chemistry-based company founded in China in 2000, and AppTec Laboratory Services, Inc., a U.S. company founded in 2001 with biology-based expertise.[a] WuXi Pharma-Tech rapidly expanded its services over a decade, offering discovery chemistry services in 2001, process development in 2003, GMP manufacturing in 2004, bioanalytical chemistry in 2005, service biology in 2006, and finally toxicology and formulation in 2007.[b] AppTec Laboratory Services contributed a broad range of testing services for the biotech and medical device industries. It has about 4,500 employees, including about 3,500 scientists; most have advanced degrees.[c]

The company's client list includes most of the major pharmaceutical and biotechnology companies. WuXi AppTec has received awards from leading pharmaceutical customers, including GSK (2009), Lilly (2009), Takeda (2009 and 2008), Pfizer (2008), Genentech (2008), Millennium (2008), Merck, AstraZeneca, Novartis (2007), and other companies.[d] WuXi is a relatively younger and smaller CRO company, compared to its global peers. It has attracted major pharmaceutical companies by providing quality service in a timely manner. The company is now moving from being a preferred supplier to potentially adopting a partnership model by providing fully integrated services (see Figure 5-7). WuXi's customer base has improved substantially since 2007 as a result of the AppTec acquisition, and its customer concentration is now in line with that of global peers. About 80% of its revenue comes from relationships with American companies, 15% from European companies, and 5% from Japanese companies.[e]

Its primary China-based facilities include a 1,006,000-square-foot R&D center in the Waigaoqiao Free Trade Zone in Shanghai, a 71,000-square-foot small-scale cGMP (current good manufacturing practice) clinical manufacturing facility and a new 222,000-square-foot large-scale cGMP manufacturing plant in the Jinshan area of Shanghai, a 253,000-square-foot R&D center focused on discovery chemistry in Tianjin, and a 314,000-square-foot preclinical toxicology facility in Suzhou. The company's acquisition of AppTec provides it with a U.S. presence and know-how in biologics and medical device testing, including three FDA-registered facilities. These U.S. facilities include an 82,000-square-foot R&D and manufacturing facility in St. Paul, Minnesota; a 51,000-square-foot testing facility in Atlanta, Georgia; and a 75,000-square-foot R&D and testing facility in Philadelphia, Pennsylvania.[f]

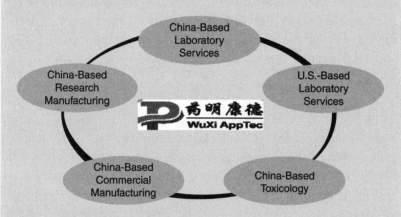

Figure 5-7 WuXi AppTec business model

Reproduced by permission from Ron Aldridge, Director of Investor Relations, presentation at 20th Annual UBS Global Healthcare Services Conference, New York, 8 February 2010.

In April 2010, U.S.-based Charles River Laboratories and WuXi PharmaTech signed a definitive agreement under which Charles River and WuXi would combine in a cash and stock transaction valued at approximately $1.6 billion. The combined company, which would retain the name Charles River, was to offer an expanded portfolio of products and outsourced services to multinational pharmaceutical, biotechnology, and medical device companies and academic and government institutions that increasingly seek the flexibility to access high-quality, early-stage expertise from chemistry to manpower from one global company.[g] However, on July 29, 2010, following opposition from investors and proxy advisory firms, Charles River Labs ended the deal and paid WuXi a $30 million break-up fee.[h]

In March 2010, WuXi PharmaTech announced it had reached an agreement with Johnson & Johnson Pharmaceutical Research & Development, a division of Janssen Pharmaceutica N.V. (JANSSEN), to collaborate in the area of preclinical services.[i]

Sources:

a-d, f. See company website, www.ir.wuxipharmatech.com

    e. WuXi PharmaTech Cayman, Beijing Gao Hua Securities Company Limited, 15 October 2009.

    g. "Charles River Laboratories and WuXi Pharmatech to Combine," WuXi, 26 April 2010.

    h. "Charles River, WuXi End Deal after Opposition," Reuters, 29 July 2010.

    i. "WuXi PharmaTech Enters Collaboration with J&JPRD," WuXi, 1 March, 2010.

Central Europe and Russia

Central Europe has been one of the more attractive destinations for clinical trials, with Poland, the biggest country in the region, among the largest players. Most leading Western CROs have a presence in the country, in addition to local CROs. Poland and other new E.U. members have reliable regulatory systems, moderate costs, and good medical expertise. About 450 clinical studies are performed each year in Poland, with 30,000–40,000 patients participating and expenditures by sponsors exceeding 700 million PLN.[52] Clinical trials are popular with patients who are frustrated with the inefficient public healthcare service and, therefore, willing to participate in new drug trials. Although the quality of Polish trials is considered to be high, critics argue that physicians benefit at the expense of the public healthcare system, which is not adequately remunerated for the trials. A recent inquiry by the State Audit Office (NIK), which inspected 13 hospitals, found that individual physicians gained the most from conducting clinical trials for sponsors—often at the expense of hospitals, which either made very little from the trials or indirectly subsidized them. On average, a physician made 5,900 euros for each patient involved in the trial. New legislation is planned that would regulate clinical trials contracting with public hospitals.[53]

As costs in central Europe have been increasing, Russia is emerging as a new "hot" destination, not just for some preclinical work (chemistry), but also for clinical trials. Russia is third in the A.T. Kearney ranking of attractiveness, just behind China and India and ahead of Brazil. Russia is a large and rapidly growing pharmaceutical market and has a sizeable population of more than 140 million citizens—most of whom are treatment naïve. It has some expertise and an improving infrastructure to conduct competitive clinical trials. In spite of the heterogeneous geography of the investigational sites, the average patient enrollment rates are ten times higher than in the United States and Europe, and only a fraction of the potential patient pool has been tapped so far. The most sites are in Moscow (184), then Saint Petersburg (114), and Novosibirsk (32).

Russian-based organizations are working hard to build up the country's image in terms of quality and reliability, not just cost competitiveness. More than 50 CROs are operating in Russia, which accounts for nearly half of the total number of clinical trials approved in the country in 2006. Leading international CROs such as Quintiles, Parexel, and ICON have a strong presence. Other market leaders include P.S.I., ClinStar Europe, and Evidence, which all specialize in clinical trials in Russia and Eastern Europe. Together the six market leaders account for more than 50% of the market. According to the data provided by Parexel analytics, the average cost per patient in Eastern Europe is 28% lower than in Western Europe, and 47% lower than in the United Kingdom.[54]

Sponsors wanting to outsource trials to Russia have several options. They can rely on international CROs operating in the country or hire a Russian CRO with local staff. Russian-based CROs make a strong case for using local CROs to perform trials in Russia, especially if local staff and local labs are used. Some sponsors do not trust Russian labs, preferring to use central laboratories located elsewhere.

This substantially increases the cost of the trials because of transportation expenses and lab fees. Russian websites claim that tests performed by Russian labs are five times—and, in some cases, up to eight times—less expensive, on average, than those performed by foreign labs. Lab costs are a small fraction of total clinical trials costs; the lion's share are the CRO fees. Russian websites provide numbers showing that local CRO services performed in Russia and Eastern Europe cost at least four times less, on average, than those provided by the local staff of international CROs, and more than five times—and up to nine times—less expensive than those provided by international staff.

For example, according to the website of a Russian provider, running a phase III trial with 300 patients enrolled in Russia could save companies up to $4.1 million in direct costs. Faster patient enrollment could generate an additional savings of a few million dollars per day in early product launch.[55]

Clinical trials conducted in Russia may be audited by the national regulator (the RZN), by sponsors, and by the FDA. According to results of FDA audits provided by Synergy Research Group, (a Russian contract research organization that has been successfully operating in Russia since 2002), Russia ranks at the top in terms of clinical trials quality among the seven pharmerging markets. Since 1995, the FDA has conducted 36 audits in Russia, resulting in only one case of a negative grade—the so-called official action indicated (OAI).[56] Such results would suggest that Russian clinical study centers are on par with ones in the West and ahead of centers in such countries as Mexico, which had a relatively high ratio of audits resulting in an OAI indication.

Latin America

Latin America conducts nearly twice as many trials as India and Russia. Figure 5-8, which traces the geographic shifts in clinical trials location, illustrates that, by 2013, China is expected to move into the number 3 position as a clinical trials destination, and Brazil is expected to move up from number 10 to number 8 globally behind the United States, Japan, China, and the large continental European nations, but ahead of Canada and the United Kingdom.[57]

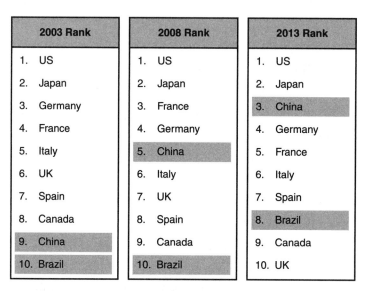

2003 Rank	2008 Rank	2013 Rank
1. US	1. US	1. US
2. Japan	2. Japan	2. Japan
3. Germany	3. France	3. China
4. France	4. Germany	4. Germany
5. Italy	5. China	5. France
6. UK	6. Italy	6. Italy
7. Spain	7. UK	7. Spain
8. Canada	8. Spain	8. Brazil
9. China	9. Canada	9. Canada
10. Brazil	10. Brazil	10. UK

Figure 5-8 The changing geography of clinical trials

Reproduced with permission from IMS Health; MIDAS, "Changing Geography of Clinical Trials," quoted by Burrill & Company, "Biotech 2010 Life Science: Adapting for Success," BIO International Convention, Chicago, 4 May 2010.

With a population of more than 520 million, comparable to that of Europe, Latin America is larger than the United States. It has 90 million people living in just seven large metropolitan areas: Mexico City, São Paulo, Buenos Aires, Rio de Janeiro, Lima, Bogota, and Santiago. Most of this large population is treatment naïve. The large metropolitan areas have modern hospitals and well-trained medical staff. Like Asian competitors, Latin American CROs claim lower recruitment delays than in Europe and the United States.[58]

Intrials is a good example of the emerging CROs from Latin America. It is a full-service contract research provider headquartered in São Paulo, Brazil, and has operations in Mexico, Chile, and Argentina. It boasts 400 world-class investigational sites and conducts all phases of clinical trials, two-thirds of which are phase III trials. Intrials works with pharmaceutical and biotechnology companies, as well as global CROs in a broad range of therapeutic areas.

The Future of Clinical Trials

As we noted at the end of the previous chapter, the anticipated progress in basic knowledge of diseases and in pathophysiology is expected to impact both the discovery and the development process of new drugs. Figure 5-9 presents a vision of the development process of the future.

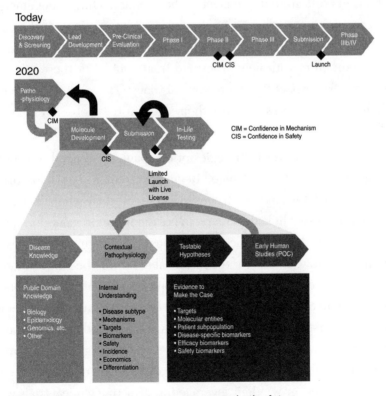

Figure 5-9 Clinical trials development process in the future

Reproduced with permission from PricewaterhouseCoopers

New knowledge and technologies, such as drug modeling, may enable companies to speed up some aspects of preclinical and clinical trials. However, they will not eliminate the need to establish the safety and efficacy of drugs and treatments in a scientific manner, especially at times when regulatory standards are being tightened around the world. The application of new technologies might enable the process to take less time and consume fewer resources while providing more accurate information.

Our analysis enables us to draw several conclusions and make some predictions about the likely impacts of the globalization of clinical trials. We made the case for the attractiveness and the indispensability of locating trials in emerging economies. As we pointed out, lower costs are but one facet of the situation. Only in big emerging economies can we find treatment-naïve populations of the size needed. Localized clinical trials can also be an important condition for market entry with new drugs and treatments. For these reasons alone, we can expect that more clinical trials (CT) will be performed in emerging countries and that their share in the global CT market will grow.

Regulatory approval strategies of companies will need to evolve as national regulations change. Regulatory requirements for drug approval will determine which clinical studies are done where, because approval is closely linked to market access and to the value for commercialization. Although the attractiveness of emerging markets will continue to grow, at least for the foreseeable future, the United States and Japan are expected to remain the top two destinations for clinical trials, in spite of their high costs. This is because, from both a pricing and an IP perspective, the two countries are expected to remain very attractive. However, emerging economies will use regulatory approvals as one of their key strategies if they want to become research hubs. As their markets grow, their leverage for attracting clinical trials will increase.

Technological progress is not the only factor that can help biopharma achieve its objectives of a more timely and less costly drug-development process. The globalization of clinical trials has the potential of making this happen. Although the cost advantages of an emerging economy location for discovery and testing are obvious, the efficiency aspect may be less apparent. With easy access to large and cooperative patient populations, it becomes possible to speed up trials by enlarging the pools of patients being tested. Higher patient-retention rates also help with speed and efficiency. And as more of the complex trials are undertaken in the new locations, the capabilities of the local CROs must grow.

Shifting more complex trials to emerging economies entails a huge transfer of CT technology from the developed nations. Indian, Chinese, and other CROs are learning fast and developing new capabilities to undertake more difficult trials and deliver them to world standards. As local companies grow and their appetite for development of new drugs also increases, the emerging CROs are venturing first into the more expensive phase III trials, which have traditionally occurred in the West, and will eventually move into new drug discovery. The higher standards of CT in the emerging countries will help push local regulators to adopt FDA and EMEA standards.

Coupled with the rapid growth in emerging drug markets, these developments will further integrate and globalize the industry with win–win opportunities for companies from the West and the East.

6

Accelerating Innovation:
Bioparks, Technology Zones,
and Emerging Clusters

"We should be cautious about sinking our resources into expensive infrastructure, especially if someone else wants to do it for us...."

—An executive from a Western high-tech company

Advantages of Locating in "Traditional" Industrial Clusters

Famous technology clusters such as Silicon Valley in the United States, Cambridge in the United Kingdom, and Munich in southern Germany have caught the imagination of the public and attracted attention from politicians, journalists, and business leaders. Clusters are sometimes seen as a solution to competitiveness, a way to attract foreign direct investment, and a means of providing high-paying jobs. Local governments, in particular, see clusters as a "must" of contemporary policy. What clusters can do and what they cannot is sometimes not well understood, and political leaders' uninformed attempts to use the "magic" of clusters can lead to disappointment. Before we launch into a discussion of this complex topic, we need to clarify some basic terms related to the concept of clusters and how they relate to global R&D. Clusters are sometimes confused with special economic zones, industrial or science parks, and similar entities. Consider some basic definitions:

- **Industrial park**—Simply an area zoned and planned for the purpose of industrial development.
- **Science park**—An area with an agglomeration of institutions dedicated to scientific research. If this research is dedicated to commercialization of inventions, the area may be called a **technology park.**
- **Special economic zones**—Areas with well-developed business and communication infrastructures that attract companies through various combinations of tax and/or tariff incentives and subsidies.

Since the Middle Ages, European craftsmen and traders have tended to group together. It simply made sense for the tanners or blacksmiths to locate on the same street or in the same district. Whether for making wine, crafting ceramic tiles, or producing clocks, industries in Europe and America have traditionally tended to cluster around certain locations. Some of those clusters, such as the cork-making cluster in Portugal and the tulip cluster in Holland, have been around for decades or even centuries. Others, such as the entertainment cluster of Los Angeles, are more recent.

Michael Porter defines regional clusters as "geographically proximate group[s] of interconnected companies and associated institutions in a particular field, linked by commonalities and complementarities."[1] Porter and others suggest that successful regional clusters are associated with international competitiveness in various industries.[2] Locating in a cluster offers companies various advantages, such as improved access to suppliers and personnel; to information and technology; and to needed institutions such as consultants, schools, infrastructure, or providers of financing. Agglomeration of companies operating in similar or related industries builds up "complementarities." For example, different products that companies in the zone offer complement each other in meeting customer needs—for example, makers of different car components for an automotive plant. Agglomeration also promotes intense local competition, thus improving productivity and quality. Geographically dispersed companies do not enjoy these colocation advantages.

As various regions and cities in the developed world experienced deindustrialization, decline, and unemployment, public authorities saw the power of clusters as a method of stimulating regional revival. Such strategies have been employed quite effectively in Europe. The German city of Wolfsburg successfully revived itself by re-creating its automotive-manufacturing cluster after Volkswagen built a state-of-the-art plant there as the "anchor investor." This investment then attracted a range of suppliers and related firms to the region, reviving employment and economic growth. Other countries have successfully employed such lead or anchor investor strategies, including emerging economies in Asia and Latin America. Clusters find synergies with local vocational schools, research institutes, and universities when they specialize in research directly relevant to the industry and develop programs for training specialized manpower that cluster companies need. In this way, they lay a foundation for multigenerational traditions of craftsmanship in the field.

In traditional industries, innovations tend to be limited to incremental product and process improvements. Breakthrough innovation, on the other hand, actually *creates* entirely new industries. This type of breakthrough innovation tends to happen in high-technology clusters, such as Silicon Valley.

The Mystery of Innovative Clusters

High-tech innovation clusters such as Biotech Bay and Tel Aviv are very different from traditional industrial clusters. Anyone who has driven around Silicon Valley or visited the high-tech cluster between

Harvard University and Massachusetts Institute of Technology in Cambridge, Massachusetts, can attest to how these special places grip the visitor with fascination and excitement. Even if as a tourist you just go to the bars and restaurants that high-tech workers, scientists, and inventors frequent, you will pick up some of the creative buzz and likely overhear conversations about the next new big technology that will change our lives. Not surprisingly, the world is jealous of American high-tech clusters. Many international companies, as well as national authorities representing government bodies from around the globe, feel they need a presence here, even if only to watch, absorb, and learn about the future. Everyone wants to know what may be the next stream of inventions, new products, and services that will spread globally and potentially change entire industries, as well as our lives. No wonder, then, that the world is fascinated by clusters, especially of the high-tech variety.

Entirely new industries based on science tend to agglomerate around universities and research labs, especially if those institutions employ lead "star" scientists and have large populations of specialized researchers, including "postdocs." Networking among the community of those scientists is critical to the discovery process. Academic entrepreneurship occurs as scientists create startup companies designed to commercialize the inventions. So-called "knowledge spillovers" occur among those dynamic complementary firms. Supporting industries, including Venture Capital (VC) firms, consultants, specialized suppliers of equipment, and IT services, spring up around the emerging cluster to service its needs. Innovation is close to the science, but unlike in the case of traditional clusters, production and distribution need not be.

Exactly why certain clusters emerge and grow to become highly successful yet others fail remains partly a mystery. Researchers have been struggling to discover the "secret" of what makes clusters work and how policymakers can somehow help create innovative clusters. What role does geography play, and how can it influence innovation?

Audretsch and Feldman's research showed that *innovation* is more spatially concentrated than *production*.[3] Moreover, firms located in innovative clusters tend to be systematically more innovative than firms located elsewhere. Economists use the concept of increasing returns to scale to explain agglomeration and its persistence.[4] Economies are resulting from intraindustry specialization; labor market economies are resulting from large pools of skilled workers and from intense communications among firms located in the same area. Local sources of knowledge determine the development of new products, but only in areas with *already large accumulations of knowledge*.[5] However, access to such knowledge (through knowledge transfer and spillovers) requires active involvement by interested parties in the knowledge-generation process and also strong competencies to develop knowledge that others discovered.[6] Researchers who have studied clusters point to "the extreme diversity of their structure, logic and dynamics."[7]

How are clusters born? Klepper hypothesizes that the outcome may be a combination of chance and companies spinning off new firms.[8] Klepper's argument relies on the idea of the cumulativeness of innovative processes. Thus, just as clusters may "cause" innovation, an original innovation may create a cluster.

The development of clusters is a complex process of construction of competencies.[9] In science-intensive fields such as biotechnology, a strong scientific base is fundamental to clustering but is not a sufficient condition.[10] The willingness and ability to exploit such knowledge for economic purposes is just as important; this includes innovative entrepreneurial activities organized through rules that govern academic involvement in commercial activities, close university–industry relations, a strong IPR regime, and VC availability.

Zucker and Derby show that the *presence of star scientists* explains the formation of new firms and their performance more than *academic research*.[11] The presence of star scientists leads to start-ups and agglomeration. However, in general, clusters appear to form around concentrations of academic excellence rather than cities.[12] Local presence of large corporations does not emerge as an ingredient of innovation clusters, although linkages between small firms and big pharmaceutical corporations are a crucial component of developing a biotechnology industry.[13] In summary, it is worth quoting the following conclusion by Orsenigo:

> As much as agglomeration forces are influenced by structural initial conditions, *processes* are the essence of what clusters are made of. The factors that lead to the genesis of a cluster are different from those that later sustain it. Clustering is the outcome of processes of construction and co-evolution rather than the automatic effect of specific preconditions or agglomeration factors.[14]

No Silver Bullet: The Stupendous Challenges of Building Innovative Clusters

If we want to see clusters develop, should we rely on market forces to form clusters spontaneously, or should we use policy and planning? As the literature review suggests, and as we shall see more clearly by the end of this chapter, building innovative clusters is an extraordinarily complex task. So many difficult conditions (which we call "cluster enablers") must be met just to start a cluster, let alone sustain it. Moreover, assembling all the "preconditions," difficult as that is, offers no guarantee of sustainable success. As the research on clusters in developed economies suggests, clusters often behave mysteriously. Creativity and invention are scarce and fickle. Planning for their emergence seems to be part science, part art, and part luck.

Although great innovative clusters become international as they develop, a good starting point in thinking about clusters is to think locally. Often the local authorities most eagerly push for cluster creation. Ramanelli and Feldman show that around 75% of human biotherapeutics firms founded in the United States between 1976 and 2002 were of local origin[15]—that is, they were spun off not only from institutions (especially universities), but also from other companies in the same geographic area. Successful clusters continue to exhibit a high growth rate of new firms, whereas unsuccessful ones do not.[16]

As we have already pointed out, the American experience suggests that early, successful clusters developed "almost spontaneously." But as we noted earlier, even in the case of Silicon Valley, public policy played a part. First in Europe and, increasingly, in the emerging economies, one observes a great effort to implement policies at the national and regional level that would help foster high-technology development. As Orsenigo writes: "The development of successful clusters has been achieved ... through wildly different approaches—there is no single way to success. On the other hand, failure is pervasive irrespective of the policies adopted."[17] Another expert, Maggioni, suggests that European policymakers have tended to overemphasize capacity building in academic institutions and infrastructures as determining the success of innovative industrial clusters at the expense of firm-based/micro-level incentives aimed at increasing the endogenous growth of a cluster.[18] In other words, without entrepreneurship, clusters will not develop. In Europe, we see a number of interesting cases of cluster failure, and we witness the great difficulties biotechnology clusters faced as they developed.

Orsenigo specifically describes the past case of the Lombardy biotech cluster's failed development.[19] In this case, failure was associated with the lack of "most of the basic preconditions for the take-off of innovative activities," such as the scientific and industrial bases, organizational structures linking science to industry, venture capital, and IP rights. Innovative activities clustered but did not "take off." The cluster failed to reach critical mass also because of its heterogeneity, or lack of technological focus.[20]

Finland is credited with having created perhaps the most advanced environment for the knowledge economy in the world and appears to be ahead of Italy. Yet this by no means guaranteed automatic success for its quickly emerging biotech sector. Shienstock and Tulkki pointed out that the Finnish biotech industry did not enjoy the same success as the country's IT industry.[21] Despite heavy state investment in biotech research, the industry was thwarted by shortages of highly qualified scientific staff, the small size of the local market, the small size of existing firms (lack of large powerful firms), and a regulatory environment that was not friendly to biotech.

Another problem with creating new clusters is simply competition. Too many cities and regions trying to attract a limited number of new high-tech ventures means that many efforts will fail, resulting in a proliferation of science and technology parks that have failed to attract private companies. As new clusters form around the world, competition intensifies and puts pressure on existing clusters as well, which have to remain dynamic or decline.

A useful way to look at cluster emergence is with the help of a "life cycle" model of birth, growth, maturity, and decline.[22] The model represented in Figure 6-1 proposes a set of benchmarks that allow for the evaluation of a cluster's competitive position on a scale from "weak" to "international leader." The authors of this model also see cluster development as a "life cycle" from emergence to growth, maturity, and "aging." They rank Singapore as an "emerging cluster" and Boston, Massachusetts, as "mature"; with Berlin and Ile-de-France categorized as "growing." As key quantitative criteria, they use numbers of employees in the biomedical sector, number of life science researchers in public institutions, and number of start-up companies in life sciences. That last measure should be regarded as a key indicator of a cluster's emergence beyond being a typical science park, which simply agglomerates scientific labs and universities. Additional criteria include industrial tissue, infrastructure, financing, and international visibility.

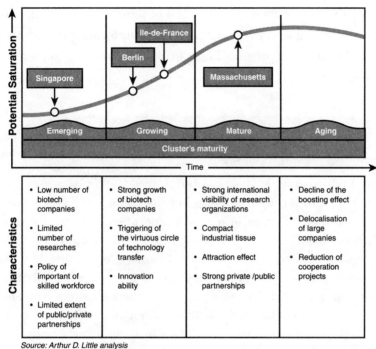

Figure 6-1 Cluster maturation phases

Reproduced with permission from D. Brown, F. Deneux, E. Halioua, and F. Le Verger, "Coming Together—Success Through Clustering," Prism 2 (2005): 9–31.

The life cycle model of cluster growth emphasizes comprehensive, in-depth development of cluster capabilities across many criteria. This implies the need to develop a strategy of sustainable international competitiveness of the cluster based on distinctive competencies that are publicized to the outside world, that provide visibility, and that attract investors. Those achievements become the hallmarks of a mature cluster.

Since the cited study, Singapore, which is discussed in the following sidebar, has made a lot of progress along the dimensions that the model suggests. Its most modern cluster, BioPolis, has moved much closer to the category of a "growing cluster." At the same time, many bioparks, as well as science and technology zones, have been started in emerging economies, all competing vigorously with each other. In the next section, we review the efforts of emerging economies to build policy-driven innovation clusters. Most of those efforts are still in the stage of creating *science bioparks* rather than forming true clusters, but evidence shows progress being made—with remarkable success, in some cases.

Tracking the Progress of a Polish High-Tech Cluster Built from Scratch: The Wroclaw Research Center EIT+

The Polish economy has enjoyed some of the strongest economic growth on the continent, but the country still lags behind most European nations in terms of innovation and high technology exports. Despite low spending on R&D, the country's science results—measured by the number of works cited relative to gross domestic product per capita—are above average (ahead of Italy, Japan, and Ireland, for example). Ambitious local governments that are aware of their communities' potential are taking steps to develop innovation-driven economies in their regions instead of waiting for the central government to act.

Of several Polish initiatives to build high-technology clusters, Wroclaw's EIT+ stands out as the most ambitious—and most promising. Located in Lower Silesia, in southwestern Poland, near Germany and the Czech Republic, the city of Wroclaw is one of the country's leading centers of science and learning, with more than a dozen universities and technology institutes. The city is known for its dynamic mayor, Rafal Dutkiewicz, who makes innovation a priority. Working with the regional government, Dutkiewicz's office attracted more than 5 billion euros in foreign direct investment between 2000 and 2008. Leading multinationals that have located in the region include LG, Toshiba, Philips, HP, 3M, VW, Google, and Bosch. Wroclaw is following up on this success with ambitions to become a leading center of high tech in Central Europe.

In 2007, a group of visionary scientists, engineers, and administrators founded the Wroclaw Research Center, EIT+ Ltd., as a joint venture among city authorities, regional government, and Wroclaw's universities. Shareholders include five of the largest universities in the area, the municipality of Wroclaw, and the province of

Lower Silesia. The initiative has raised more than 200 million euros in funding from the Polish government and the European Union, to fund research projects and new science facilities.

EIT+ simultaneously manages several large-scale research projects aimed at commercializing leading converging technologies: IT, nanotechnology, and biotechnology. These research projects include BioMed (biotechnology and modern medical technology), NanoMat (use of nanotechnology in advanced materials and drugs), and the ICT Research Center (which encompasses telecommunications and information technologies).

EIT+ has a startup company incubator and also oversees the construction of a state-of-the-art science and technology park at Pracze, a suburb of Wroclaw. Pracze aspires to attract technology entrepreneurs and multinational R&D investment, and to thus create the high-tech cluster of Wroclaw. The campus at Pracze will consist of 40 newly built specialist research and technological laboratories covering approximately 23,000 square meters (about 250,000 square feet). With funding of approximately 140 million euros, in the years 2013–2014, the Pracze campus will be the home of certified laboratories affiliated with EIT+ projects, with participation from IBM, the Fraunhofer Institute, the Leibniz's business incubator (an R&D center for optical fibers and cell transplantation), the Center for Applied Mathematics, and others. Also planned are student hotels, guesthouses, a music hall, sports facilities, and restaurants. The campus aims to harbor broad collaboration by researchers from diverse fields, creating a unique community able to work on converging technologies.

In the conservative environment of traditional European academia, getting diverse academic teams to work together on large applied projects while coordinating with local government is hard enough. Similar investments in science parks located in other Polish cities often result in additional laboratory capacity being dedicated to purely academic projects run by politically influential scientists or in simply leasing out the new laboratory space to the highest bidder.

EIT+ stands out because it manages the large-scale R&D projects more effectively than competing initiatives, while at the same time moving ahead with the construction of the new laboratory infrastructure. The R&D projects are coordinated with scientists from different disciplines and institutions working together toward commercially applicable innovations under a philosophy of technology convergence. EIT+ has set for itself the goal of starting at least ten spin-off companies based on its research results. To do this, EIT+ has to manage the research projects in a pragmatic and flexible way, terminating unpromising avenues and moving teams to projects nearing completion.

EIT+'s capabilities and vision have been recognized: It has attracted major funding and forged international partnerships. All these are crucial milestones in the development of a cluster. However, EIT+ must still prove that its research is not only generating patentable inventions, but also attracting startup companies that want to commercialize them and private-sector R&D investors that want to buy into the creative network. The real test will be to attract private-sector investments. EIT+ is perhaps halfway to launching a true innovation cluster, but it is making impressive progress ahead of its competitors in the region.

Sources: www.eitplus.pl and personal interviews by the author.

Agglomerations and Clusters in Emerging Economies

Emerging economies from Taiwan and Brazil to Thailand have developed successful industrial clusters in various industries, from automobiles to eyewear. India is well known for its software clusters in Bangalore and Mumbai. Rio de Janeiro is known for its oil and gas exploration cluster anchored around Brazil's energy giant, Petrobras. All the new life science players among the emerging economies that we identified in Chapter 2, "The Race for the Best National Innovation

System," are spending considerable resources to support the creation of life science clusters and industries in an accelerated fashion.[23]

As in some of the European countries mentioned earlier, the emerging economies, especially in Asia, have pursued a planned approach of rapid life science industry development based largely on public spending. Policies incorporate the creation of clusters that are expected to become focal points of innovation and to also attract outsourced R&D. Policymakers realize that, without public support, market forces alone will not suffice. At the same time, they grapple with the complexity of the task, realizing that success can be elusive, progress can be slow, and failures are common.

Josh Lerner, author of the previously cited *Boulevard of Broken Dreams*, is among the harshest critics of wasteful government intervention to promote entrepreneurial high-tech start-ups. His book cites Malaysia's unsuccessful effort in 2001 to create BioValley, a planned biotech cluster with three life science research institutes: commercial, educational, and residential facilities on a 2,000-acre site with a public expenditure of more than $150 million. Somewhat ironically, BioValley was built on the site of Entertainment Village, Malaysia's failed attempt to create a version of Hollywood. By April 2004, only three companies had signed contracts to locate in BioValley, which earned itself the nickname "Valley of Bio-Ghosts." Companies apparently preferred to locate in the better planned and equipped BioPolis, in nearby Singapore.[24]

A small city-state that has tried to emulate Singapore's success is Dubai. Its strategy has been to provide a base for technology companies doing business in the Middle East, Africa, and India. By 2006, the Dubai Internet City had attracted affiliates representing a quarter of the world's top 500 companies. Dubai then tried to replicate this success by creating Dubai Healthcare City, Dubai Biotechnology and Research Park, Dubai Knowledge Village, and Dubai Media City. Results have fallen short of expectations, however. Even Dubai

Internet City has few R&D and new innovation-based companies. Many global companies have come to Dubai, but they have done so to spread innovations made elsewhere. Dubai has not created any thriving innovative clusters; instead, it has built large, successful service hubs.[25] This example highlights the truth that it is far easier to build up a manufacturing or service hub than to create a true innovation cluster.

Although we do not know the optimum path leading to viable innovative life science clusters, policymakers in emerging economies can learn from the experience of the more developed countries, some of which we described earlier. Leaders with the determination to provide the resources needed for an innovative cluster do not always seem to realize how difficult a task they face. Although we still do not have in the emerging economies innovative clusters that can compete with, say, Biotech Beach or Biotech Bay in California, several emerging economies do have large science parks that boast state-of-the-art infrastructure and world-class research facilities. The best of them have become attractive destinations for not only advanced manufacturing sites, but also organizations that perform clinical trials and collaborative or outsourced R&D. Emerging economy policymakers see such international investments as key milestones in the process of gradual upgrading; in time, the bioparks could become true innovative clusters.

In the following sections, we first provide an overview of science and technology parks initiatives in the new player economies: India, China, and Brazil. We also look in some detail look at the two success stories: the biotech clusters of Shanghai, China, and BioPolis, in Singapore. Both appear to be well on the way to eventually becoming successful innovative clusters able to attract international investments as well as domestic start-up companies. We also describe the case of a new-generation minicluster, the Advanced Institutes of Convergence Technology (AICT) in Korea.

Life Science Parks in New Player Economies

Major emerging economies from Brazil to China are investing heavily in developing new life science parks. The scale of these investments is stupendous: Both India and China each have approximately 100 parks in various stages of development; South Korea is in the process of adding new highly specialized technology parks, while many other nations such as Taiwan, Malaysia, and Thailand are following suit.

India

The Indian government in Delhi is committed to developing biotechnology and supports the efforts of local governments to build bioparks. The government promotes these major biotech hubs in the country:

1. **Southern region**—Hyderabad, Bangalore, Chennai, Kerala
2. **Western region**—Maharashtra, Gujarat
3. **Northern region**—NCR region, Lucknow, Punjab

In its eleventh 5-year plan, the government proposed to set up 10 biotech parks with incubators.[26] In 2008, the government announced plans to set up at least 20 new bioparks throughout the country.[27] The ambitious national vision could transform India into a "biotech superpower." The major currently operational bioparks are Shapoorji Pallonji biopark in Hyderabad, ICICI Knowledge park in Hyderabad, Lucknow biotech park in Lucknow, TICEL biopark in Chennai, and International Agri biopark in Pune. Genome Valley, a biocluster in Hyderabad, is the first of its kind in the country; the area houses two bioparks and several biotech companies.

Facilities that these bioparks offer range from manufacturing facilities to warehouses and machinery engineering and maintenance. Many parks offer incubation services to occupants. Several companies that started off in the bioparks have clinched lucrative investment deals from foreign companies. Shantha Biotech, one of the oldest biotech companies in India housed in the Genome Valley, is one such example. Many other companies that are well-known names in the Indian biotech world, such as Biocon, Jubilant Biosys, have also benefited from bioparks.

Figure 6-2 shows a map of the currently operational and planned bioparks, as well as approved special economic zones (SEZs) in the country.[28] Given the size and potential of India, even if only a minority of the sites are successful, India could indeed become one of the biotech superpowers of the world.

South Korea

As noted earlier, South Korea has ambitious plans to become more than just a high technology manufacturer. It wants to become an innovation leader and also a significant world player in basic science research. Science parks and technology clusters are a key instrument in making this policy happen. In the area of life science, South Korea is pursuing a tightly planned and structured approach.

The nation has an elaborate network of 4 regional bioareas and 25 bioclusters. The Korea Bio Hub Center (KBHC) is one of the most recent government initiatives to further strengthen the biotech infrastructure in the country and help it converge into a life sciences leader. The KBHC was founded by the Bio-Max Institute at Seoul National University with the help of the Ministry of Knowledge Economy. The project, undertaken in July 2004, was to be completed by June 2009. The budget for the project is $29.6 million, and 25 organizations are participating, including 9 bioventure centers and 16 Regional Technology Innovation Centers.[29]

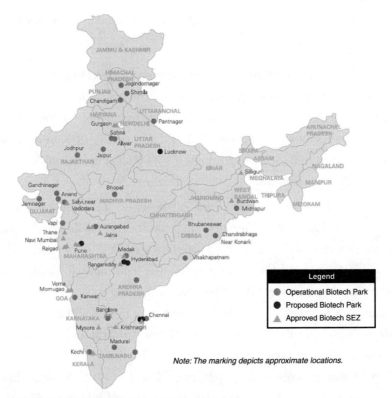

Note: The marking depicts approximate locations.

Source: Cushman & Wakefield Research, January 2008

Figure 6-2 India: Biotech parks, operational, planned, and SEZ

Reproduced with permission from "Pharma Summit 2008: India Pharma, Inc.—An Emerging Global Pharma Hub," KPMG & CII report, September 2008. Available at www.kpmg.com/Global/en/IssuesAndInsights/ArticlesPublications/Documents/Pharma-summit-2008.pdf.

The four regional bio areas and their specializations are listed here:[30]

1. **Seoul**—Biopharma, bio product

2. **Daejeon**—Biomedicine, health/medical care, Oriental herb medicine, animal resources, functional foods

3. **Ganwon**—Bioenvironment/bioprocesses, marine resources, bioenergy, biohealth industry, functional materials, biochemicals, marine bioresources, traditional biomaterials, herbal medicine

4. **Jeolla**—Novel natural materials, biofoods, bioagriculture, plant/marine resources

Major universities and institutes involved in R&D in life sciences include Gacheon University and Yonsei University, Korea Research Institute of Bioscience and Biotechnology (KRIBB), National Institute of Toxicological Research, Catholic University of Korea, Korea Institute of Science and Technology, Korea University, Seoul National University, and Korea Basic Science Institute.[31]

Osong Bio Technopolis is one of the latest additions to Korea's bioclusters. Located in Chungcheongbuk-do, central Korea, it would cover an area of 4.6 million square meters, with 36.3% for production, 16% for R&D, and the rest for residence, commercial, public, and other support facilities. About 16 universities and colleges are close to the area. A few agencies, including the Korea Food and Drug Administration and the Korea Center for Disease Control and Prevention, are scheduled to move into the complex by 2010.[32] To date, more than 54 Korean companies, including CJ and LG Life Science, have said they will move to the complex, investing $1.1 billion (as of October 2007).[33] VGX Pharmaceutical, a U.S. drug developer, is investing $200 million to establish an Asian regional headquarters in the complex. Four U.S. and Canadian companies invested a total of $260 million in foreign investments in the complex.[34] Investing companies can lease space in the Bio Technopolis at an annual fee of approximately $1.65 per square meter for a maximum of 50 years. For investment scale of above $30 million, leasing is free of charge.[35]

Among Korean clusters, until recently (that is, by 2007), only Seoul had made it to the top ten non-U.S. biotechnology clusters. Among those top ten were three Japanese clusters (Tokyo, Ibaraki, and Osaka), two Canadian clusters (Vancouver and Toronto), two British clusters (Cambridge and London), and a cluster apiece in Rehovot, Israel, and Paris, France.[36] According to the cited author, Lara Marks, South Korea is most advanced among emerging Asian countries in terms of patent/inventor counts for the period 1972–2006, but it is still behind such countries as Israel and Switzerland. Nevertheless, such backward-looking analyses should not induce a sense of complacency among Americans. Given the investments that emerging Asia is making, more successful clusters are likely to emerge.

Building a Next-Generation High-Tech Hub in Northeast Asia

Advanced Institutes of Convergence Technology (AICT) in Gwanggyo Techno Valley, Korea: A New Generation Specialized Mini-Cluster

Established in 2007, the AICT and the Gwanggyo Techno Valley (GTV) are located in Gyeonggi province, near the capital Seoul. More than 50% of Korea's population and much of its industry and intellectual infrastructure are located in the province. This recently established "mini cluster" combines the features of a research center, business incubator, and learning institution. It has chosen to specialize in the convergence of key technologies deemed crucial to the future of the competitiveness of the Korean economy. The mission of AICT is to combine cutting-edge research on convergence technology with the education of a new generation of innovators trained in interdisciplinary science and engineering—all with the purpose of creating a "next generation high-tech hub based on convergence technology applications." Several key research institutes from Seoul National University (SNU) have been relocated to the GTV campus to combine with AICT and the Graduate School of Convergence Science and Technology (GSCST): the Korea Advanced Nano Fab Center (KANC), the Gyeonggi Bio-Center, and the Gyeonggi Small & Medium Business Center (GSBC). All are located in the valley, to provide a comprehensive infrastructure to conduct convergence technology research and business development (see Figures 6-3 and 6-4). GTV is close to large multinational companies such as Samsung, Hyundai, SK, and KT, as well as many high-tech SMEs. With this strategic location, GTV can act as a "corridor" or "lynchpin" connecting other technology clusters situated near Seoul and in other parts of the country.

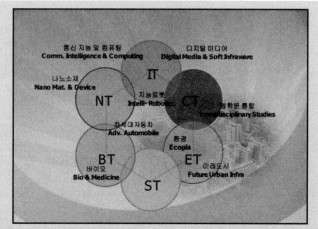

Figure 6-3 Research map at Advanced Institutes of Convergence Technology (AICT)

Reproduced with permission from L. Marks, "Beyond the United States International Biotechnology Clusters," Silico Research Ltd., April 2007.

Figure 6-4 Gwanggyo Techno Valley

Reproduced with permission from L. Marks, "Beyond the United States International Biotechnology Clusters," Silico Research Ltd., April 2007.

Locating the research institutes away from the main campus of SNU has the advantage of starting a new organizational structure with minimal or no boundaries between disciplines or departments.

Such a configuration encourages fresh thinking outside the traditional boundaries and allows new ideas to develop from intermixing traditional disciplines. This is further enhanced by experts working in many jointly appointed teaching and research positions.

The six institutes cover convergence technology areas such as nanotechnology, biotechnology, IT, green smart systems, transdisciplinary studies, and technologies for living together. An example of a topic under study is the future of books and impacts on culture. The Technologies for Living Together Program searches for convergence technology solutions to help the disabled and the aging population. Through the process of providing seed funding by the AICT and assistance with moving from early planning to the pilot stage of technology development, the Bio Convergence Institute won a 10-year, $100 million government grant to develop key technologies for fast and low-cost drug development. Companies can participate in this process and work as partners in establishing Centers of Excellence, with member researchers from the various participating organizations. Overseas institutes are also welcome to join or invest in these Technology Centers of Excellence. For example, a light-emitting diodes (LED) Research Center was formed with support from a global LED company to work together on key technological issues and to identify new applications that require convergence of disciplines (including industrial design, psychology, and human sensory perception).

AICT believes that convergence technology is the key to successful future innovation and sees South Korean companies well suited for this new phase of global competition. Many recent examples show how this is already happening. Samsung Electronics has been leading the digital convergence evolution, having successfully introduced many digital functions, such as digital imaging and MP3 in cellphones. Apple has brought the digital platform to another level by seamlessly integrating user-friendly interfaces and software contents with attractively designed hardware. In the biotechnology area, Pacific Bio Sciences has successfully developed the next-generation genome-sequencing platform by ingeniously combining biotechnology with nanotechnology. The intelligent automobile is an excellent example of a convergence platform that brings together mechanical technology with electronics and wireless communication technologies. Upcoming electric vehicles will have even more diverse convergence technologies that include totally new power train concepts and electronics interfaces.

Dr. Eugene Pak, a director of the AICT, explains the new educational philosophy: *"In educating a new generation of innovators using convergence technology (CT), basic disciplines of science and engineering will need to be taught perhaps even at a deeper level. This is because you cannot have true innovation with just a team of generalists. Learning to define a clear end goal and identifying critical constituent disciplines or technologies would also be very important so that an appropriate team of experts can be brought together to meet the end goal. Teamwork, communication, and deeper understanding of other disciplines will increasingly be important. An environment should be created to allow free exchange of ideas that encourage new and innovative concepts to develop from diverse backgrounds."* AICT has invited professionals from industry to work as a team with professors, researchers, and students.

AICT is designed to serve South Korea's national development goals. As Dr. Pak puts it, *"Korea's vibrant economy today enjoys a strong manufacturing base in consumer electronics, information and communications technology (ICT), automobiles, construction, and ship building. The next step is to become even more competitive with what's already strong, mainly in hardware, then go further with creatively combining software, design, and contents that lead to market-creating killer applications and services. The basis to achieve this is 'convergence technology.'"* AICT is being developed to compete and collaborate with the best convergence technology centers in the world, such as MIT Media Lab, Stanford's Bio-X in biotechnology, the Robotics Institute of Carnegie Mellon University, and the Cambridge University Technopole Cluster.

As for the future of clusters, Dr. Pak believes, *"They will continue to play an important role for innovation as technologies become more complex and diverse. Networking of innovation centers with the world-class production or manufacturing clusters will also be important in meeting the future market demands in a more timely way. In this regard, international cooperation of innovation clusters will play an important role."*

Sources: Information and images from L. Marks, "Beyond the United States International Biotechnology Clusters," Silico Research Ltd., April 2007; also based on interviews conducted by the author with Dr. Eugene Pak, Director of AICT, November 2010.

Brazil

Asia is not the only continent investing in cluster formation. Top-performing industrial clusters in Brazil include metal mining and manufacturing, agricultural products, chemical products, automotive, and aerospace. Agricultural products and their exports are still the most important for the country.

Medical devices and biopharmaceuticals are still in a state of infancy but are showing signs of vigorous growth. The Brazilian government has started to build a comprehensive framework of infrastructure for the life sciences sector. Brazil has several life sciences parks comprising incubators and research and academic institutions designed to act both as an effective support system for new and existing life sciences ventures and as a platform for foreign life sciences players to set up business in the country.

The "clusters" have a tiered structure. The states of São Paulo and Minas Gerais are the biggest clusters, accounting for around 73% of the total number of biotechnology companies in the country. On the second tier lie the states of Rio Grande do Sul (6.6%) and Rio de Janeiro (6.1%). On the third tier are Pernambuco (3.3%) and Paraná (2.8%). The next tier is populated by nine other states, which account for 0.55% to 1.1%. The first three tiers account for almost 92% of the total number of biotechnology companies in the country, with the first tier accounting for almost 73%.[37]

Generic manufacturers dominate the bioclusters, although a few firms have ventured into innovation and drug discovery. International contract research organizations (CROs) and biopharma companies also are showing signs of increased interest in Brazil. For example, Amgen recently decided to start an R&D center in São Paulo. The two biggest Brazilian bioclusters are these:[38]

1. **Minas Gerais**—The first life sciences cluster of the country was established in the state of Minas Gerais. The state accounts for almost 30% of the total biotechnology companies in the country.[39] Belo Horizonte, its capital, was the first planned city of the country. It houses three universities, including the University of Minas Gerais, and the Biominas Foundation, which has supported more than 30 biotech companies and introduced more than 20 to the market. The capital city houses 15.5% of the country's biotechnology companies; Uberlândia, another prominent location in the state, houses 5.6%.[40]

2. **São Paulo**—The state of São Paulo accounts for around 42% of the nation's biotechnology companies.[41] It is also home to several life sciences academic and R&D institutes, including the Butantan Institute, a vaccine supplier to the Brazilian Program for National Immunization (PNI), and Intrials, a clinical trials research organization. Campinas is one of the most important biotechnology locations in the state, accounting for around 14.1% of the country's biotechnology companies. The city of São Paulo has 9.9%, and Ribeirão Preto, another prominent biotech location, houses 7.0%.[42]

The country has several universities engaging in research activities in life sciences. University of São Paulo, University of Campinas, Paulista State University, and the Federal University of São Paulo are some of the major academic institutions that became involved early on in research in the areas of biodiversity, genomes, animal toxins, and health and medicine.

China

With China's economy doubling every nine years, the bio-pharmaceutical industry in China is also expanding rapidly.[43] The 12th Five-Year Plan expresses the creation of an innovation economy, with biotechnology as one of the targeted industries.[44] The Chinese government has been making huge efforts to stimulate the development of life science–based business by building science parks and technology zones.

As Figure 6-5 shows, China has more than 100 bioindustry parks above the provincial level, 53 at the national level. The Chinese bio-industry parks serve as a central location for developing biotechnology and pharmaceuticals, while promoting and supporting future development. Fifty-one bioindustry parks in locations such as Beijing, Shanghai, and Jilin, and in 16 provinces and cities, had an average investment scale exceeding $49 million, annual production value approximating $123 million, profit payments and tax turnover exceeding $20 million, and a total number of employees exceeding 130,000, with an average of 2,500 employees per park.[45]

Enterprises that have entered the bioindustry parks cover almost all sectors of biotechnology, such as traditional chinese medicine (TCM), the fermentation industry, biological pharmacy, farming biotechnology, biochips, and stem cell research. For instance, with a total export of about $85 million by 2003, the Zhongguancun Life Science Park represents a complete biological medicine industrialization chain, from test tube to clinic. At the city level, Beijing Bioengineering & Pharmaceutical Industrial Park is located in the Beijing Daxing Zone and facilitates accelerated conversion of technological and biological science achievements. In Shanghai province, Zhangjiang High-Tech Park National Shanghai Biological Medicine Industry Base mainly develops biological medicine and microelectronic information. In Guangdong province, Guangzhou International Biological Island focuses on TCM modernization and functional gene research.

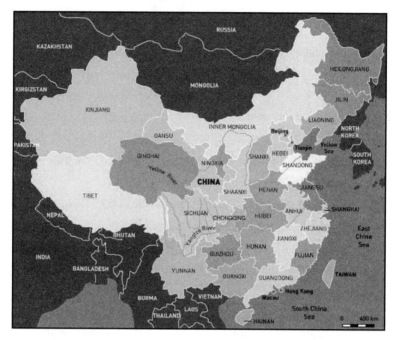

Figure 6-5 Bioindustry park distribution in China's provinces (number of parks)[46]

The most prominent park, with promising prospects for international investment–based expansion, is Zhangjiang High-Tech Park, near Shanghai, which is discussed later in the chapter.[47]

Two Emerging Cluster Success Stories: Singapore and Shanghai

Singapore and Shanghai are examples of two emerging clusters that show promise of success. Singapore, a city of several clusters, is smaller than Shanghai and provides an image of stability, quality of life, and an outstanding business environment. Shanghai, on the other hand, is home to 91 R&D centers, which is nearly double that of Singapore.

Singapore Biopolis and Tuas Parks

As you learned in Chapter 2, Singapore, a small city-state and an almost perfect contrast with giant China, has achieved a lot in a relatively short time in terms of developing an advanced life science–based industry. Companies that have opened international R&D centers in Singapore include Genelabs Diagnostic, Becton Dickinson, Lilly Systems Biology, PharmaLogicals Research, Novartis, and GlaxoSmithKline.

Major corporations with clinical research organization in Singapore include Novo Nordisk, Quintiles, and Covance.

The city-state of Singapore is a city of clusters. It has six agro-bioparks and two major bioclusters, BioPolis and Tuas Biomedical Park, in addition to a number of biomedical educational and research institutions.

Tuas Biomedical Parks I and II are located in Western Singapore and are also easily accessible from Malaysia. The second major biomedical park to be formed was BioPolis, which opened in September 2003 and is better known than Tuas. BioPolis was built with an investment of $300 million and launched as a part of a broader cluster-development program called "One-north." BioPolis Phase 1, a 185,000-square-meter campus, opened in October 2003 and houses more than 2,000 researchers from five biomedical research institutes under the Agency for Science Technology and Research (A*STAR) and research laboratories of global biotech and big pharma companies. BioPolis Phase 1 is about 90% occupied. BioPolis Phase 2 was completed in 2007 and adds around 37,000 square meters to Phase 1. An additional research space of 440,000 square feet area is expected to be complete by 2010.

Among the facilities provided are incubators for start-ups, plug-and-play facilities (ready, fitted-out lab space), and shared facilities and services for corporate and academic researchers. A stem cell bank is also in the process of being set up. These new facilities have attracted a limited number of biotech startups and several of the leading big pharma companies, including GlaxoSmithKline, Lilly, Novartis, Schering-Plough, and Abbott. Among emerging biotech companies housed at the Biopolis are PharmaLogicals and SGAUSTRIA (formerly Austrianova).[48] Over the past two decades, Singapore has built up a comprehensive network of educational and research institutions specializing in biomedical research and training:[49]

- 1987: Institute of Molecular & Cellular Biology
- 1990: Bioprocessing Technology Centre (BTC)
- 1993: Centre for National Products Research
- 1996: Bioinformatics Centre
  Lilly–NUS Centre for Clinical Pharmacology
- 1998: Centre for Drug Evaluation
  Kent Ridge Digital Labs
- 2000: Johns Hopkins–NUH Centre
  Singapore Genomes Program (SGP)
- 2001: SGP renamed Genomes Institute of Singapore
- 2003: BioPolis, biomedical research hub
  Novartis Institute for Tropical Diseases
  Institute for Bioengineering and Nanotechnology,[50] opened by A*STAR
- 2007: Duke–NUS Graduate Medical School

All seven of Singapore's biomedical public research institutes participate in BioPolis. Today more than 4,300 researchers carry out biomedical sciences R&D, and companies can tap the annual pool of more than 8,500 science and engineering graduates from local universities.

Shanghai Zhangjiang High-Tech Park

Among the leading Chinese biotechnology parks, the Shanghai Zhangjiang High-Tech Park, also known as "Drug Valley," is perhaps the most successful. Although it is still developing rapidly and is by no means "mature," the park has so successfully attracted private-sector R&D and start-ups that it can be considered a potential world-class innovation cluster.[51]

Shanghai Zhangjiang High-Tech Park was established in July 1992 and was developed as a national-level scientific park dedicated to high-technology development. However, no real development began until 1996, when the agreement of National Shanghai Biotechnology and Pharmaceutical Industry Base (NSBPIB) was signed and influenced key research institutions to resettle in the park. As of 2008, Zhangjiang High-Tech Park occupied 2,500 hectares, with two biomedicine zones totaling 300 hectares—about 30 times larger than Singapore's Biopolis area—dedicated to life science companies.[52] The number of employees exceeded 11,200, 2% of which had Ph.D.s by the end of 2008.[53]

This policy-driven park is successful for a variety of reasons, mostly because of strong support from the park's administration, state government, and municipal government. Governments are replacing the role that venture capitalists play in private sector-driven clusters.

In addition to strong logistics support, warehousing facilities, bonded facilities, incubators, and other services that make the park an attractive location, the government provides tax incentives and other subsidies. For example, companies that export more than 70% from the zone pay a tax rate as low as 10%, whereas the standard tax rate for foreign corporations is 24% and for domestic companies is 28%.

As of 2008, more than 130 organizations and companies had established R&D centers inside Zhangjiang, including Novo Nordisk, Roche, GlaxoSmithKline, Dupont, Hutchinson Whampoa, Amway China, Honeywell, National Biological Chip Center, Rohm, and Haas

Electronic Materials.[54] We profile a number of these investments in the next chapter.

Organizations inside the park have many innovative drugs and products in advanced phases of development. More than 200 biological medicine projects have been started.[55] Shanghai's biopharmaceutical growth over the past five years has been 15%, and already by 2005, sales of the city's biopharma industry exceeded $3.4 billion. Shanghai boasts some of China's best research institutes and hospitals, such as Shanghai University of Traditional Chinese Medicine, Shuguang Teaching Hospital, Shanghai Institute of Materia Medica Chinese Academy of Sciences (SIMM), National Human Genome Center (CHGC), and National Center for Drug Screening (NSCDSER).[56]

Chinese CRO growth is outpacing that of the industry, and CROs are prominent in Shanghai. As noted in Chapter 5, "Globalization of Clinical Trials," a growing number of foreign CROs are also establishing operations in China and are present in the cluster.

However, some factors are still missing from Shanghai Zhangjiang High-Tech Park. Advanced management skills and serial high-tech entrepreneurs are in short supply. Research on the cluster shows that more networking takes place between the biotech companies and the government than among the biotech companies themselves. Such an exclusive and closed nature of networks makes it more difficult for companies to benefit from innovation and competition, as compared with world-class clusters.[57]

Shanghai Zhangjiang High-Tech Park and Singapore BioPolis Compared

Shanghai Zhangjiang High-Tech Park and Singapore BioPolis have a common background, as shown in Table 6-1. Both grew as a result of top-down government policies to become, in a relatively short time, major agglomerations of bioscience manufacturing, research, and development. The incentives used to attract foreign MNCs include tax benefits and other incentives, such as public research facilities and a highly educated workforce. The presence of anchor firms in the newly created cluster and of significant research institutes and hospitals was a magnet for startups and supporting firms to facilitate and sustain cluster growth.

Table 6-1 Comparison between Shanghai Park and Singapore Hub[58]

Clusters	Shanghai Zhangjiang High-Tech Park[59]	Singapore Biopolis Biomedical Science Hub[60]
Foreign R&D Centers	Approximately 91 R&D centers.	More than 50 companies carrying out biomedical R&D, which included discovery, translational, and clinical research in 2010.[61]
Biotech Startups	In 2008, 294 biomedical start-ups.[62]	More than 130 venture capital firms located in Singapore.[63]
Other Major Companies from Other Industries	More than 150 IC design and production firms in Zhangjiang HIDZ. Top semiconductor manufacturers such as AMD, Free Scale, and IBM have established businesses in the zone. Semiconductor Manufacturing International Corp (SMIC), Hongli Semiconductor, and Hua Hong NEC are the three major IC producers in the zone. The total production capacity of the three companies accounts for 50% of China's total.[64] Many well-known software enterprises, such as Microsoft, Bi Bo, SONY, and Kyocera Electronics, have a presence.[65]	3M, Becton Dickinson, HillRom, Siemens, Thermo Fisher, Welch Allyn, and AB Sciex.[66]
Number of CROs	More than 40 CROs.[67]	Core base of 20 leading CROs in Singapore.[68]

(continued)

Clusters	Shanghai Zhangjiang High-Tech Park[59]	Singapore Biopolis Biomedical Science Hub[60]
Number of Manufacturing Plants	In 2010, 42 domestic and international first-class pharmacy plants.[69]	50 commercial-scale manufacturing facilities in 2010.[70]
Number of New Drugs	229 new drugs developed and 207 new drugs under research (127 innovative drugs and 44 in clinical tests in 2008).[71]	31 approved new drug applications in 2005.[72]
Number of Public Research Institutes/ Universities/ Hospitals	8 national institutes in 2008.[73]	More than 30 public-sector institutes in 2010.[74]
Human Capital (Science Base)	Policy-planned workforce; government actively attracting world-renowned researchers and local returnees after studying abroad. 11,221 employees in biomedicine, as of 2008. 136 DBFs, as of 2004.[75]	Attracting worldwide scientists and local star talents to Singapore after university graduation. As of 2008, A*STAR staffed by 2,620 researchers, with a concentration of 103 researchers per 10,000 labor force.[76] 30 DBFs in 2004.
Financial Incentives	Favorable tax incentives (foreign 24%, domestic 28%) and low rent fees.[77] Attract foreign MNCs and, recently, provide services as CROs.	Favorable corporate tax rate, reducing from 20% to 18% in 2008. R&D and education support with ten years of tax exemption for projects of strategic importance. Zero percent tax on start-ups for the first three years or the first $100,000, 9% thereafter on the next $290,000.[78]
Patents	Small but emerging. As of 2009, 7,946 international patents applied for, representing a growth of 29.7% from the previous year.[79]	Growing. As of 2008, 1,581 patents applied for, 730 awarded.[80]

Compared to the enormous potential of the China talent pool and market, Singapore is tiny. It cannot even approach the pool of treatment-naïve patients for clinical trials that China has. Shanghai as a city is several times bigger than Singapore, which is also a more expensive destination to do business in. Yet Singapore enjoys an impeccable image of stability, quality of life, and good business environment. Singapore's wide use of the English language offers a low barrier for researchers from Europe and the United States to enter—and leave—BioPolis. BioPolis is also likely to forge collaborative ties with the neighboring Malaysian biotech cluster, opening the possibility of access to Malaysia's resources.

On the other hand, the language barrier in China means reliance on a bureaucracy of go-betweens and intermediaries. Although the policy-driven strategy has served China well in creating the life science parks, the top-down process of "picking and choosing" projects for the government to support only means pleasing government officials, perhaps at the expense of private industry networking.

Concluding Remarks

As the literature on clusters points out, even wealthy developed nations have trouble replicating the success of large existing biotech clusters such as San Francisco and Boston. Many European cities have tried this, with only limited success. Can the emerging economies succeed? The answer lies not in trying to emulate the American clusters, but in adopting a realistic approach that takes competition into account and is grounded in the local ecosystem. We can expect that initiatives based on crude imitation are likely to fail; others that wisely make use of local competitive advantages may succeed—perhaps not in creating a world-class innovation cluster, but in founding a sustainable industrial cluster or science park that will attract investment.

Although China, India, South Korea, and Singapore have many of the most important emerging bioparks, many have been built elsewhere in Asia alone; additional ones are being built or are planned around the world. Taiwan has more than a dozen well-funded life science parks, and nations such as Thailand and Malaysia are in the process of building bioparks that they hope to develop into clusters to attract international R&D from big companies and innovative start-ups. Emerging economies in Latin America and Central Europe are following suit. Russia has announced the creation of a major biomedical park outside Moscow at Skolkovo.

So at a time when most Western governments are struggling with budget cuts, leading emerging economies are making huge investments in scientific infrastructure and are increasingly able to offer lab facilities that are as good as or better equipped than the ones in the West. As some Western economies are struggling just to maintain their funding for science,[81] fast-growing emerging economies (which we noted in Chapter 1, "Power Shifts in Global R&D and Innovation") are accelerating spending. In the coming decade, we can expect the science infrastructure in these new player economies, often in the shape of dedicated parks, will grow more rapidly than in the developed Western nations.

The proliferation of new capacity for R&D in many parts of the world means that, as never before, multinational companies will have plenty of options in choosing the optimum location for their R&D, whether they decide to establish a fully owned facility, set up a joint venture, or outsource. The competition to attract R&D type investments among the existing and emerging clusters is already enormous and likely to get stronger. Only the most competitive clusters will be able to attract significant international R&D from the world league of companies.

But even if many science parks and emerging clusters do not immediately succeed in attracting high-profile multinationals or exciting startups, they will add to the national capacity of emerging economies to perform scientific research in modern laboratories. Some of those modern labs will undertake government-funded research;

others will become available for rent—eventually attracting domestic and foreign clients who may not be doing state-of-the-art research, but simply need good lab space at a competitive price to perform routine work. This has started to happen in Central Europe, where, for example, companies from Western Europe have moved some of their routine lab work to newly built science parks, simply to save money by employing technicians and scientists at lower wages.

Pfizer used to have R&D facilities in ten different countries. It has been consolidating them into countries that it deems to be strategic: the United States, Japan, United Kingdom, China, and South Korea.[82] Even big companies will not open facilities in every new science park coming online. Deciding to locate a large research laboratory in a country is a major decision and a long-term commitment to building networks of collaboration. A location needs to have world-class facilities, access to world-class science, and entry into a major growing market. Shanghai appears to be meeting all three conditions. Leading multinationals, including Pfizer and Novartis, appear to have recognized South Korea's massive efforts to join the top league of knowledge-based economies. Smaller, less-developed countries recognize the level of competition and have chosen to develop "niche" clusters, such as Thailand's specialization in aqua cultural biotechnology related to shrimp production.

In the global knowledge economy, companies and central and local governments are constantly looking for better ways to accelerate innovation. How effective are clusters as "accelerators of innovation" in the life science–based business? G. Steven Burill, one of the leading American biotechnology gurus, believes that clusters will actually be less important in the future.[83] The growing capabilities of IT and communications technology make global networking ever easier. A well-connected company may not need to locate in a particular cluster to reap most of the advantages of networking in the future. Nevertheless, countries such as China, which are committed to building up a broad science infrastructure, will likely continue to invest in clusters.

Others will look for "innovations" in the innovation game. One way may be to build smaller, more specialized, "new generation" mini-clusters that combine selected converging technologies with a unique educational approach similar to the Korean AICT exhibited earlier. As we will see in the next chapter, international companies show continued interest in locating their activities in the most competitive emerging clusters. Those such as Zhangjiang are likely to thrive.

7

Company Strategies of Global R&D Collaborations: From West Meets West to West Meets East

"The success of our FIPNet strategy is inextricably tied to the success of our partners, and our network is only as strong as our partners."

—John Lechleiter, CEO, Eli Lilly and Company[1]

Global Biopharma Industry Changes As It Interfaces with New Players

The biopharma industry used to be a club of companies from the United States, Europe, and Japan. Those companies are often classified into distinctive groups. The most important group is the so-called "big pharma," the top dozen or so truly big global players. The second group includes the smaller "mid pharma" companies. The generics companies and the newly arrived large biotechnology (biologics) companies form two more categories. Japan's large pharmaceutical companies are sometimes classified as a separate category, called "Japan pharma." Those Japanese firms tend to be smaller than the biggest multinational from the United States and Europe. No Japanese company is in the first league of global big pharma.

In terms of globalization, the top dozen or so largest industry leaders are of greatest interest to us. These are the industry trendsetters. They have big market shares and broad product portfolios. Their size allows them to devote sufficient resources to undertake large-scale R&D on an international scale. The top biologics companies are also big and are significant R&D players, but they tend to have narrower product portfolios and are less globalized than the big pharmas. The biotechnology companies have not been around as long as big pharma in international markets and thus have fewer contacts and less global experience. Although Japanese pharma companies are important in Asia, they tend to be regional rather than global players and have relied mostly on internalized R&D strategies with little use of outsourcing. Although the largest German pharmas are among the group of global leaders, most are smaller than the biggest American or British multinationals and have been more cautious in their approach to globalization.

The lead group of large multinational pharmas is committed to R&D globalization, but these companies approach it in different ways. Some companies have been much quicker than others in moving away from traditional in-house models of R&D to an open model. In building new models of innovation, some companies emphasize setting up a network of wholly owned global R&D centers, while others rely more on risk/reward–sharing partnerships with other companies or universities.

In this chapter, we start with a discussion on GlaxoSmithKline (GSK) and AstraZeneca, two U.K.-based companies that recently have been visibly shifting their R&D capacities from the developed West to Asia. The two leading Swiss companies Novartis and Hoffmann-La Roche have pursued more gradual strategies. Novartis combines a range of approaches to global R&D with a far-sighted strategy of finely balanced diversification. We treat Novartis as a trendsetter for two reasons: It is currently the industry's fastest-growing company and it is an innovation leader in the number of attained new molecular entity approvals.

As trendsetters, we also consider Lilly and Merck. Lilly stands out as a company that has committed itself to the concept of FIPNet, which stands for the "fully integrated pharmaceutical network." The network relies on outsourcing and embraces the entire value chain, from R&D, with strongly externalized or outsourced discovery, clinical trials, and development; through manufacturing; to marketing and sales. Merck has also drastically transformed its R&D strategy from one based on in-house research to a model that takes advantage of global risk/reward partnerships.

Growing sales in emerging markets, streamlined R&D structures with incremental capacity invested in the emerging markets, and an externally generated R&D portfolio have become the industry standards for global pharmaceutical companies. All the big pharma companies have been moving in this direction, albeit some faster than others. Changes at Pfizer and Sanofi-Aventis, two giants, are good illustrations of this trend. R&D capacity, especially in Europe, is being restructured and sometimes downsized just as capacity in emerging markets in Asia and other continents is being rapidly expanded. In the last part of this chapter, we take a look at Boehringer Ingelheim, a Germany-based pharma company that, until recently (together with Sanofi-Aventis and the Japanese pharmas), was among the "reluctant globalizers" of the industry. However, that has changed; all those "reluctant globalizers" have recently been establishing partnerships with emerging economy companies or founding R&D centers in Asia.

The activities of global pharmas in the emerging economies are accelerating a long-term transformation of the global industry structure by activating new players, both large and small. Through the impact of collaborations, joint ventures, acquisitions, and also competition from the big Western firms, a range of highly capable new players is emerging. This includes large international companies such as Ranbaxy and Dr. Reddy of India, companies that often started out as generics producers but have been moving into new fields, including original drug development. On top of that, a variety of strong medium-size players are also emerging, especially in China and India. They are the multinationals' partners in manufacturing, clinical trials, and discovery. These medium-size companies have been growing rapidly, often combining manufacturing and contract research organization (CRO) services within a diversified business model. A prominent example is the Indian star company Biocon, which recently entered into a strategic agreement with Pfizer for worldwide commercialization of insulin products. We profile several of the new players in this chapter and show how collaborations with big international players are shaping them.

Downsizing R&D Capacity in the West While Growing It in the East: The Cases of GSK and AstraZeneca

The two leading British-based pharmaceutical companies, GSK and AstraZeneca, have been under pressure to cut costs and improve their performance. Both of these seasoned companies have been adding to their R&D capacity in Asia, while downsizing some of their R&D activities in the West.

GlaxoSmithKline: A Seasoned Global Player Shifts R&D Capacity in Favor of Asia

GSK is Britain's largest public drug company, formed from the acquisition in 2000 of Glaxo Wellcome and SmithKline Beecham. GSK is a major global healthcare group, with operations in 120 countries and its corporate head office in London and its U.S. headquarters in Research Triangle Park, North Carolina.[2] At the end of 2009,

GSK had 99,913 employees, 21,011 of which worked in Asia (including China) and 5,169 in Latin America. GSK is a global player; the United States is its leading market, followed by Europe and then the emerging markets. Its portfolio of products for major disease areas includes asthma, cancer, virus control, infections, mental health, diabetes, digestive conditions, and consumer healthcare.[3] Facing sales declines and strong pressures to cut costs, GSK has been cutting its overall R&D outlays and trying to improve its efficiency by shifting capacity to Asia. GSK and its predecessors have especially extensive experience working in India, dating as far back as 1919.[4] GSK is currently the leading foreign pharmaceutical company in the country.

GSK pursues a global approach to R&D, with laboratories in the United States, Canada, and several European countries. Like its competitors, GSK has been adding R&D capacity in emerging markets while reducing some of its R&D potential in Europe.[5] In announcing its Q4 2009 earnings in February 2010, GSK stated that it was aiming to deliver an additional annual pretax saving of $500 million by 2012; half of that is set to come from R&D, with a significant proportion of the savings derived from a "reduction of infrastructure."[6] GSK has proposed ending R&D activities across several sites, from the United Kingdom to Italy and Croatia. Furthermore, the company intends to stop preclinical development at its site in Mississauga, Canada, and neurosciences drug activity in Harlow, U.K. In addition, GSK is abandoning research in select central nervous system areas, including depression and pain.[7]

With the reduction of funding for internal R&D, GSK plans to source more drugs from outside its own labs; it already farms out 30% of its discovery research activities, or more than 80 projects, to its 47 partners.[8] The overall goal is to bring in new drug candidates through option-based agreements, such as buying the rights to license an early-stage drug candidate later in its development. In September 2010, GSK decided to include outsourcing as part of a broader initiative to simplify clinical development and significantly increase R&D

productivity. CEO Andrew Witty outlined the change and announced that GSK would "reduce the number of CROs it [works] with to increase efficiency and productivity."[9] (GSK's selection of Parexel and PPD as partners is in keeping with the current trend for big pharma to form closer links with one or two top-tier CROs.)

GSK is an active player in outsourcing and partnering. With 67 deals, the company was the most active in-licensor during 2008–2009.[10]

As one of the first multinational companies to fund pharmaceutical research and development in China, GSK's total R&D investment in China has exceeded RMB1 billion in the past 20 years. The research focus adheres to the disease control priorities set by Chinese government, including the areas of infections, diabetes, oncology, and respiratory diseases. Along with economic development and increased health care in China, GSK is planning to develop a more comprehensive and robust R&D strategy to bring in China as a key strategic center for GSK global R&D in the near future by such initiatives as these:

- GSK has established Clinical Research Centers in China, with more than 200 drug-development projects conducted in collaboration with more than 30 leading medical universities and hospitals.

- GSK is a clinical research leader in China in developing medicines for hepatitis, asthma, diabetes, oncology, and mood disorders.

- Recently, the company further boosted the R&D investment in China with an emphasis on cancer prevention and treatment.

- GSK set up an OTC R&D organization in Tianjin in 2003 and a global R&D center in Shanghai in 2007.

- Substantial investment is still dedicated to drug discovery and genetic research in leading medical universities and the Chinese Academy of Science. A collaboration program in the field of combinational chemistry with the Shanghai Institute of

Materia Medica (SIMM) under the Chinese Academy of Sciences has continued for more than ten years.

• GSK reached an agreement with Shenzhen Neptunus to develop influenza vaccines in China.

GSK also has R&D centers in Romania and South Africa, as well as some notable collaborations in Singapore. GSK already has sizeable research operations in Bombay and Bangalore, and employs 2,400 people in India, where it controls 5.9% of the pharmaceuticals market. In 2007, GSK signed an outsourcing deal with Tata Consulting Services (TCS), of India, to establish a drug development support facility in Bombay.[12] Under the terms of the deal, TCS supports GSK's global clinical research and development program by providing outsourced data management and medical trial reporting services. The arrangement created nearly 100 new jobs on an existing site and was worth more than £10 million. GSK reportedly picked TCS as a partner because of "its strong record in knowledge process outsourcing and operational excellence."[13]

GSK has forged strategic alliances with the large Indian pharmas. The collaboration between GSK and Indian-based Ranbaxy was established in 2003.[14] Ranbaxy, India, prides itself on its drug-discovery and drug-development capabilities. Its 1,400 scientists also research new drug-discovery and drug-delivery systems. The company is collaborating with GSK and Merck on preclinical testing. In particular, its partnership with GSK is based on risk/reward and milestones for toxicity, pharmacokinetic, and selectivity analysis on a GSK drug candidate.[15]

In June 2009, GSK and Dr. Reddy's agreed to develop and market selected products across an extensive range of emerging markets. The agreement with Dr. Reddy's is to develop and market prescription pharmaceutical products across India and a number of other emerging markets in Africa, the Middle East, and Latin America.

Dr. Reddy's

Dr. Reddy's Laboratories, Ltd., (trading as Dr. Reddy's), founded in 1984 by Dr. K. Anji Reddy and headquartered in Hyderabad, India, has become India's second-biggest pharmaceutical company.[a] The group's major product lines include antibiotics, pain relievers, ulcer medicines, antidepressants, and cardiovascular drugs. Dr. Reddy's major activity also is exporting bulk actives, branded formulation, and generic formulations to more than 100 countries, including the United States, the European Union, Latin America, the Commonwealth of Independent States (CIS) countries, China, the Middle East, Japan, South Africa, and Southeast Asia. The company employs more than 7,000 staff, of which over 1,100 work outside India.[b] It has developed more than 190 medications and 60 active pharmaceutical ingredients for drug manufacture, diagnostic kits, critical care, and biotechnology products.[c]

International subsidiaries are located in the United States, the United Kingdom, Russia, and Brazil, with joint ventures in China (named Kunshan Rotam Reddy Pharmaceuticals Company, Ltd.)[d] and South Africa (named Venturepharm, Ltd.).[e] The company has a U.S. FDA-approved, modern manufacturing unit in India. The company has R&D centers in Hyderabad, India, and Atlanta, Georgia.[f]

In its first overseas acquisition, in 2002, Dr. Reddy's acquired two small British generic drug companies, BMS Laboratories and its subsidiary, Meridian Healthcare. With this acquisition, the pharma major ventured into the European market, which it had been eyeing for some time.[g] In 2004, Dr. Reddy's gained access to drug-delivery technology platforms in the dermatology segment through its acquisition of U.S.-based Trigenesis Therapeutics.[h] In 2005, Dr. Reddy's acquired Roche's APU business at the state-of-the-art manufacturing site in Mexico, with a total investment of $59 million.[i] In March 2006, Dr. Reddy's Lab's acquired a German generic firm Betapharm for 480 million euros in one of the biggest overseas acquisitions by an Indian pharma company.[j] Betapharm is the fourth-largest player in the German market, which is the largest generics market in the world after the U.S. market.[k]

In September 2005, Dr. Reddy entered into a co-development and commercialization agreement with Denmark-based Roeoscience A/S for the joint development of Balaglitazone. In 2006, it entered into an agreement with U.K. ClinTec International for the joint development of an anticancer compound, DRF 1042. That same year, it collaborated with the National Cancer Institute in Maryland and with Argenta Discovery Limited for Chronic Oberstructive Pulmonary Disease.[l]

Dr. Reddy's formed a strategic alliance with GSK on June 15, 2009, to develop and market more than 100 products in emerging markets. This partnership will combine its portfolio of quality branded pharmaceuticals with GSK's extensive sales and marketing capabilities.[m] Dr. Reddy will manufacture the product, which then will be licensed and supplied to the GSK market, including Latin America, Africa, the Middle East, and Asia Pacific. This alliance is expected to make a meaningful contribution to Dr. Reddy's revenues for 2 to 3 years.[n]

In 2010, the family-controlled Dr. Reddy's denied that it was in talks to sell its generics business in India to U.S. pharmaceutical giant Pfizer, which had been suing the company for alleged patent infringement after Dr. Reddy's announced that it intended to produce a generic version of Atorvastatin, marketed by Pfizer as Lipitor, an anti-cholesterol medication. Dr. Reddy's was already linked to U.K. pharmaceuticals multinational GSK.

In October 2010, Dr. Reddy's expanded its portfolio in Russia and CIS countries through in-licensing deals. It entered into an agreement with Cipla limited, India, for exclusive marketing rights to a portfolio of over-the-counter and prescription products in the Russian and Ukraine markets.[o] The company also entered into an agreement with U.K.-based Vitabiotics, Ltd., for a range of nutraceutical products for Russia and select CIS countries.[p] The agreement gives Dr. Reddy's exclusive marketing rights to two of Vitabiotics' leading products: Jointace and Dietrim. Vitabiotics will supply these products on a long-term basis from its facilities in Europe.[q]

Sources:

a, e. Dr. Reddy's Laboratories, from Wikipedia. Available at en.wikipedia.org/wiki/Dr._Reddy's_Laboratories.

b. "Employment—Dr. Reddy's Laboratories," Dr. Reddy's Laboratories, Ltd., 2009. Available at www.drreddys.com/sustainability/ec-employment.html.

c. "Asian Health Newsletter," *Business Development Asia* 20 (August 2000). Available at www.bdallc.com.

d. "Dr. Reddy's Laboratories in South African Partnership," SiliconIndia, 8 November 2003. Available at www.siliconindia.com/shownews/Dr_Reddys_Laboratories_in_S_African_partnership___-nid-21685.html.

f. "Dr. Reddy's Reckoner: A Business Snapshot, 2007–2008," Dr. Reddy's Laboratories, Ltd., 20 May 2008. Available at www.drreddys.com/media/pdf/Reckoner_Q4FY08.pdf.

g. "Dr. Reddy's Signs Definitive Agreement to Acquire BMS Laboratories and Meridian Healthcare U.K.," Business Wire, 12 March 2002.

h. "Dr. Reddy's Acquires U.S. Company for $11 M," SiliconIndia, 7 May 2007. Available at www.siliconindia.com/shownews/Dr_Reddys_acquires_US_company_for_11_M___-nid-24085.html.

i. K. Barnes, "Dr. Reddy's Expands into Mexico," Outsourcing-Pharma.com, 11 November 2005. Available at www.outsourcing-pharma.com/Clinical-Development/Dr.-Reddy-s-expands-into-Mexico.

j. "India's Dr. Reddy's Beats Rivals with 480M-Euro Bid for Betapharm of Germany," ThePharmaLetter, 27 February 2006. Available at www.thepharmaletter.com/file/77794/indias-dr-reddys-beats-rivals-with-480m-euro-bid-for-betapharm-of-germany.html.

k. N. Kresge and A. Kirchfield, "Ratiopharm Gives Teva 'Last Ticket' to German Generics Market," *Bloomberg Businessweek*, 18 March 2010. Available at www.businessweek.com/news/2010-03-18/ratiopharm-gives-teva-last-ticket-to-german-generics-market.html.

l. "Dr. Reddy's, Argenta Discovery Announce R&D Collaboration," *Hindustan Times*, 2 February 2006. "Dr. Reddy's Laboratories, Ltd.," *Bloomberg Businessweek*, 18 February 2011. Available at http://investing.businessweek.com/research/stocks/snapshot/snapshot.asp?ticker=881725.

m, n. T. Staton, "Glaxo, Dr. Reddy's Team Up in Emerging Markets," FiercePharma, 15 June 2009. Available at www.fiercepharma.com/story/glaxo-dr-reddys-team-emerging-markets/2009-06-15.

o, p, q. "Dr Reddy's Enters Pact with Cipla, Vitabotics to Market Drugs," *The Economic Times*, 25 October 2010. Available at http://economictimes.indiatimes.com/news/news-by-industry/healthcare/biotech/healthcare/Dr-Reddys-enters-pact-with-Cipla-Vitabiotics-to-market-drugs/articleshow/6810067.cms.

AstraZeneca's Restructuring and Outsourcing of R&D to Asia

AstraZeneca spends more than $4 billion per year and employs more than 11,000 people in its R&D organization. In 2009, worldwide sales of AstraZeneca products totaled $32.8 billion.[16] The company has undertaken one of the most far-reaching programs of restructuring and employment downsizing in the industry.

The company has announced employment cuts on a worldwide basis (roughly 8,000 positions), which would constitute one of the biggest industry "shake-ups" in history. The job cuts will likely result in the loss of 1,500 jobs in the United Kingdom, as well as 3,500 posts from its other R&D facilities worldwide.[17] According to Chief Executive David Brennan, the plan is to "outsource more of AstraZeneca's research and development function—a division largely defined as the heart of any pharmaceutical company. However, AstraZeneca's plan is to outsource much of that work to pharma-emerging markets such as China."[18] The chief executive reportedly has mentioned to U.K. media:

> As the majority of our employees are in the U.K., the U.S., and Europe, you could expect more job cuts there.[19]
>
> Between 2007 and 2009, the company made around 12,600 job reductions with annualized benefits of $1.6 billion by the end of 2009, rising to an anticipated $2.4 billion by the end of 2010. In early 2010, the company announced a further 10,400 reductions over the next four years, with an additional annual benefit of $1.9 billion forecast for year-end 2014, with approximately half of these benefits realized by 2011. The company is expected to counter some of these job reductions by increasing staff numbers in biologic product development and operations in emerging markets.[20]

AstraZeneca's annual report for 2009 summarized the R&D strategy as follows:

As part of our strategic expansion in important emerging markets, we continue to strengthen our research capabilities in Asia Pacific. Investment continued during 2009 at our 'Innovation Centre China' research facility in Shanghai, which opened in 2007. Our research facility in Bangalore also continues to grow with capital investment supporting increases to R&D resources in India. Both facilities are increasingly involved in development activities. In 2009, we invested $4.4 billion in R&D (2008: $5.2 billion; 2007: $5.2 billion), $764 million on acquiring product rights (such as in-licensing), and additionally approved $329 million of R&D capital investment to strengthen our resources in line with our strategic objectives.[21]

R&D Centre, Bangalore, India, was created in 2001, on the heels of a $15 million investment by AstraZeneca.[22] Its mission was to discover new chemical entities for the treatment of infectious diseases of the developing world. It is the only tuberculosis-dedicated research center in the world. The Bangalore facility does business under two identities—AZPIL (AstraZeneca Pharma India Limited) and AZIPL (AstraZeneca India Private Limited)—and is engaged in marketing, R&D, PR&D, manufacturing, and clinical trials.[23] AZPIL currently employs more than 1,400 people.[24]

AstraZeneca Innovation Center China (ICC) opened its lab facilities in Zhangjiang Park, near Shanghai. The ICC was established in 2006, with an initial $100 million investment by AstraZeneca as one of the main global R&D facilities of AstraZeneca. The ICC is part of the AstraZeneca investment initiative in China that has a presence in 23 locations around the mainland and employs more than 3,000 employees.[25]

More recently, AstraZeneca has been signing drug discovery research partnerships with Asian companies. Jubilant Life Sciences Limited India forged a research collaboration agreement with AstraZeneca in 2009.[26] Under the shared risk-reward collaboration, which will initially focus on the neuroscience area, Jubilant aims to deliver a steady stream of discovery programs to fill AstraZeneca's preclinical pipeline.

The Importance of Early Entry and Deep Commitment to China's Emerging Market: The Success of the Swiss Pharmas Novartis and Hoffmann-La Roche

The two major Swiss pharmas, Novartis and Hoffmann-La Roche, have both achieved well above-average success in the industry. What is remarkable about both companies is that they were early movers in Asia, with a long-term view and gradual approach to expansion. As a result, they have been able to establish productive partnerships on that continent.

Novartis Finds an Exquisite Balance to Become an Industry Leader

Novartis, a global pharmaceutical company headquartered in Basel, Switzerland, was created in 1996 through the merger of Ciba-Geigy and Sandoz. With 99,830 employees, sales for 2009 of $44.267 billion, and R&D expenditure at $7.469 billion, Novartis is one of the big global pharmas. But it stands out among its peers (see Figures 7-1 and 7-2).

Novartis has pulled off a rare trick: It is well diversified without having lost any of its powers to innovate. It currently has four main divisions: branded prescription pharmaceuticals, vaccines and diagnostics, generic prescription pharmaceuticals (Sandoz), and consumer healthcare.

Focus on innovation leads to success

Number of US FDA new molecular entity approvals for selected companies, 2000 - Dec. 22, 2009

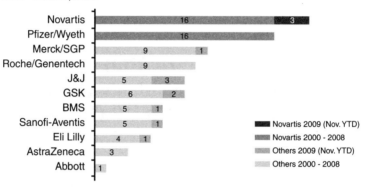

Notes: Novartis includes co-developed or co-marketed products from CIBA Vision, QLT, Idenix, Genentech; Pfizer includes products from Pharmacia, Upjohn, Parke Davis, Wyeth, Merk includes products from Schering, Berfex, Organon; Roche includes products from Genentech; J&J includes products from Janssen, Centocor; RW Johnson; Xolair® is included in both the Roche-Genentech data and the Novartis data; Source: FDA

1. | Novartis 2009 Annual Results | January 26, 2010

Figure 7-1 Focus on innovation leads to success
Reproduced with permission from Novartis.

Pharma tops competitors in IMS sales growth

	Nov YTD Growth in LC% vs PY	YTD Sales (USD bn)	YTD Market Share MS%	vs PY%
Novartis Pharma	11.6	24.9	3.8	0.2
Roche	11.4	28.6	4.4	0.2
Lilly	9.0	17.8	2.7	0.1
AstraZenca	8.9	30.1	4.6	0.1
Bristol-Myers SQB.	6.3	12.8	2.0	0.0
Abbott	4.4	17.3	2.7	-0.1
Sanofi-Aventis	2.8	31.0	4.8	-0.2
Pfizer	0.7	37.2	5.7	-0.3
Merck & Co	-0.3	22.4	3.4	-0.2
GlaxoSmithKline	-1.9	30.6	4.7	-0.4
Wyeth	-2.1	13.0	2.0	-0.2
Johnson & Johnson	-7.4	23.4	3.6	-0.5

Source: IMS PADDS Monthly, 59 Countries Nov 09 YTD

35. | Novartis 2009 Annual Results | January 26, 2010

Figure 7-2 Novartis leads pharma sales growth
Reproduced with permission from Novartis.

With strong research capabilities, Novartis has historically generated the majority of its prescription pharma revenues from internally developed products. The company has its research headquarters in Cambridge, Massachusetts. However, to ensure continued growth, in recent years, the company has increasingly used external collaborations to enhance its late-stage R&D pipeline.

Novartis has 14 research centers[27] located in developed economies, including Cambridge, Massachusetts; East Hanover, New Jersey; Emeryville and La Jolla, California; Basel, Switzerland; Horsham, U.K.; Siena, Italy; and Tokyo, Japan. In addition, it has eight that are located in emerging economies, including Singapore, Indonesia, China, and India. Indications show that it is expanding capacity in the new emerging economy centers and curtailing some activities in developed countries such as Italy.

Novartis' outstanding track record of success with new drug approvals over the past decade testifies to the effectiveness of its R&D strategy, which appears finely balanced in centers in Europe, North America, Japan, and emerging Asia. Recently launched products and sustained expansion in emerging markets have helped position Novartis as the industry's fastest-growing company.

Novartis' commitment to conducting R&D in emerging markets is evident. Novartis has two R&D centers in China. One is located in Shanghai's Zhangjiang Hi-Tech Park; the other Chinese center is in Changshu. NIBR Shanghai has been built with associates recruited primarily from Shanghai's emerging cluster of innovative academic, biotech, and pharmaceutical research institutions. Research focuses on infectious causes of cancer primarily found in Asia and includes efforts in discovery chemistry and biomarker research. Novartis increased the number of associates at the research center in Shanghai from 160 to nearly 1,000.[28]

The Novartis site in Changshu is situated about 80 km northwest of Shanghai, near the city of Suzhou.[29] The focus of the Changshu site is on the process and analytical R&D of innovative experimental drug substances, as well as on their manufacturing technologies.

The Novartis Pharmaceutical Development site in India is located at Hyderabad. This development center integrates information sciences across all development franchises, technical research and development, drug regulatory affairs, drug safety and epidemiology, and development informatics. Novartis Hyderabad is also the site in India for vaccines and diagnostics, global marketing and sales, global sourcing, and business planning and analysis. In addition, it is the home of the Novartis Institute for BioMedical Research.[30]

Novartis has also been making additional acquisitions in India and China. On August 28, 2009, Novartis acquired an additional stake in its Indian subsidiary, Novartis India, Ltd., of up to approximately 39% from public shareholders.[31] Novartis also reached an agreement to acquire an 85% stake in the Zhejiang Tianyuan Bio-Pharmaceutical Co., a Chinese vaccines company, for approximately $125 million cash, subject to regulatory approvals in China.[32] Zhejiang Tianyuan Bio-Pharmaceutical Company's net sales doubled to approximately USD 25 million in 2008 compared to 2006.[33]

Korea and Thailand offer examples of how Novartis places bets on biotechnology start-ups in Asia. Novartis Korea was created in 1997 through the merger of Sandoz Korea (established in 1984) and Ciba-Geigy Korea.[34] It is among the top five producers in the country and plans to invest KRW50bn ($52.1 million) over the next 5 years in its local operations.[35] Since 1984, Sandoz has been present in South Korea, when it formed a joint venture with Dong Wha.[36] In late 2007, the $550 million the Novartis Venture Fund (NVF), operated by Swiss Novartis, entered the Korean equity market. The fund aims to expand its presence across Asia, starting with the Korean biotechnology industry. In October 2009, Novartis announced a five-year plan to invest $100 million in South Korea.[37] The money will support the development of new drugs in local bioscience start-ups.

Novartis today has among the fullest pipelines of new drugs. It also has strength in all its market segments: prescriptions, vaccines and diagnostics, generics, and consumer healthcare. Novartis was among the first to establish a presence in the emerging markets (such as Sandoz India in 1996) and to build R&D capacity in Asia (Singapore tropical disease R&D unit in 2003). The company's far-sighted and finely balanced strategy has put it in a position of strength that is the envy of its rivals (see Figure 7-3).

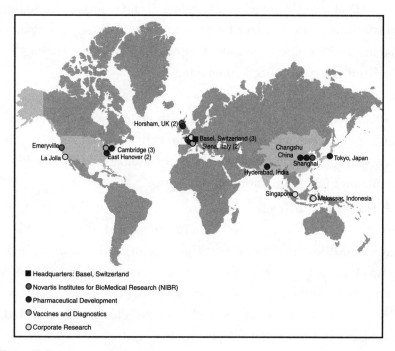

Figure 7-3 Novartis global footprint
Reproduced with permission from Novartis.

Hoffmann-La Roche: A Pioneer in China with Creative Partnerships

Roche is smaller and less diversified than Novartis, but it sells diagnostic and monitoring equipment as well as original drugs. Worldwide, the group employs more than 80,000 people.[38] Roche's two divisions, Pharmaceuticals (CHF 39 billion sales in 2009) and Diagnostics (CHF 10 billion sales in 2009), are both market leaders.[39]

Roche's pharmaceutical research focuses on inflammatory diseases, bone diseases, disorders of the central nervous system, cancer, metabolic disorders, and viral illnesses.[40]

For new products and manufacturing processes, global spending on R&D by the Roche Group amounts to CHF 5.7 billion annually.[41] Every year, the Group spends around CHF 5 billion on pharmaceutical R&D alone, which includes Genentech and Chugai.[42] More than 50 scientific and commercial collaborations with biotech companies and universities have been sought out to complement and strengthen the Group's dynamic R&D capabilities.[43]

"The Group's innovation model also includes Roche spin-offs like BioXell, set up in 2002, and the biotech company Basilea Pharmaceutica—as potential drug development partners."[44] Licensing agreements that give Roche access to new drug candidates and technologies are another important part of its strategy.

Hoffmann-La Roche's R&D centers are located in Basel and Rotkreuz, Switzerland, as well as in Indianapolis, Indiana, and Pleasanton and Palo Alto, California.[45] The company added Shanghai to its network as early as 2004, after starting commercial activities in the country earlier than its competitors. In Shanghai, Zhangjiang High-Tech Park is home to both Shanghai Roche Pharmaceuticals, Ltd., and Shanghai Roche R&D Center (China), Ltd.

Shanghai Roche Pharmaceuticals, Ltd., was founded in 1994 and was Roche's first joint venture in China.[46] It was dedicated to providing a wide variety of prescription drugs encompassing key therapeutic areas such as oncology, virology, and transplantation.

Opening 10 years later, in October 2004, the Roche R&D Center (China), Ltd. (RRDCC), was one of Roche's first wholly owned R&D centers in Asia.[47] It is also one of Roche's global pharmaceutical R&D facilities, and its activities focus on lead generation and optimization for medicinal chemistry research while also providing key support to Roche's business development strategy in China.[48]

Roche is leveraging its China presence to seek out new business opportunities and achieve synergies between its own R&D centers and technology start-up companies in the area of diagnostic and scientific equipment operating in China, such as CapitalBio, ChemPartner, and BioDuro.

Shanghai ChemPartner (ChemPartner) was founded in 2003 and is one of the leading contract research organizations, providing discovery biology, medicinal chemistry, drug metabolism/pharmacokinetics (DMPK), process R&D, toxicology, pharmacology, analytical development, formulation, and contract manufacturing services to more than 120 pharmaceutical and biotech companies worldwide. Headquartered in China, ChemPartner has overseas business development operations in Boston, Massachusetts, and Copenhagen, Denmark. The company currently has a team of over 1,000 scientists, including more than 100 senior scientific leaders with extensive industry experiences gained from leading global pharmaceutical and biotech companies.[49]

The "Pure" Pharmas: Lilly and Merck As Leaders in Radical Partnering

Eli Lilly and Merck stand out as undiversified, "pure" pharmaceutical companies with very strong traditions of research-based innovation. The companies have been transforming their "in-house approach" to innovation into a model that is network-based. In this sense, they have been experimenters in creating new systems of innovation based on risk- and reward-sharing partnerships, many of which are made with new, emerging-market companies.

FIPNet: Eli Lilly's Radical Model of Networked Innovation

Eli Lilly was founded in 1876, became publicly traded in 1955, and became known as a leader in diabetes treatment after launching the world's first commercially available insulin in the 1920s. Lilly is a "pure pharmaceutical company." It divested its medical device and diagnostics business more than a decade ago and focuses almost exclusively on the development and sales of original prescription drugs (the exception is animal health products, which provide the company with a small fraction of revenue).

Smaller than lead pharma players such as Pfizer or GSK, Lilly finds itself in the same predicament as many of its peers: It faces major losses of revenue resulting from patent expirations of its key products. These have either already occurred (as in the case of Prozac) or are about to happen during 2011–2014 (for example, with Zyprexa and Cymbalta). Internal R&D was the company's source of growth in the past, and those successful products were the result of the company's discoveries made through in-house R&D.

The challenge ahead of the company today is the looming crisis of sales loss and how to find new sources of revenue and growth. As Lilly CEO John Lechleiter explains, to manage those challenges, the company "is transforming itself from a fully integrated pharmaceutical company to a fully integrated company network or FIPNet."[50] The company is changing the way it operates in all areas, from investment and R&D to manufacturing, marketing, and sales. This long-term strategy is designed to make the drug-discovery process more efficient, with heavy use of outsourcing. Unlike some of its competitors, Lilly has not used quick acquisitions as short-term fixes to revenue problems.[51] It is making long-term investments in changes that will enable it to prosper in the future after the patent expiry crisis. The company is moving away from relying on internal product sources to betting on external product sources. The company has chosen codevelopment as a primary basis of growth in the years to come. Outsourcing many components of R&D, along with several other business functions, such as data management, sales, and marketing, is the way to cut costs and combat the decline in sales expected from 2011. Two strategic acquisitions (ICOS and ImClone) complement the approach.

Partnerships underpin novel methods of molecule discovery with up-and-coming players from India and China. In 2007, Lilly signed risk-and-reward sharing agreements with Nicholas Piramal and Suven Life Sciences of India and with Hutchinson MediPharma, based in China. In the case of Piramal, the company will develop molecules from Lilly's discovery pipeline all the way to phase II of clinical trials. As the drug candidates make progress, Piramal receives milestone payment plus, ultimately, royalties—if the drug makes it to market. Similar deals for early stage molecules were made with Suven and Hutchinson.

Lilly uses a "virtual drug development network" called Chorus to manage 15 molecule-development programs that all occur outside the company.[52] Chorus has a lean staff of fewer than 30 scientists who design, plan, and oversee discovery and development work. The Chorus model has delivered results on 14 molecules, 6 of which have led to successful proof-of-concept decisions that saved the company $100 million.[53] Chorus has itself proven to be a highly efficient vehicle for discovery. It has been able to achieve savings by accelerating the time it takes to reach "proof of concept" by as much as a year, at half the average industry cost.[54]

Following up on the early successes, Lilly is extending the codevelopment model further by making a joint venture deal with one of India's leading CROs, Jubilant Organosys.[55] The deal includes the right for Lilly to exercise first negotiation on non-Lilly assets developed within the joint venture—those sourced by Jubilant and other third parties.

Another step toward the externally driven discovery model is Lilly's "open source" R&D platform. Under this initiative, the company tests, free of charge, compounds that outside researchers submit in disease areas of interest. In return, the company retains first rights to negotiate a licensing or codevelopment agreement with the submitting party, which receives ownership of the study report if no agreement results and can publish the data. This system has been attractive enough to draw 130 universities and biotechnology companies from 21 countries to participate since the program was launched in June 2009.[56] The company has received multiple submissions and is in the process of evaluating thousands of new molecules.

FIPNet also encompasses clinical trials and toxicology. In both domains, new partnership models are also being devised. The company sold its own lab facilities located in Greenfield, Indiana, to the CRO Covance, with whom the company had worked before and has a long-term outsourcing relationship. For chemistry services, Lilly chose to work with a Chinese entrepreneur to create ShangPharma, which will work exclusively for the company. The full extent of Lilly's network-based R&D system can be appreciated by looking at its diagrammatic representation in Figure 7-4.[57]

FIPNet is a comprehensive system. In addition to discovery collaborations and the use of functional outsourcing for preclinical and clinical trials, FIPNet makes ample use of equity-based investments and partnerships. Lilly established Lilly Ventures and Lilly Asian Ventures with a combined capital of $300 million. These were joined by a new venture capital fund, Health Care Ventures.[58] The funds have started investing in biotech, healthcare, and medical technology companies around the world, and have enabled the creation of companies with capabilities important for the operation of FIPNet, such as HD Biosciences of Shanghai. The venture capital (VC) fund gives Lilly preferential access to new, high-quality molecules, to advance their development. Further partnering is taking place with private investment funds.

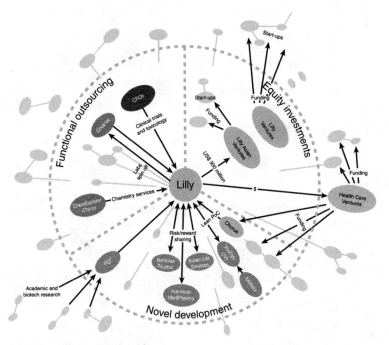

Source: Ernst & Young and Eli Lilly and Company

Figure 7-4 Lilly's R&D FIPNet

Reproduced with permission from "Beyond Borders—Global Biotechnology Report 2010," Ernst & Young, 2010, 23.

What makes the FIPNet model remarkable is its consistency and radicalism, as well as Lilly's commitment to partner with the new players from the pharmerging markets (see Figure 7-5). The industry is observing Lilly's progress with the model with a great deal of interest, and some companies are replicating elements of FIPNet's pioneering codevelopment partnership model. Lilly is betting that its new "innovation engine" will yield superior results. As John Lechleiter points out, whether this happens largely depends on how well the company manages partnerships. As he states, "All partners—Lilly included—must demonstrate flexibility, open and honest communication, collaboration, and a steadfast commitment to common goals."[59]

Legend: ● Sales Office ▲ Manufacturing ■ Research

		Chile	●	Honduras	●	Mauritius	●	Singapore	● ■
		China	● ▲ ■	Hong Kong	●	Mexico	● ▲	Slovak Republic	●
		Colombia	●	Hungary	●	Netherlands	●	Slovenia	●
		Costa Rica	●	Iceland	●	New Zealand	●	South Africa	●
		Croatia	●	India	●	Norway	●	Spain	● ▲ ■
		Czech Republic	●	Indonesia	●	Pakistan	●	Sweden	●
		Denmark	●	Ireland	● ▲	Panama	●	Switzerland	●
Algeria	●	Dominican Republic	●	Israel	●	Peru	●	Taiwan	●
Argentina	●	Egypt	● ▲	Italy	● ▲	Philippines	●	Thailand	●
Australia	● ■	El Salvador	●	Japan	● ▲ ■	Poland	● ■	Tunisia	●
Austria	●	Estonia	●	Kazakhstan	●	Portugal	●	Turkey	●
Belgium	●	Finland	●	Korea	●	Puerto Rico	● ▲	Ukraine	●
Bosnia-Herzegovina	●	France	● ▲	Latvia	●	Romania	●	United Arab Emirates	●
Brazil	● ▲	Germany	● ▲	Lebanon	●	Russia Federation	●	United Kingdom	● ▲ ■
Bulgaria	●	Greece	●	Lithuania	●	Saudi Arabia	●	United States	● ▲ ■
Canada	● ■	Guatemala	●	Malaysia	●	Serbia and Montenegro	●	Venezuela	●

Figure 7-5 Lilly global locations

Reproduced with permission from Eli Lilly and Company website, www.lilly.com. Copyright © 2010 Eli Lilly and Company.

Merck's Radical Partnerships: Moving from Internally to Externally Driven R&D

Merck is one of the great leaders of the global pharmaceutical industry. It employs approximately 100,000 people worldwide and invested $5.8 billion in R&D in 2009. With the recent acquisition of Schering-Plough, Merck becomes the second-biggest prescription drug company, behind Pfizer. The merger will improve both Merck's drug pipeline and its competitive market position.

Even before the merger with Schering-Plough, Merck was repositioning itself strategically and undergoing significant restructuring to face problems associated with patent expiry and high costs. The company emphasized the role of emerging markets for future sales growth, expanded its low-cost manufacturing base, and started shifting its reliance on in-house R&D to a system of innovation that took advantage of external collaborations and partnerships. A growing share of these partnerships was forged with companies from China and India.

In 2010, Merck phased out production in eight manufacturing plants, consolidating its manufacturing capacity to 77 facilities worldwide. The company also decided to close down 8 of its R&D sites in Europe and North America, consolidating its R&D centers to 16 facilities across the globe. All the lab closures took place in high-cost destinations and included Montreal, Quebec; Boxmeer, Schaijik, and Oss in the Netherlands; Newhouse, Scotland; Odense, Denmark; Waltrop, Germany; and Cambridge, Massachusetts.[60]

Since 2005, Merck has been busy expanding its network of partnerships. An increasing number have been forged with emerging players and are not just confined to toxicology, chemistry, or clinical trials. Several of those have been contracted to WuXi PharmaTech of Shanghai. In 2006, Merck in-licensed an experimental diabetes drug, GRC 8200, which was in phase II of clinical trials, from Glenmark, India, paying $39 million up front.[61] (Merck dropped this particular initiative after deciding to move into other disease areas.)

Since then, Merck has been entering into a number of value-sharing deals with partners from India and also China that include risk and reward–sharing features and milestone payments predicated on the progress of drug candidates (see Figure 7-6). The company created a value-sharing partnership with Advinus India to develop metabolic disease treatments. The agreement provides milestone payments of $74.5 million.[62] Advinus carries out research until phase II of clinical trials and is eligible for royalties once Merck commercializes the drug. Merck has also concluded a value-sharing agreement with Nicholas Piramal and one on preclinical trials through phase II with Ranbaxy. Both companies are leading Indian players. In addition, Merck formed a partnership with Orchid Pharmaceuticals in 2008. This started with an exchange of scientists from the two companies who shared an interest in antifungal compounds and, over time, also became a risk-sharing agreement.

In China, other than the deal with WuXi PharmaTech, Merck has worked with ShanghaiBio on a project in clinical oncology research in which ShanghaiBio collected tissue samples indicative of four types of cancer for use in clinical trials. Using its expertise in microarray, the company also provided Merck with gene expression analyses. Merck retains intellectual property rights to the results of this research because it will perform the final analysis of the gene panels itself.[63]

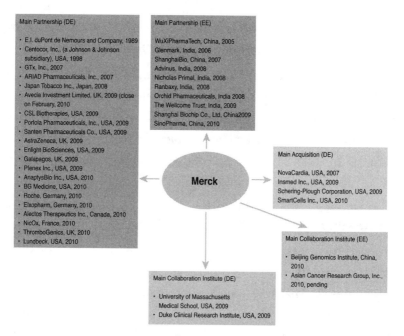

Figure 7-6 Merck & Co. collaborations and mergers and acquisitions with developed and emerging economies[64]
Key: DE = Developed economies; EE = Emerging economies.

Advinus of Bangalore

Advinus is a new-generation Indian CRO specialized in discovery, preclinical, and early phase clinical R&D work. Founded in 2005 by an Indian entrepreneur with extensive experience in the international pharmaceutical industry, it employs 600 people and has worked with both large Indian pharmaceutical companies and international companies such as Merck and GSK. Tata, a large Indian conglomerate, has invested $10 million in the company. In the discovery end of its business, Advinus targets three major disease areas: metabolic disorders, inflammatory diseases, and orphan (neglected) diseases such as malaria, dengue fever, and tuberculosis, which occur primarily in underdeveloped countries.

Advinus has a vision of moving beyond providing preclinical and clinical trial services. It plans to become a developer of original drugs from discovery all the way through phase IIb of clinical trials. At that point, the drug candidate would be sold to pharmaceutical companies for full development. This is the business model underlying its partnership with Merck. Advinus carries out research as far as phase II, after which Merck assumes control for phase III and commercialization of the drug. Advinus is eligible for milestone payments as the drug candidate progresses through the pipeline. Advinus also has a partnership with Drugs for Neglected Diseases Initiative (DNDi), a not-for-profit drug research organization based in Switzerland,[a] and AgilityBio, a division of U.S. BioImagene, Inc., with preclinical development services offered by Advinus.[b]

Advinus' pharmaceutical-development Bangalore operation is located on an 8-acre campus with 220,000 square feet of modern facilities. This business offers an end-to-end preclinical to early clinical development platform for pharmaceutical product development. The corporation has more than 275 professionals.[c]

Sources:

a. "Company News: Advinus Therapeutics and DNDi Join Forces on Drug Discovery and Development for Visceral Leishmaniasis (Kala Azar)," Advinus Therapeutics, 11 October 2007. Available at www.advinus.com/view_news.asp?id=122.

b. "AgilityBio and Advinus Announce Partnership," BioImagene, 23 October 2008. Available at www.bioimagene.com/news_articles/press_releases/press_release_10232008.html.

c. "About Us," Advinus Therapeutics, 2008. Available at www.advinus.com.

The Giant: Pfizer

Pfizer, the world's largest pharma company, has maintained its clout due to its determined policy of streamlining operations globally, accompanied by a policy of making selective acquisitions. Recently, Pfizer has decided to rely more on externally sourced products and has become more open to partnerships and R&D collaborations.

Pfizer: A Conservative but Far-Sighted Giant

Founded in Brooklyn, New York, in 1849, Pfizer, Inc., is still headquartered in New York. With a revenue of $50.0 billion in 2009 and 116,500 employees worldwide in 2010,[65] it is the biggest global pharma company. Like other companies in the industry, Pfizer has been actively streamlining and restructuring itself, refocusing its drug portfolio, and looking to emerging markets as sources of growth. Before its Wyeth acquisition, the number of its manufacturing sites and R&D centers had been reduced by more than 40%, from 78 to 46 and from 15 to 9, respectively.[66]

Pfizer Global Research and Development facilities support both the BioTherapeutics and Pharma Therapeutics R&D organizations. In 2009, the company invested 7.7 billion USD in new drug discovery, a value that corresponds to approximately 15% of the company's global revenues. For 2010, the estimated investment in this area is $9.6 billion.[67]

R&D locations around the world have been reduced from a presence in ten countries to six countries: the United States, the United Kingdom, and Japan for the developed countries, and China, Korea, and Singapore for the rapidly developing countries. While some of the R&D labs in the United States, such as the one in St. Louis, Missouri, are being closed or sold, new R&D centers in China are being opened up.[68]

Pfizer was an early entrant into the China market, ahead of some of its rivals. First established in 1983, Pfizer's operations in China (known by its Chinese name, "Hui rui") initially targeted the relatively affluent east-coast cities, such as Beijing and Shanghai.[69] Now the operations are present in around 170 areas, with manufacturing facilities located in Dalian, Suzhou, and WuXi, and corporate sales offices located in most major cities around the country.[70] The company has invested more than $500 million in its China operation.[71] Pfizer is actively involved in discovery, development, and manufacturing. Its operation in China engages in sales and marketing and manufacturing. It is also active in R&D through partnerships with CROs and local academic research institutions. Pfizer also conducts clinical trials supporting its local and global drug development.

In 2005, Pfizer inaugurated an R&D center in Shanghai to provide technological support to its global operation, particularly its business in China and the rest of Asia. In 2005, the Shanghai center had 14 employees; by the summer of 2009, that number had grown to 342.[72] Then on October 12, 2010, Pfizer announced that its second, new R&D center, this time in Wuhan, is up and running.[73] First this site was reported as a support center for phase I through phase IV clinical studies from around the world, but Pfizer also designed the facility to be specialized in radiation biology. The Wuhan center currently has 40 employees, which will grow to 200 by 2012.[74] Biolake (Wuhan National Bioindustry Base) is the location of Pfizer's new center. With a population approaching 10 million, Wuhan is the largest city in central China.[75] This is the first R&D facility that Pfizer placed in central/western China, bringing the number of Pfizer Labs in China to four, in addition to its Shanghai R&D center.[76]

By 2014, Pfizer can expect to generate approximately 28% of its sales from externally sourced products.[77] Pfizer had the second-highest in-licensed total in 2009, after GSK and just ahead of third-highest Sanofi-Aventis. Also in 2009, Pfizer tied with GSK as the company with the second-highest number of out-licensed agreements, behind AstraZeneca.[78]

Former CEO Jeffrey Kindler has indicated that Pfizer's "monolithic" approach to drug R&D is a thing of the past. He has laid out plans to carve $3 billion out of the newly merged Pfizer-Wyeth company's budget for R&D,[79] as the company shifts away from its traditional reliance on in-house projects and opens itself up more to partnerships and collaborations. While partnerships and collaborations with U.S. companies remain important, an increasing number is concluded with emerging economy companies and universities as well.

In October 2010, Pfizer and India's largest biotechnology company by revenue, Biocon Ltd., agreed to a licensing deal in which Pfizer would pay $350 million for the rights to commercialize Biocon's diabetes treatment products. The deal is the latest in which Pfizer is tapping a third party for a potential new drug, as its own pipelines have suffered in recent years from a lack of blockbusters.[80]

Biocon

Biocon started out as a company in India that sought to provide affordable treatment of diabetes for the Indian market, as imported insulin was simply too expensive. With success as an insulin producer, Biocon grew rapidly and diversified. Today it is a fully integrated healthcare company that delivers innovative biopharmaceutical solutions. Biocon India is incorporated as a joint venture between Biocon Biochemicals, Ltd., of Ireland and an India entrepreneur, Kiran Mazumdar-Shaw. It was founded in 1978. It was included in "The Best Under a Billion" listing by *Forbes* in 2009[a] and, in the same year, was judged the best listed company in the Asia Pacific region by BioSingapore, based on its market capital, sound business model, and excellent management team.[b] Employing 4,500 people,[c] Biocon is the 7th-largest employer among the top 100 global biotechnology companies.[d] Between 2005 and 2010, Biocon entered into more than 2,200 high-value R&D licensing and other deals within the pharmaceuticals and biopharmaceutical space.[e] In July, Biocon reported that its fiscal first-quarter profit had climbed 33%, helped by better performances from its bio-pharmaceuticals and contract-research businesses[f] (see Figures 7-7 and 7-8).

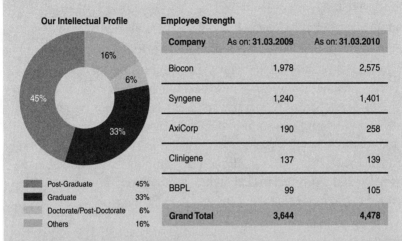

Our Intellectual Profile

Post-Graduate	45%
Graduate	33%
Doctorate/Post-Doctorate	6%
Others	16%

Employee Strength

Company	As on: 31.03.2009	As on: 31.03.2010
Biocon	1,978	2,575
Syngene	1,240	1,401
AxiCorp	190	258
Clinigene	137	139
BBPL	99	105
Grand Total	**3,644**	**4,478**

Figure 7-7 Biocon personnel profile

Reproduced with permission from "Emerge: New Opportunities for BioPharmaceuticals—Biocon Annual Report 2010," Biocon, May 2010. Available at www.biocon.com/docs/AR10-BIOCON.pdf.

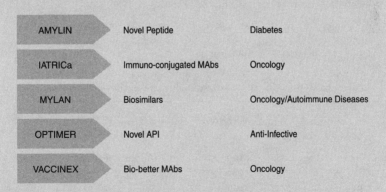

AMYLIN	Novel Peptide	Diabetes
IATRICa	Immuno-conjugated MAbs	Oncology
MYLAN	Biosimilars	Oncology/Autoimmune Diseases
OPTIMER	Novel API	Anti-Infective
VACCINEX	Bio-better MAbs	Oncology

Figure 7-8 Biocon Global Alliance: research and codevelopment

Reproduced with permission from "Emerge: New Opportunities for BioPharmaceuticals—Biocon Annual Report 2010," Biocon, May 2010. Available at www.biocon.com/docs/AR10-BIOCON.pdf.

Biocon has multiple R&D collaborations with Mylan, Optimer, Amylin, and Vaccinex, which are making steady progress. Syngene, which is part of the group, has entered into synergistic research partnership with Endo Pharmaceuticals. Syngene is working toward jointly discovering and developing novel biological drug molecules to fight cancer. Endo will retain all rights to molecules developed, while Syngene will receive research fees.

The global biosimilars market is expected to be worth $19 billion by 2014.[g] Biocon has the requisite technical and operational expertise to develop, take to market, and innovative Biocon's first growth drivers: BioSimilar insulin and mAbs. Biocon has a development and manufacturing strategy for a distribution network. For emerging markets, Biocon has adopted a common go-to-market pathway for all its products. This includes launching in India first, then moving into emerging markets, and eventually entering developed markets.

Sources:

a. "Biocon Among 20 Indian Companies in Forbes 'Best Under a Billion' Tally," MSN News, 24 September 2009. Available at http://news.in.msn.com/business/article.aspx?cp-documentid=3230334.

b. "BioSingapore Presents the 2009 Asia Pacific Biotechnology Awards," BioSpectrum: Asia Edition, 19 March 2009. Available at www.biospectrumasia.com/content/190309sgp8935.asp.

c, f, g. "Emerge: New Opportunities for BioPharmaceuticals—Biocon Annual Report 2010," Biocon, May 2010. Available at www.biocon.com/docs/AR10-BIOCON.pdf.

d. "Biocon Awards," Biocon, 2008, 2010. Available at www.biocon.com/biocon_aboutus_awards.asp.

e. "Biocon Net up 33 percent in First quarter," The Economic Times, 23 July 2010. Available at http://economictimes.indiatimes.com/news/news-by-company/earnings/earnings-news/Biocon-net-up-33-percent-in-first-quarter/articleshow/6206142.cms.

Pfizer is increasingly relying on acquisitions and collaborations with CROs to fill the company's drug-development requirements. About 50% of these needs are filled through acquisitions.[81] Concerned for its intellectual property, Pfizer built trusted relationships with only a few companies and initially avoided collaborations involving its most sensitive intellectual property. It is now using its CRO partners for more of the complex work. One such partner is WuXi PharmaTech, one of China's largest CROs, which Pfizer contracts to perform lab services and custom synthesis work. Unlike Merck, at least in Asia, Pfizer has been slow to negotiate risk-sharing relationships with outside firms and has relied mostly on acquisitions and CROs for drug discovery—although there has been a change in that policy recently. In addition, Pfizer's Shanghai R&D center, with more than 200 employees, supports Pfizer's global clinical development.[82] Pfizer plans significant expansion of R&D, especially in oncology and in types of diseases common in Asia.[83]

Pfizer has also decided to add leading Chinese universities to its network, a network that includes University of Wisconsin–Madison and University College, London.[84] In March 2009, Pfizer China announced that it would invest RMB 3 million to establish the Peking University Pfizer Quantitative Pharmacology Education Center in conjunction with the Peking University Health Science Center (PUHSC). The center aims to train staff in quantitative pharmacology as part of Pfizer's program to support the development of the medical and healthcare systems in China.[85] In July 2009, Pfizer announced a partnership with Fudan University to establish a graduate program in Clinical Data Management and Statistical Programming. In Shanghai, the Pfizer China Research and Development Center has become an integral component of Pfizer's worldwide pharmaceutical development program. The center collaborates with leading academic researchers and top institutes in China, including Peking University, Tsinghua University, Shanghai Jiaotong University, and multiple institutes of Chinese Academy of Sciences.[86]

Pfizer's commitment to Korea stands out. In 2007, the company announced a memorandum of understanding to invest KRW 300 billion ($269.2 million) in South Korea through 2012, to help advance R&D.[87] This is the largest investment plan ever made by the pharmaceutical industry. After the January 29, 2010 merger was approved by South Korea's Fair Trade Commission, Pfizer Korea integrated its operations with Wyeth Korea.[88] Korea's approval process for trials is shorter than in most Asian countries, and Pfizer is now conducting around 90 multinational clinical trials in Korea, covering a wide range of therapeutic areas.[89] Pfizer has had a strong interest in Latin America as well. Pfizer Mexico began its operations in 1951 and now has products in major therapeutic areas. The Pfizer Science Institute was established in Mexico to promote medical science, scientific development, and research.[90]

Until now, Pfizer has relied on acquisitions and its own R&D centers around the world. It recently announced a modification of its strategy toward partnerships. In a program called "Global Centers for Therapeutic Innovation," the company will launch partnerships with academic centers, with the objective to speed up drug-discovery efforts. Pfizer will establish local centers at each partner site where university and company researchers will work together on new compounds and drug candidates. Pfizer will fund the early phases of research and clinical trials development. It will offer milestone payments and royalties, as well as equal IP rights and publication rights to the universities, in exchange for the rights to commercialize drug candidates. The first partner will be the University of California in San Francisco. Other partnerships with universities from the United States, Europe, and Asia will follow in 2012. The strategy is about a more efficient and accelerated manner of translating science into novel proofs of mechanism, as Pfizer's president of worldwide R&D puts it.[91]

The Germans, the French, and the Japanese Follow the Trend

Known as the "Pharmacy of the World," Germany was first to develop the pharmaceutical industry and become its world leader until approximately the middle of the past century. Although the

German biopharmaceutical industry is still strong, the VBA, the national industry association, has lost its international leadership position (for example, in 2005, only 6 out of 140 newly approved drugs were developed in Germany).[92]

France has also been making efforts to stay in the top leagues of the pharmaceutical industry. A study commissioned by Leem, the French pharmaceutical industry association, estimates that 32,000 pharmaceutical jobs will be at risk in France between 2005 and 2015.[93] The leading French pharma, Sanofi-Aventis, has been slower than some of its rivals to globalize its R&D strategy, but it has moved decisively since 2009. In 2009, Sanofi-Aventis announced a major reorganization of its R&D model, creating a leaner, more efficient, and more focused organization. By 2010, more than 60% of the company's development portfolio consisted of vaccines and biologics drugs, and 55% of this portfolio consisted of projects originated by external R&D.[94]

The vast majority of Sanofi-Aventis R&D sites are still located in the developed countries of Europe and in the United States, but the company has had sites in China since 2005 and recently added one in India.[95] Consider its current R&D sites:

- In France, 11 sites. The largest, in terms of surface area, are in Vitry/Alfortville, Montpellier, Chilly/Longjumeau, and Toulouse.

- In other European countries (Germany, United Kingdom, Hungary, Spain, and Italy), 5 sites. The largest is in Frankfurt, Germany.

- In the United States, 6 sites. The largest is in Bridgewater, New Jersey.

- In Japan, R&D is represented in Tokyo.

- In China, the main R&D operations are located in Shanghai, with a Clinical Research Unit in Beijing.

The Japanese pharmaceutical market is the second largest in the world, and the country has a substantial pharmaceutical industry, with 20 companies that have sales of more than $500 million. However, according to Catenion, a Western consultancy, the Japanese pharma industry is suboptimal in size, is uncompetitive, and suffers from a "broken model" of innovation and risk management.[96] Traditionally, Japanese pharma companies have relied on in-house R&D. The challenge is to build highly competitive R&D machines. Japanese clinical trial sponsors spend only about 11% of total development costs on outsourcing, compared with 24% globally.[97] Nevertheless, Japanese companies have moved toward R&D models based on a global organization and on partnership with universities and outside companies. Dainippon Sumitomo Pharma's global R&D system is composed of centers in the United States, China, the United Kingdom, and Japan. The company is committed to creating global products through a global approach to innovation.[98] Mitsubishi Tanabe Pharma is following a similar global approach to drug development, with bases in Europe and the United States in addition to Japan.[99] To survive in the global marketplace, Japanese pharmaceutical companies will have to globalize their operations even further.

Boehringer Ingelheim

Boehringer Ingelheim, founded from a small tartaric acid factory and headquartered in Ingelheim am Rhein, Germany, is a group of privately held companies since 1885, dedicated to researching, development, manufacturing, and marketing products of high therapeutic value for human and veterinary medicine. As one of the world's 20 leading pharmaceutical companies, the group consists of 142 affiliated companies in 50 countries, 41,534 employees, and 12,721 million euros in net sales.[100] Geographically, 49% of net sales have been generated in the Americas, 31% in Europe, and 20% in the Asia, Australasia, and Africa (AAA) regions. The company spent 17.4% of net sales on R&D in 2009,[101] and its corporate motto has steadfastly been "Value through Innovation."[102]

With its strong core competencies already in R&D and manufacturing capabilities, Boehringer Ingelheim traditionally relies heavily on its own internal R&D effort for discovery and development and collaborates with other major pharmaceutical companies.[103] As such, the company has followed a strategy of fueling future growth through early-stage R&D agreements instead of acquiring late-stage or marketed products. Emphasizing such strategy, the company states following its March 27, 2007, financial results, "We don't buy sales. We buy R&D."[104]

A lot of the R&D budget goes to pay for clinical trials, the vast majority of which Boehringer Ingelheim conducts in Europe and North America. However, the share of Central Europe, Asia, and Latin America is significant and exceeds 20% for phase I through III trials. For the location of its R&D, the company still relies on Europe and America, but it is adding new centers in China and Latin America.

Boehringer Ingelheim R&D Locations

DE (6)	EE (3)
Biberach, Germany	Mexico City, Mexico
Ingelheim, Germany	Shanghai, China (CoC)
Vienna, Austria	Buenos Aires, Argentina
Milano, Italy	
Ridgefield, Connecticut, USA	
Laval, Canada	
Tokyo, Japan	

DE = developing economies; EE = emerging economies

In 2009, Boehringer Ingelheim announced a 100 million euro expansion plan to not only double the plant production capacity, but also build its new R&D Center of Competence (CoC) in Shanghai. By August 2010, more than 20 highly qualified organic and analytical chemists had been recruited for the CoC.[105] Furthering the expansion plan into Southeast Asia, Boehringer Ingelheim also entrusted Sinopharm to be its sole distributor in China.[106] With offices in Shanghai, Beijing, Guangzhou, Chengdu, Hangzhou, and Nanjing, the company currently has 1,800 employees; that number is expected to rise to as many as 7,000 in the next 5 to 6 years.[107]

The venerable Boehringer Ingelheim has capitalized on its private, family owned status to pursue long-term objectives. It has steadfastly held to its motto and invests heavily into R&D through internal R&D expenditure, acquisition, and strategic partnerships. It has also created a venture fund to nurture small biotechnology firms.

Conclusions

In the past several years, we have seen a huge acceleration of multinational company expansion of R&D activities in emerging economies, especially in Asia. By 2010, practically all the leading large pharma multinationals had opened up significant R&D facilities in emerging Asia—about two dozen purpose-built laboratory facilities have opened in China and India alone since the turn of the century. In addition, numerous academic research grant programs, strategic alliances, or acquisitions by Western pharmaceutical companies have been taking place. One can say that the center of gravity of global R&D in biopharma has been gradually shifting away from the West, in the southeasterly direction. What just a few years ago were mostly small, experimental R&D centers dealing with tropical diseases or clinical trials coordination have become rapidly expanding key hubs of companies' global R&D networks dealing with cancer, neurological diseases, Alzheimer's disease, biomarker research, and other cutting-edge topics. Many of the new Asian-based R&D centers have grown large and are staffed with hundreds of scientists from both the West and the East, working together on critical research challenges in therapy, diagnostics, and medical technology development.

The activities of the new centers, many of which have chosen to locate in the new bioparks, have stimulated the growth of local universities, pharmaceutical and biotechnology companies, CROs, and companies specialized in discovery or technology development. Some of these emerging multinational corporations were founded by local entrepreneurs; others are branches or subsidiaries of Western firms that found it highly profitable to operate in the emerging market or to enter into joint ventures. Some of these medium-size companies grew and prospered to become small multinationals.

Over time, the sum of all those new West–East collaborations will have profound consequences on the quality of science and the innovation capacity of the host countries, unleashing virtuous cycles of growth and progress. Success with new products and processes created by mixed teams of researchers will stimulate even more investment and collaboration with firms from the West. The next tier of medium-size biopharma companies from the United States and Europe will follow the lead of the top multinationals and become more active in the key emerging markets.

How soon are we to expect significant global competition from the new breed of Indian and Chinese biopharma companies? Although some of these companies, such as Ranbaxy, have become serious international players, especially in generic drugs, none has yet reached the critical size to become a direct competitor to the leading American or European multinationals. The barriers to entry into the proprietary drug industry are too huge. Nevertheless, in time, the most successful of the new larger Chinese or Indian players may be in a position to acquire an ailing Western multinational and then graduate to the status of a global competitor. For now, the new players present excellent opportunities for mutually profitable trade and collaboration, with benefits to consumers and investors in both developed and developing economies.

The rapid emergence of the new players and their integration with global companies have started to transform the way the global R&D system works. This process, as we shall see in the next chapter, is creating a new paradigm of global innovation in the life sciences-based business.

8

The Future: The Expanding
Universe of Global Innovation

"The world is our lab now."

—Dr. John E. Kelly III, Director of IBM Research[1]

Knowledge Drives Economic Development and Becomes the Foundation of Power

For most of human history, controlling territory and other natural resources meant effective power and control of economic life. With the Industrial Revolution, this began to change. Today small nations without physical resources can command great wealth. The battles and power struggles of this century are increasingly about knowledge and technology. Since the 18th century, when the Industrial Revolution started in Britain, the world has witnessed successive changes in the "techno-economic paradigm." Interdependent and mutually supporting technological innovations drove each new wave. Mark Dodgson, et al., describe five such "waves of technological development"[2] since the 1770s as being driven by a set of "key factor industries":

1770–1840	Early mechanization—cotton and pig iron
1840–1890	Steam power and railways—coal and transport
1890–1940	Electrical and heavy engineering—steel
1940–1990	Fordist mass production—energy
1990–now	Information and communications technology—microelectronics

The rapid growth of lead economic sectors accompanied each of these waves. For example, textiles, waterpower, and canals flourished during the first wave; computers, software, IT services, and telecoms were the fruits of the fifth wave.

With each stage of technological development, knowledge acquires growing importance relative to the physical factors of production and becomes more complex. We do not yet have a commonly accepted name for the "next big wave." The new lead sectors will likely be biotechnology, space/satellite, and environmental technologies. Once those technologies mature, we can expect dramatic shifts in industry structures and in supply-and-demand conditions. More such dramatic shifts will follow as new knowledge is developed and applied in the marketplace.

As difficult as it is to measure the impact of the knowledge economy on gross domestic product (GDP) and its growth, there is broad agreement that this impact is already profound and continues to grow. Intangibles, intellectual capital, innovation, and particularly talent are all difficult to measure—especially if we rely on economic measurements rooted in ideas developed during the era of the old industrial economy. National Statistical Offices tend to be conservative, but some countries are beginning to rely on economic indicators that reflect the laws of the global knowledge economy.

New Zealand's Department of Labor has determined that knowledge-intensive sectors of the private-sector economy have been generating a steadily increasing proportion of national GDP since the mid-1990s. If public knowledge-intensive sectors are added, the total proportion of GDP generated by the knowledge economy of the country by 2008 was 45.5% and appeared to be increasing further.[3]

Policymakers in developed economies now accept that about half of the GDP is generated by the knowledge economy that includes the core science-based industries. This ratio is expected to increase in the future, to a point where the majority of the GDP of advanced economies will be driven by knowledge-intensive industries and over-all GDP growth will also depend increasingly on innovation and on new emerging industries that did not exist even a generation ago. Knowledge stimulates industry, and knowledge production has itself become an industry. As we have been stressing throughout the book, securing conditions for an internationally competitive innovation-based knowledge economy has become a strategic political objective for both developed and emerging economies.

In this chapter, we look at the evolution of the modes of innovation in industrial countries during the twentieth century, from closed to open systems. We then present a new paradigm of global R&D as the new meta-idea for innovation in the twenty-first century. We conclude with the prediction that global R&D, in which emerging economies play highly significant roles, is likely to come about sooner than we may have expected.

Earlier Models of Corporate Innovation: From the 1950s to 1990s

The Industrial Revolution eventually lead to the emergence of large national and multinational companies in the West. In a number of industries, such as chemicals, electrical machinery, and pharmaceuticals, these companies depended on R&D for new products and competitive processes.

At the turn of the twentieth century, it was considered usual for industry to outsource research to universities or independent research scientists.[4] Even in the pharmaceutical industry, this was considered the most appropriate method for conducting scientific research until World War I.[5] Not until the interwar years did substantial in-house R&D laboratories became common in leading industrial countries such as the United States, Germany, and the United Kingdom. (A hundred years later, companies are returning to the idea of outsourced R&D and the closed innovation model is becoming obsolete.)

Large R&D departments grew during the interwar years and then, for most of the twentieth century, became one of the most important forms of innovation in Western industrialized nations.

This in-house "closed" innovation model was based on several principles:

- The firm investing in its own R&D is best able to recruit the most qualified people for the job.

- To profit from R&D, firms must undertake and complete the entire process, from development to product sales.

- If the R&D lab comes up with an invention, the firm is best positioned to get it to market first, thus ensuring the best returns on R&D investment

- Firms should control their own IP and prevent their competitors from profiting (first mover advantage rules).

- Firms that come up with the best new ideas and products will win the competitive battle.

The closed model worked relatively well for a time. However, the competition to find optimum innovation processes became especially intense after World War II. Various authors describe the period from the 1950s to the end of the century as consisting of five successive phases (or "generations") of innovation. Each successive generation was supposed to be an improvement on or expansion of the previous model.[6]

The **first-generation** innovation process (see Figure 8-1) assumes that innovation is a linear process, beginning with scientific discovery; passing through invention, engineering, and design; and leading to manufacturing, marketing, and commercial sales of the product or process. This model, which became prevalent in the 1950s and '60s, was based on the idea of *research push*. New inventions and products came about as a result of scientific breakthroughs that subsequently became commercialized. No feedback was needed; the most important issue was how managing R&D to ensure a steady stream of scientific breakthroughs leading to new products.

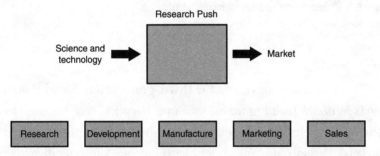

Figure 8-1 First-generation innovation process

Reproduced with permission from Mark Dodgson, David M. Gann, and Ammon Salter, *The Management of Technological Innovation, Strategy, and Practice, Second Edition* (Oxford: Oxford University Press, 2008).

This overly simple model completely ignored customers and market demand as factors that influence innovative activity. In the 1960s, the **second-generation** model of innovation (see Figure 8-2) started to be adopted. It was also a linear model, but it was based on the completely opposite idea of *demand pull*—the recognition that *customers and markets* drive demand for new products. Company marketing departments are best positioned to find out what customers want and then to use this knowledge to drive innovation.

Rothwell argues that both linear models were simplistic.[7] Their application varied across industry. Research push may describe what went on in science-based businesses such as nuclear energy, while demand pull may help explain innovations taking place in mass consumer products, such as detergents.

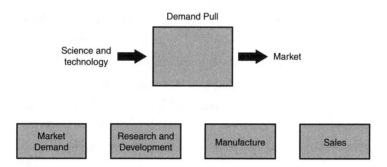

Figure 8-2 Second-generation innovation process

Reproduced with permission from Mark Dodgson, David M. Gann, and Ammon Salter, *The Management of Technological Innovation, Strategy, and Practice, Second Edition* (Oxford: Oxford University Press, 2008).

The idea that brings about the **third-generation** model of innovation is *feedback* (see Figure 8-3). Communication and feedback loops actually link science and technology push with the pulls exercised by markets. The job of management is to manage those feedback loops and to promote integration among R&D departments, design and engineering units, and the sales and marketing research units.

The **fourth-generation** innovation process evolved as a result of more competition among companies as they pursued the goals of coming to market in the timeliest way with high-quality new products that would delight customers (see Figure 8-4). Time became a factor in competition, as did a company's ability to ensure quality standards but also tap customers and suppliers for ideas for improvements. At the same time, companies realized there was value in building horizontal research alliances. Even closer integration among departments was required, and cross-functional teams were often deployed. New advanced technologies such as computer-aided design and computer-aided manufacturing (CAD/CAM) and intranets helped the innovation process at all phases of design, manufacturing, and product testing. Companies sometimes began participating in collaborative

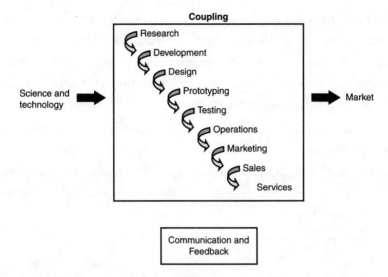

Figure 8-3 Third-generation innovation process
Reproduced with permission from Mark Dodgson, David M. Gann, and Ammon Salter,
The Management of Technological Innovation, Strategy, and Practice, Second Edition
(Oxford: Oxford University Press, 2008).

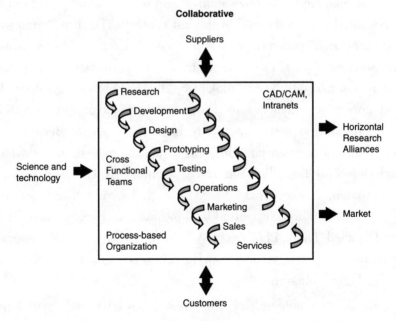

Figure 8-4 Fourth-generation innovation process
Reproduced with permission from Mark Dodgson, David M. Gann, and Ammon Salter,
The Management of Technological Innovation, Strategy, and Practice, Second Edition
(Oxford: Oxford University Press, 2008).

R&D with their industry competitors, such as in the famous American Sematech initiative. All these developments helped accelerate innovation, but they also made management more complex and required greater coordination among company departments. Dodgson called the fourth-generation innovation process "collaborative."

As we observe the evolution of corporate innovation systems, we see a process of gradual opening up and an increase in the role of collaboration, of alliances and partnerships. The opening really happens in what is referred to as fifth-generation innovation; this next phase started around 1990.[8]

Turn-of-the-Century Developments: Innovation "Opens Up" for Good

The opening of the innovation system was a gradual process that accelerated toward the end of the last century. The fifth, "strategic and integrated" phase of innovation (see Figure 8-5) differed from the previous phases because it occurred in a concurrent, not sequential, manner. The fifth wave took place at a time of much greater risk and uncertainty than before, resulting from globalization, greater competition, and new waves of technological change. Because of the nature of such an environment, organizations need to cultivate high levels of flexibility and responsiveness. As Dodgson writes, "[R]esearch, development, design and engineering take place in concurrent iteration, supported by 'innovation technology' in a fluid model called 'Think, Play, Do.'"[9] What distinguishes the fifth-generation innovation process most from the previous stages is "strategic and technological integration."

Until the nineteenth century, new knowledge and inventions came about mostly as a result of individual creativity. Brilliant inventors—many of whom were dedicated enthusiasts rather than "career researchers," perhaps working with a group of apprentices or assistants—made crucial contributions. With the advent of the research university, knowledge advanced within traditional academic "disciplines," with peer review providing quality control within a community of experts in a specialized field. Although the discipline-based professional academic model worked well for most of the twentieth century, this traditional mode of knowledge creation may become one of several competing ones in the present age of the global innovation race. Authors such as Gibbons, et al., believe that, in addition to traditional modes of knowledge production based on *disciplines*, a new, highly contextual and broader *transdisciplinary* form of knowledge creation is emerging.[10] This new model is driven by the goal of *rapid application* and occurs within networks of knowledge producers linked by communications and information technology. Accountability is based on economic success, and creativity is a group phenomenon.

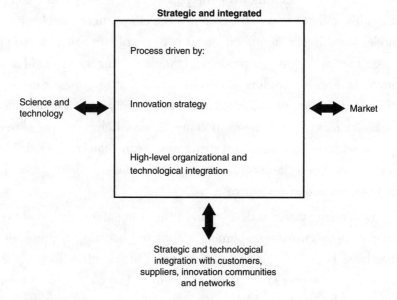

Figure 8-5 Fifth-generation innovation process

Reproduced with permission from Mark Dodgson, David M. Gann, and Ammon Salter, *The Management of Technological Innovation, Strategy, and Practice, Second Edition* (Oxford: Oxford University Press, 2008).

This new "mode" of knowledge creation has the potential to overcome the silo effects of traditional disciplines, which can often delay new ideas and inventions that transcend disciplinary constraints. Such silo effects can be powerful and can occur not just within traditional universities, but often in corporate laboratories as well. Moving to the new model of innovation was not just a matter of transcending discipline boundaries, but also one of learning to interact with customers, suppliers, and innovation networks.

Knowledge Explosions and Why the Closed Innovation System Started to Fail

Before we describe how the modes of innovation began evolving further, we first need to explain why the model of "closed innovation" has been withering over the past decade. Henry Chesbrough and other authors[11] make the case that the closed innovation business model faced declining effectiveness because of two facts: the rising costs of technology development and the shortening life cycles of new products. Shorter product life cycles mean that revenues from new products likely are decreasing. Higher R&D costs also make it harder for companies to justify innovation investment. Relying on the closed system with vertical command structures became uneconomical. The open innovation system offered a way out of this double whammy of higher costs and lower returns.

Leveraging external development can bring about both cost and time savings. Divesting, spinning off, or out-licensing technologies that have been developed in-house but can be utilized externally are welcome sources of additional revenue. The old world of technology exchange that relied on brokers and patent attorneys was not an efficient market for innovation. The closed nature of such a limited market made valuations difficult and kept transaction costs high. Companies were tempted to "hoard" unneeded technology instead of selling it. Chesbrough estimates that 75% to 95% of patented technologies are simply "dormant"—that is, lying "on the shelf," unused.[12] Opening to a market in innovation should greatly improve technology utilization rates and create win–win situations for buyers and sellers.

The dominant model of twentieth-century corporate (and, to some degree, university) innovation, which has been termed the "closed innovation" model, is giving way to more open and porous systems.[13] Open innovation is sometimes confused with such ideas as open source software development—as in the case of the Linux operating system, "know-how trading systems," or distributed innovation—which relies on large Internet-linked communities of inventors solving problems. These different systems share a common idea: In many industries and walks of life, *users* are the originators of most novel innovations "because they experience novel needs well ahead of manufacturers."[14] Studies by Eric von Hippel have showed users' dominant role in originating innovations, reflecting the fact that knowledge is not only distributed, but also "sticky." By "sticky," we mean that moving knowledge between locations is relatively difficult and extremely costly. Shifting the locus of innovation to where it is "the stickiest"—that is, where users actually are, makes sense in terms of facilitating innovation.[15]

Knowledge is not only sticky, but also has been growing in quantity exponentially. Inevitably, no matter how hard they try, even large and wealthy organizations cannot keep up with all the knowledge relevant to their business. As Karim Lakhani and Jill Panetta put it, "[M]ost of the needed knowledge resides outside the organization." The two authors nicely illustrate this with an example taken from the life sciences. From 1955 to 2005, the number of academic papers published in the life sciences increased approximately six-and-a-half-fold, from 105,000 to 686,000.[16] Even in the relatively narrow and obscure field of tissue engineering, for instance, 17,044 individuals authored 6,131 academic papers between 2004 and 2006.[17]

This explosion in the sheer quantity of knowledge alone called for a new way of organizing innovation in the knowledge-based industries. Companies could not do it alone, and new divisions of labor had to arise. By using open business models, organizations can leverage many more ideas and create value by incorporating them from outside in different ways (for example, by in-licensing). On the flip side, out-licensing knowledge to business partners or clients enables the organization to make more efficient use of its own knowledge when it deems that it either cannot or does not need to commercialize that knowledge. As Henry W. Chesbrough puts it, "[W]ith innovation markets, ideas can flow out of places where they do not fit and find homes in companies where they do."[18]

The open innovation model more efficiently generates innovation because it captures more talent, creativity, and new ideas than would be possible inside even a large organization. Good ideas and inventions can come from some surprising places—not just from R&D labs, but also from other organizational units, customers, suppliers, joint venture partners, and even the public. Customers as well as amateur inventors have been successfully tapped to solve problems typical for consumer product industries. But can outsiders really contribute significant innovations in advanced science-based industries such as pharmaceuticals or biotechnology?

Opinion is mixed, but the case of InnoCentive.com (an organization spun off from Lilly's Internet incubator) shows some promising success stories. Instead of solving a scientific problem in their own labs, high-tech companies can elect to post the problem on the InnoCentive website, with a cash prize for a solution that can range anywhere from $5,000 to $100,000. Problem posters and prospective solvers can remain anonymous. The firm seeking the solution chooses the best entry and, in return for the prize, acquires all IP rights. InnoCentive is a knowledge broker with a global network of more than 100,000 scientists and engineers. The idea is not only to save money, but also to generate options for many diverse solutions. You may think that scientists who lack large labs or expensive equipment would be unable to make significant contributions. Apparently, this is not the case. Computer simulations can help solve many problems, and individual inventors often have complex equipment at home, especially now that powerful scientific devices are accessible and affordable even to individuals with relatively modest resources. More than 50 company labs have used InnoCentive to post hundreds of problems. Scientists from around the world look over these problems, and usually about ten submit a solution. The overall results are worthwhile; about one-third of the posted problems find solutions based on a new and unexpected approach that the company lab was unable to generate.[19]

The idea of open innovation is that company business models should be built around getting returns from exploiting ideas often generated outside, not just trying to seek first mover advantage with their own inventions. The importance of innovation has increased, and firms are paying more attention to the best ways to use their resources to not only create their own inventions, but also take advantage of innovation elsewhere. Consequently, firms need to create capabilities to profitably absorb innovations made outside. Because innovation "resides" in extensive networks of innovators, company absorption capabilities are a function of managing partnerships and network transactions.

The Outsourcing and Offshoring Revolutions: From IT to R&D

A parallel development taking place alongside open innovation was the emergence of outsourcing and offshoring. This trend started with IT and eventually spread to R&D, although early forms of R&D outsourcing were practiced much earlier. Eastman Kodak's landmark deal made with IBM on October 2, 1989, is often considered the beginning of the era of IT outsourcing.[20] The next step, known as

IT "offshoring," took the process of outsourcing to low-cost nations. This stage started around 1995, with Indian companies offering to fix problems associated with the Y2K situation.[21] Within a short time—by around 2000—the huge success of IT offshoring led to companies offshoring IT-enabled services, or ITES (sometimes also known as business process outsourcing, BPO, or knowledge process outsourcing, KPO).[22] ITES included a range of services, from such lower-end services as call centers, data entry, and medical transcription to highly complex tasks such as equity research, CAD/CAM, patent filing, medical diagnosis, web design, and engineering design. By 2009, although the two top outsourcing companies were American (Accenture and IBM), several Indian providers, such as Tata, Wipro, and Infosys, found themselves among the top ten.[23] Offshoring today has become a well-established, pervasive business practice; industry leader Accenture employs more personnel in India than in the United States.[24] Outsourcing and offshoring are rapidly spreading to other industries and business functions, most notably to R&D. In just two decades, information and communication technologies have enabled a true revolution in the high-value-added international trade in services.

The Twenty-First Century: The Expanding Universe of Global R&D and the Emergence of the Sixth-Generation Innovation Process

The twenty-first century brings the expansion of innovation-driven industries to the large emerging economies. The resulting new levels of competition have started to transform the entire market for knowledge and inventions into a more global market that is growing in new directions. Rising R&D expenditures in the public and private sectors (with growth largely coming from the emerging economies) are leading to increases in the *supply* of knowledge, which has become a global industry in itself. In turn, the global competition—especially in the technology-driven industrial and service sectors—keeps *demand* for new knowledge increasing continually. Indeed, a global scramble for marketable innovations has arisen, as industries in "hot" science-related fields such as energy, biopharmaceuticals, new materials, and electronics maneuver for advantage. In this race, a variety of institutions operate in a broad range of geographical destinations that strive to create new knowledge. This expanding range includes private firms, consultancies, government laboratories, and universities of all kinds. All these organizations are competing to find faster and more efficient paths to new knowledge—knowledge that can be turned into new or better products and services for worldwide consumers.

Before the next "model" or "generation" of innovation began to appear, companies had to accept first the open business model philosophy and then the idea of global offshoring. Global R&D advanced more rapidly in some industries than in others. As in biopharma, the significant expansion of global engineering R&D (which increasingly embraces emerging economies) is relatively recent, dating back to approximately 2005.[25] After IT, the global sourcing of engineering R&D grew strongly, with revenue in 2008 estimated at $8.3 billion and expected to reach from $40 billion to $45 billion by 2020. In spite of the recent slowdown in the global economy, the thirst for competitive innovations is so strong that overall spending on engineering R&D increased by 12% just from 2008 to 2009.[26] Multinational companies have been forced to seek fuel efficiency, new energy sources, and green, environmentally friendly technologies. They are also seeking benefits from technological convergence and are keen to enter emerging markets. Outsourcing engineering R&D (ER&D) and design to emerging market providers, who continue to upgrade their skills and improve their performance, can help with market entry, tap scarce skills and ideas, and cut costs.

Not surprisingly, India wants to follow up its success with IT and ITES outsourcing by becoming the global leader for high-value-added engineering design and R&D services. The same Indian business association that is credited with furthering the country's success with IT outsourcing (NASSCOM) recently conducted a study with

Booz & Company entitled "Global ER&D: Accelerating Innovation with Indian Engineering."[27] The report recognizes that the ER&D industry has developed into a global services industry with a highly competitive group of providers, many located in emerging economies. India is emerging as a leader in this industry, and the report expects the country to capture a huge 40% share of global revenues within a decade and to create more than five million well-paying jobs. Competitors include China, in second place, followed by Central Europe, ASEAN, Brazil, and North African destinations.

The United States is the most aggressive market for Indian ER&D services, presently contributing more than 60% of revenues. As other players start using Indian providers, the American share is expected to decrease to less than 50%. The European share is expected to reach 30%, while the rest of the world (including Japan, which is expected to belatedly join the global outsourcing game) will make up 25%; India itself will reach 10% to 15%. Indian providers are working on innovative solutions in such sophisticated industries as hybrid automotive technology, aerospace, telecoms, electronics, and medical devices. They are expected to become specialized in developing new low-cost products tailored for the needs of emerging economies (so-called "frugal innovation"). To a large degree, success depends on developing and managing collaborative partnerships between the low-cost providers and the sponsoring multinational companies (MNCs). The cited report argues that Indian providers have developed so fast that today they have the complex skills to work with even the most demanding U.S. and European companies.[28]

An example of a huge project that relied to a greater extent than ever on radical global research, engineering, and manufacturing was Boeing's Dreamliner aircraft. The Dreamliner project was so qualitatively different that we can speak of it as a milestone in the progress toward fully globalized innovation, technology integration, and distributed manufacturing.

Strategic integration here meant working across disciplines and also working with an unprecedented number of suppliers and subcontractors to deliver a breakthrough design for the most fuel-efficient commercial aircraft ever. Technological integration meant combining expertise in composite materials, wing design, electronics, and metallurgy for the planes. This type of technological integration was enabled by such inventions as CAD, computer modeling, and simulation. The idea was to facilitate time to market, which, in the case of the Dreamliner (and also the giant Airbus 380), initially failed to happen, resulting in costly delays. The sheer complexity of coordinating so many suppliers from around the world overwhelmed management, creating incompatibilities and costly delays. At the end of the day, however, the new Boeing 787 is a most impressive plane, and airlines have placed multiple orders.

The Dreamliner project showed the need for different suppliers of highly complex parts—engines, wings, fuselage, avionics, and so on—to coordinate their efforts at the level of technologies developed and applied when making the plane. As the experience of both Airbus and Boeing demonstrates, such highly complex coordination is enormously difficult to implement, especially across cultural, organizational, and national lines. In fact, Boeing decided to more closely vertically integrate some of the suppliers of Dreamliner parts, to ensure tighter control. In spite of the delays, we can expect that lessons have been learned; problems will be debugged and efficiencies from global collaboration eventually will be realized. Other complex industries will learn from this situation.

In the pharmaceutical and biotechnology industries, the strategic and integrated approach to innovation and R&D has seen growth since the 1990s, with a huge expansion of external innovation partnerships with biotechnology companies and specialized providers of genomics research, bioinformatics, combinatorial chemistry, and high-throughput screening. In her 2004 book *Outsourcing R&D in the Pharmaceutical Industry,*[29] Bianca Piachaud lists 25 specialist providers of genomic research. All the firms listed at that time were from the United States. Similarly, until a few years ago, most providers of combinatorial chemistry expertise and services were U.S. or West European firms. A list of academic research partnerships in six therapeutic areas funded by GlaxoWellcome included six universities or research institutes from the United States, four from the United Kingdom, and one each from Sweden and Australia.[30] A similar focus on developed-world companies emerged in the book's list of CROs with clinical development expertise. However just six years after the book was published, so much has changed—especially in the geography of collaborative partnerships.

The leap to a global perspective that embraces emerging economies (a development we call **sixth-generation innovation**) came after 2005 and began to grow quickly. We documented extensively in the previous chapter how the networks of partnerships and R&D collaborations among the leading biopharma companies have become more international and have also been strategically reoriented to the key new players in emerging economies. Thus, the new key dimension of this sixth-generation innovation is the *scale and scope* of its globalization. The new strategic and technological integration embraces customers, suppliers, innovation communities, and networks from "new player" innovation economies. We suggest, therefore, that, in several technology intensive fields, including advanced industries such as biopharmaceuticals, we are witnessing the emergence of such a *sixth-generation innovation process.*

Around the year 2005, several important events reached what, with hindsight, are likely to be viewed as historic tipping points. Most of these events occurred in the emerging economies. In the 2000s, most large emerging economies decided on national strategies of building knowledge economies. They streamlined their innovation systems and committed substantial and growing resources to R&D. A crucial and symbolic development was India signing TRIPS in 2005.

By that year, most key emerging economies had committed to play by the international rules governing intellectual property. The third development was the maturing of international trade in IT-enabled services, which began to encompass not just business processes, but engineering R&D, complex design, and offshored research. Information and communications technologies had become sufficiently robust to support the collaboration of globally distributed teams working on complex work.

As the economic weight of emerging economies continued to grow, multinational companies in technology-based industries saw their future prospects increasingly tied up with the rapidly growing emerging markets. It made sense not just to sell there, and but also to manufacture there—and the next logical step was to add R&D activities. Expanding R&D investment and collaboration with emerging economies also began to be good business. Thus, the "Western" universe of R&D started to expand and transform itself into a global one. The network of global R&D collaborations is growing; more "nodes" are being added to it, and the relationships among the "nodes" are changing. The universe of global R&D has truly expanded—the center of this universe is shifting, and new "celestial bodies" have joined.

In the life science–based business, the old universe was confined to players from the developed world that might be represented as looking something like Figure 8-6.

The great universities and government laboratories (and the often more specialized independent research institutes) of the rich, developed world were at the center of this system, providing the basic science discoveries that were transformed into products through the applied research efforts of the for-profit corporations. As the system opened up, highly specialized innovative start-ups and CROs began to play important roles in applied research. To a large degree, the entire system was a "club," with membership confined to the transatlantic community of developed nations, along with wealthy Japan and Australia.

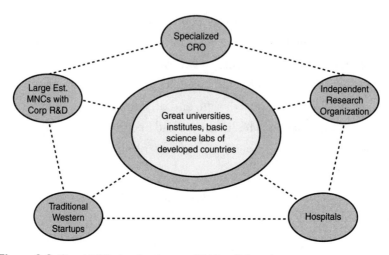

Figure 8-6 The old "Western" universe of R&D collaboration

Players from the wealthy West will continue to play important roles for a considerable time. However, the dynamics of the system have changed and we can clearly see the outline of a bigger and more diverse system emerging. In this expanded system, new world-class science labs and universities from the emerging world begin to play roles comparable to those of Western centers of basic science. Scientific institutions from Korea, China, and India have already started to play more important roles in global science. Thus, a new, larger, and more diverse "core" of institutions generating basic science is emerging.

New, successful MNCs with business plans to create innovative products are venturing onto the global business scene, as are new innovative start-ups from the emerging world. New players such as Dr. Reddy's, Glenmark, Ranbaxy, and Hutchison MediPharma are active and attractive partners for joint ventures, codevelopment, and collaboration with the established players in biopharmaceuticals.

I am not suggesting that science from the emerging world will somehow supersede Western science. Instead, I am suggesting that a new, richer, more mutually profitable phase of collaboration is arriving: a phase of intense, complex partnerships among the old and new players. Most of the new players do not yet have the full capabilities to take a drug from discovery through all the steps of development and ultimately to global commercialization. Most still have to rely on Western firms for some vital parts of the value chain, especially for financing the expensive phase III trials and for the global launch and marketing of the drug. However, in most other parts of the biopharmaceutical global value chain, the new players have strong capabilities and are not only competitive, but also essential partners—they can offer services at a fraction of Western costs and also supply ideas and, increasingly, intellectual property.

Most of the new players today are undertaking original proprietary research. The share of India and China in pharmaceutical applications filed through the World Intellectual Property Organization Patent Cooperation Treaty (WIPO PCT) is currently only around 14%, but it has been rising quickly.[31] The new players have already had success with new proprietary drugs and have many drug candidates in the pipeline. They have faced steep learning curves and will likely achieve success. Much of the success with new drugs, therapies, and medical devices will come about as a result of deeper collaborations with the established MNCs from the West.

The new, expanded universe of global R&D is the enabling context of sixth-generation innovation, as shown in Figure 8-7.

Sixth-generation innovation is quite new and has just started unfolding. Buying into this system is not simple or easy, and it presents company management with numerous new challenges. Companies will encounter problems and difficulties with making this new system function smoothly, and detailed solutions (often on a global scale) will need to be worked out. But the underlying forces that shape the new system are powerful and the benefits are attractive. Visionary leaders in several industries have emphasized that we need to innovate how we will innovate in the coming decades.

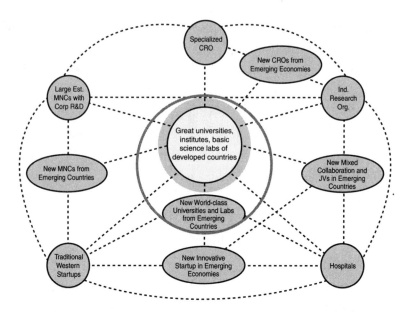

Figure 8-7 The new, expanded universe of global R&D

Sixth-Generation Innovation in Other Industries: IBM Navigates the R&D Universe Successfully

Companies that are embracing sixth-generation global innovation include such leaders as Intel and IBM. Andrew A. Chien, Vice President for Future Technologies Research at Intel, says, "We'll have more and more global research .... We have an imperative to reach out and tap that power."[32] Similar to other high-technology companies, IBM has realized that performing R&D alone is simply too expensive and ineffective. The company reinvented its approach to R&D and created a strategy based on radical collaboration, designed to produce more and better innovation more efficiently for the same or for less money. "Radical collaboration" refers to large-scale joint ventures in which IBM wants 50% or more participation from its partners. Projects crucial for the company's future are selected and synchronized with the company's overall technology strategy, called "Smarter

Planet" (which includes, among others, electrical grids, semiconductors, computing, and data center management). The idea is to build a global network of "collaboratories": These joint ventures tap leading expertise in a particular technology, are staffed with 10–100 scientists, and address technology projects that are expected to bring results quickly. IBM has no shortage of interested potential partners, but it is extremely demanding in selecting the right partner. Such decisions are crucial to success and happen only after complex negotiations, which include agreeing on cofunding, on the precise research agenda, and on IP. In addition to its labs in Texas, Massachusetts, New York, and California in the United States, IBM has R&D centers in Japan, Israel, Switzerland, China, and India.

IBM is creating a $70 million semiconductor laboratory for nanotechnology research in collaboration with ETH in Zurich, a state-owned technical university that is participating in building the advanced lab facilities. The two institutions reached agreement after negotiation on how best to align their research agendas. IBM's target for the research is inventing the next-generation semiconductor switch.

IBM is also aggressively reaching out to emerging players such as the King Abdullah University of Science and Technology in Saudi Arabia (KAUST) and China Telecom Technology Research Institute in Shanghai. In the case of the KAUST, an agreement on collaboration was reached after the university bought one of IBM's supercomputers. The joint research focuses on the Red Sea and is designed to enhance oil and other mineral exploration.

Before creating a "collaboratory" with a strategic partner, IBM may enter into a more limited form of cooperation, such as information exchange or mutual visits by scientists. Some potential partners are observed and visited many times before contracts are discussed. In this way, IBM can assess the strengths and weaknesses of possible future partners. In the case of collaboration with China Telecoms, the deal works well for both sides. China Telecom profits from IBM's huge experience in database analysis. IBM gains valuable insights about Chinese customers and markets. R&D collaborations with China become an important pathway to the huge Chinese market for telecoms.

About one of every three IBM researchers today works outside the United States. with the growing number of global "collaboratories," IBM expects to see a multiplier effect from achievements with its partner institutions and from the circulation of new ideas and inventions around the globe.

Obstacles and Objections to Global R&D

As previously discussed, many business companies in the life science-based industries continue to increase their offshoring of R&D activities. In doing so, they are contributing to what we call the expanding universe of global R&D. Any new, bold experiment in complex international collaboration that combines diverse technologies, institutions, and cultures is risky and difficult. Global R&D is a radical idea that may bring enormous benefits, but it also is challenging to manage. Management in some companies may balk at the complexity and risks associated with buying into global R&D. Politicians also may object if they see domestic jobs threatened by the trend.

Sixth-generation innovation means accelerating the scale and depth of global offshoring of distributed design and research work. Global R&D means increased geographic dispersion of knowledge creation and also greater fragmentation or modularity of the value chains associated with discovery and development. Some experts believe that the trend toward deeper outsourcing of work to less costly destinations may not be beneficial for the developed countries in the longer run.

One of the harsher critics of outsourcing as applied to many high-technology industries is Gary P. Pisano, a professor at the Harvard

Business School. Pisano disagrees with the view that the United States can prosper simply by becoming a center of innovation while leaving the manufacturing of the products it designs to others. He describes this process as the U.S. "outsourcing away its competitive edge."[33] Pisano argues that competitive dynamics require R&D and manufacturing to be closely intertwined. Knowledge is transferred from R&D into production, but also the other way around: "The act of production creates knowledge about the process and the product design."[34] Although in some instances R&D and manufacturing are separable, those are the exceptions. "In the vast majority of high-tech products, knowledge about manufacturing helps you design the products and get them to market quickly," he argues.[35]

The logic of this argument is that, once manufacturing capabilities are allowed to move out of the country, design and R&D capabilities will eventually follow. The manufacturing partner learns not just to make the product, but also to improve on it; the company starts designing components and eventually learns how to design as well as make the entire product. The argument can be extended to include a company's "absorptive capacity to incorporate innovation" that may now come from suppliers who "reside" overseas. A company that has been losing its problem-solving capacity also loses its ability to appropriate knowledge (for instance, in the form of "purchased innovation").

Some managers concede that, to gain market entry, a multinational company is obliged to give something up—and that may be its manufacturing location. Steven Brown, a professor of management at Exeter Business School in the United Kingdom and an expert on manufacturing outsourcing, argues that outsourcing decisions are made on the basis of short-term financial considerations and often by CEOs who do not understand the strategic implications of outsourcing for the company capabilities in key areas such as quality and innovation. He laments the demise of the manufacturing base in the United Kingdom and sees a similar process underway in the United

States. As he writes, "Once operations capabilities are gone, they are gone forever and do not come back."[36]

The links among manufacturing, design, and R&D are much closer in engineering, machinery, and electronics than in pharmaceuticals. The principle of outsourcing itself is not to blame for hollowing out national skills. Instead, the culprit could be indiscriminate outsourcing and offshoring based in the short term, that starts to include core functions and capabilities that should "stay in the organization." That approach can potentially harm the national economy. Strategic knowledge management, which includes deciding what to keep inside and what to outsource or codevelop, should guide the organization's R&D offshoring decisions. Such decisions demand a high level of skills and experience, as well as the foresight to trade knowledge and IP to the organization's longer-term advantage—without facilitating the emergence of new competitors.

Under globalized R&D, knowledge with partners is shared and technology is transferred both endogenously and exogenously. Ever more knowledge is created as a result of creative international research collaborations. This process will enhance partners' capabilities in emerging economies, making them better suppliers and more interesting customers. The famous argument in favor of international trade that "all boats will rise" when countries trade also applies to trade in knowledge and innovation. As economists remind us, it can be to a country's advantage to give up capabilities to produce lower value-added products or services and instead concentrate on products and services that demand more knowledge and innovation-intensive skills in which a nation is more competitive. This kind of transformation through trade in knowledge can happen only in an environment that is open to trade in services, one that favors the protection of IP and supports foreign investment.

Some might argue that managing global R&D teams distributed among multiple national locations may be so complex and difficult that it outweighs any benefits.

Such a debate about the management challenges resulting from the modularity of value chains has been happening a lot within the IT industry. Other industries face the problem as well, but the IT industry has the most experience with different forms of outsourcing and offshoring. One of the controversies within the industry is whether it makes sense to outsource *product development* and, if so, for what kind of company. Even critics acknowledge that data entry, product testing, and other, simpler forms of IT work can be efficiently outsourced and offshored. Disagreement arises about the benefits of outsourcing product development, especially by innovative startup companies.

The main reason for skepticism is experience with problems resulting from development teams working on the same project but in different geographical locations and time zones. The coordination problems that arise are said to make outsourcing an ineffective strategy, for these reasons:

1. Coordinating and managing such global teams is difficult and absorbs management resources, especially many locations and teams are involved.

2. Less is more. Hiring more IT specialists at lower cost and deploying more teams does not lead to greater productivity— smaller but more highly skilled teams tend to be more productive and creative.

3. Different parts of projects need to fit tightly together. Lack of close coordination can lead to misalignments and costly rework.

4. Risk of IP dissipation is real in some countries, especially where there is high mobility of IT workers and poor IPR enforcement.

5. Shortages of IT workers with highly specialized skills lead to escalating wage rates.

6. Distance from the end users leads to a poor understanding of precise customer requirements.

These arguments could also apply to distributed R&D in biotechnology or pharmaceuticals.

The challenges are well known and have been the subject of much debate among outsourcing specialists, academics, and consultants. Many of them argue that although the problems are real, they can be resolved and the major benefits of outsourcing can be preserved. Global software teams can be made to work, and so can global R&D teams—they just need to be managed well. Such management relies on multiple components: sound strategic choices of key partners, mutual organizational learning, and partnership development. State-of-the-art communications technology helps overcome the barriers of distance. Product development, which includes R&D, should never be outsourced simply to find a lower-cost provider. The potential partner must offer a skills set that the sponsor does not have. At the same time, the two companies must have a profound understanding of the objectives of the innovative work and must agree on the philosophy of how this is to be done. If either component is missing, the deal will not result in success. Correct partner choice is only the beginning: Companies must invest in the deep day-by-day collaboration between the product owners and the distributed teams. Product managers must learn to interact with teams and provide frequent (sometimes daily) feedback across time zones. Customer and technical requirements must be communicated and shared in a timely way, to avoid incompatibilities.

The latest development tools and architectures, combined with communications technologies such as videoconferencing, greatly facilitate the process of managing distributed teams. Once experience with managing distributed teams is accumulated and best practices are learned, such teams may perform better and may be more creative than a centralized team. Why? Because team members from different locations and with different backgrounds and approaches contribute new ideas and achieve synergies vital for new product development.[37] In summary, accumulated experience and the success with globally managed software development teams strongly suggest that global R&D in biopharma can also be made to work with effectiveness and efficiency.

Nevertheless, not all companies may choose to fully participate in the global R&D system. Some companies will pursue the opportunities of sixth generation innovation, but others may be reluctant globalizers or may even try to invent strategies to *avoid* more globalization (for example, by concentrating on therapy niches of extreme complexity that are hard to replicate).

Internal company politics, the influence of internal R&D lab personnel, and simply a short-term view that focuses on revenues alone are among the internal forces of resistance to change. Embracing global R&D as an engine of future company growth requires bold visionary leadership, a willingness to take risks, and a long-term view. Effective implementation of the global R&D model requires changing incentive structures and restructuring the way research is done in the company. Instead, top management can choose to temporarily boost the bottom line by simply reducing R&D expenditures or to use aggressive acquisitions to please Wall Street.

Global R&D can also be disrupted by unexpected political developments such as terrorism or a new wave of protectionism in the West that focuses on stopping the offshoring of high-value-added services. Companies and countries will face the choice of participating or trying to stay outside the global R&D system. Even if some choose not to play, more will recognize that the forces shaping the new system cannot be reversed.

The Age of Global R&D: 2020 and Beyond

Several years ago, I was presenting my views about the coming rise of global R&D at a conference at a renowned European university. When I predicted that emerging economies would soon become important players in the global game of science and technology, I was met with skepticism. My critics said that the selected group of wealthy developed nations (primarily the United States, Western Europe, and Japan—the leaders in science) were so far ahead of everyone else that emerging economies had no chance of becoming valuable partners, let alone providing serious competition within our lifetimes. Non-Western scientific research was simply too far behind, they said. Just a few years later, this somewhat arrogant perception has been shaken up, as evidence of emerging economies' growing strengths accumulates.

During the first decade of this century, several important events have taken place. Separately, they may not have become crucial turning points, but together they amount to a major new development. In the early 2000s, a number of large emerging economies increased their R&D spending to significantly higher levels. As we noted in earlier chapters, already by 2003, Asia was spending more on R&D as a percentage of GDP than Europe; by 2008, the continent accounted for 40% of global R&D spending, well ahead of Europe, at 23.9%, and the United States, at 30.1%. Also, between 2000 and 2007, the leading emerging economies (including India, China, South Korea, and Brazil) all recognized the strategic importance of biotechnology for the future and formulated ambitious national plans for its development, with considerable funding for research. Perhaps even more significant were the decisions by two of the biggest new emerging economy players, China and India, to sign up with TRIPS and thus open the way for new waves of trade, investment, and international collaboration in R&D. India's decision in 2005 came after that of China, South Korea, Singapore, Malaysia, and Taiwan. It was especially momentous, given India's rapid emergence as a leader in off-shored R&D in a number of fields, from engineering to life science. I posit that the year 2005 will be remembered as the year global R&D took off.

Just two years after the age of global R&D started, the worst financial crisis since the 1930s hit the developed Western world. We will live with its consequences for a long time; the most profound will be the impact of the post-crisis situation on comparative long-term economic growth rates. China has set for itself the year 2020 as a target date; by this time, the country is supposed to emerge as an "innovation-oriented" society. Other emerging players have set similarly ambitious goals. Let us examine what is likely to happen in terms of economic trends between now and 2020, and how they may impact the development objectives of wealthy and emerging economies.

Most developed Western nations, including the United States, are confronting high levels of public sector debt, fiscal austerity, and relatively high levels of unemployment. Western societies are aging fast, putting additional pressures on public finances. Still, at the turn of the century, wealthy countries contributed about two-thirds of the value of the world economy at purchasing power parity. In 2010, that share shrunk to about half. By 2020, it could be down to 40%.[38] This relative decline is expected to happen as a result of slow economic growth in developed nations over the coming decade. The Economist Intelligence Unit published a forecast in March 2006 (before the financial crisis hit), predicting an average rate of economic growth of 2.8% between 2011 and 2020 for the United States, and 2.0% for the EU15 (which includes the wealthiest European economies). Japan was expected to grow only by 0.5% during this period. Meanwhile, China and India were predicted to grow by 5.1% and 5.5%, respectively.[39] Those growth rates would mean that, during 2006–2020, China would be the greatest contributor to global growth (at 26.7%), followed by the United States (at 15.9%) and then India (at 12.2%).[40] Brazil, Russia, Indonesia, and South Korea would make up approximately the next 10%.[41] Traditional European industrial powers such as the United Kingdom, Germany, and France would each contribute less than 2%, and Japan just over 1%.[42] But even these sobering growth predictions have been revised downward.

Since the financial crisis, new forecasts have become more pessimistic. Dale Jorgenson and Khuong Vu expect the potential growth rate of the G-7 group over the next decade to drop to around 1.45%, which would be the slowest growth since World War II.[43] Fiscal austerity and low growth does not bode well for R&D spending in the West. President Barak Obama has declared a national goal for the United States to start spending 3% of GDP on R&D. Europe has struggled to meet even 2%. It is hardly surprising, then, that Máire Geoghegan-Quinn, the European Union Research Commissioner, declared that Europe was facing an "innovation emergency." Europe is still a long way from meeting its goal of spending 3% of its GDP on R&D.

The earlier cited EIU report[44] included a survey of more than 1,650 executives that asked for their views on how companies and the world environment will change by 2020. The executives saw the "management of knowledge" as the area of activity with the greatest potential for productivity gains in the next 15 years. Collaboration with outside parties will become more important as a source of competitive advantage in the coming years. Executives see both trends as highly relevant to the healthcare and pharmaceutical sectors, where "cooperation will be a critical element of success" and "teams will co-operate globally on process such as product development or test analysis." The executives single out India: "with its inexpensive supply of highly trained researchers, the country looks likely to become the focus of product development and manufacturing activity in the near future, whether for Indian firms or multinational or both."[45]

One of the authorities on knowledge economics, Paul Romer, wrote in 2007, "Perhaps the most important ideas of all are meta-ideas. These are ideas *about how to support the production and transmission of other ideas.* The British invented patents and copyrights in the seventeenth century. North Americans invented the modern research university and the agricultural extension service in the nineteenth century, and peer reviewed competitive grants for basic research in the twentieth century. The challenge now facing all of the industrialized countries is to invent new institutions that encourage a higher level of applied, commercially relevant research and development in the private sector."[46] Global networked innovation is such a meta-idea for the twenty-first century.

As we saw from the content of this volume, the rise of global R&D within an open architecture of sixth-generation innovation in which new players are gaining ground is happening before our eyes. This future is arriving faster than was thought possible just a few years ago.

Endnotes

Chapter 1

1. D. Tapscott and A. Williams, *Macrowikinomics: Rebooting Business and the World* (New York: Portfolio, 2010), 164.

2. Mohamed El-Erian, *When Markets Collide: Investment Strategies for the Age of Global Economic Change* (New York: McGraw-Hill, 2008), 27.

3. *Ibid.*, 139.

4. "Innovation 2010: A Return to Prominence and the Emergence of a New World Order," The Boston Consulting Group, April 2010; 19. Available at www.bcg.com.

5. "Emerging Asian Economies: On the Rebound," *The Economist*, 15 August 2009.

6. The Boston Consulting Group, 18.

7. National Science Foundation, "Statistics: Education Degrees," National Center for Science and Engineering Statistics, April 15, 2011. Available at www.nsf.gov.

8. Economic Intelligence Unit, "Innovation: Transforming the Way Business Creates: 2007 Rankings," Economic Intelligence Unit—Cisco Systems White Paper, 2007. See also "The Global Competitiveness Report 2009–2010," World Economic Forum; Table 5.

9. *Ibid.*, 13.

10. *Ibid.*

11. Pooja Van Dyck, "Importing Western Style, Export Tragedy: Changes in Indian Patent Law and Their Impact on AIDS treatment in Africa," *Northwestern Journal Technology and Intellectual Property* 6, no. 1 (2007). Available at www.law.northwestern.edu/journals/njtip/v6/n1/8/. Eve Y. Zhou and Bob Stembridge, "Patented in China: The Present and Future State of Innovation in China," Thomson Reuters, 2008. Available at www.ip.thomsonreuters.com/media/pdfs/WIPTChina08.pdf. K. Maskus, "Intellectual Property Rights in the WTO Accession Package: Assessing China's

Reforms," World Bank, 16 December 2002. Available at www.worldbank. org. "Biomedical Science Initiative: Singapore Agency for Science, Technology and Research," A°STAR, 2009. Available at www.a-star.edu.sg/About ASTAR/BiomedicalResearchCouncil/BMSInitiative/tabid/108/Default. aspx. "Intellectual Property Office of Singapore: Overview," 2007. Available at www.ipos.gov.sg/topNav/abo/. "National R&D Program in Republic of Korea," South Korean Ministry of Science and Technology, 2003. Available at www.unpan1.un.org. "South Korea and the WTO," World Trade Organization, 2011. Available at www.wto.org/english/thewto_e/countries_e/korea_republic_e.htm. "The Story of Taiwan Science and Technology," Government Information Office of Republic of China (Taiwan), 2004. Available at www.gio.gov.tw/info/taiwan-story/science/tw_s03.html. Wayne M. Morrison, "Taiwan's Accession to the WTO and Its Economic Relations with the United States and China," CRS Report for Congress, 16 May 2003. Available at fpc.state.gov/documents/organization/23370.pdf. "Biotechnology for Wealth Creation and Social Well-being: The Way Forward," Malaysian Ministry of Science, Technology and Innovation, 28 April 2005. Available at www.mosti.gov.my/mosti/images/pdf/biotech_policy.pdf. "Malaysia: December 2001 Trade Policy Review," World Trade Organization, 5 December 2001. Available at www.wto.org/english/tratop_E/tpr_e/tp180_e.htm.

12. "Biotechnologies in Brazil," Technology Vision Group, 2011. Available at www.techvision.com/bpl/pdf/Biotechnologies%20in%20Brazil.pdf.

13. C. Enzing, et. al., "Biopolis: Inventory and Analysis of National Public Policies That Stimulate Biotechnology Research, Its Exploitation, and Commercialization by Industry in Europe in the Period 2002–2005," European Union, March 2007, FP6 Contract 514174 Final Report.

14. McKinsey & Company, "Thought Starters to Spur U.S.–India Biopharma Collaboration," *Business Monitor International,* June 2008.

15. C. Enzing, et. al.

16. McKinsey & Company, 2008.

17. M. Osborne, "The Bio-economy by 2030: Designing a Policy Agenda," *OECD Observer,* no. 278 (March 2010).

18. For more information, see www.valueline.com.

19. M. Huckman, "Genentech overtakes Pfizer—Briefly," 28 February 2009. Available at http://seekingalpha.com/article/123299-genentech-overtakes-pfizer-briefly.

20. "Convergence or Conflict?" *The Economist,* 28 August 2008.

21. For more information, see www.pharmafocusasia.com.

22. C. Myers, "Pharma Looks to Biotech for R&D Model," *Fierce Pharma,* 15 April 2009. Available at www.fiercepharma.com/story/pharma-looks-biotech-r-d-model/2009-04-15.

23. J. Plunkett, *Plunkett's Engineering & Research Industry Almanac* (Houston: Plunkett Research, 2006).

24. J. Plunkett.

25. McKinsey & Company, 2008.

26. "Next-Generation Offshoring: The Globalization of Innovation," Duke University and Booz Allen Hamilton, March 2007. A. Lewin, et al., "Why Are Companies Offshoring Innovation? The Emerging Global Race for Talent," *Journal of International Business Studies* 40, no. 8 (March 2007): 1,406.

27. "India Pharma 2015—Unlocking the Potential of the Indian Pharmaceutical Market," McKinsey & Company, 2007. Available at www.mckinsey. com/locations/india/mckinseyonindia/pdf/India_Pharma_2015.pdf.

28. McKinsey & Company, 2008.

29. "Outsourcing Strategies: The UK Outsourcing," *Management Today*, 2000, 107–128.

30. McKinsey & Company, 2008

31. B. Piachaud, *Outsourcing R&D in the Pharmaceutical Industry: From Conceptualization to Implementation of the Strategic Sourcing Process* (New York: Palgrave-Macmillan, 2004).

32. National Science Foundation, "S&E Article Output Volume: Figure 31 & Figure 33," National Center for Science and Engineering Statistics, August 2007. Available at www.nsf.gov/statistics/nsf07319/content. cfm?pub_id=1874&id=5#fig31 and www.nsf.gov/statistics/nsf07319/ content.cfm?pub_id=1874&id=6#fig33.

33. McKinsey & Company, 2008.

34. "Academic Ranking of World Universities—2008." Available at www.arwu. org/ARWU2008.jsp.

35. "World University Ranking of Engineering Schools 2009," World Science & Engineering University Portal, 2009. Available at www.universityportal. net/2007/09/world-university-ranking-of-engineering.html. Also see www. topuniversities.com/university-rankings/world-university-rankings.

36. *Ibid.*

37. "All Nobel Prizes," Nobel Prize.org, 15 February 2011. Available at www. nobelprize.org/nobel_prizes/lists/all/.

38. For more information, see E. Silverman, "Merck to Cut 7,200 Jobs, Close to 3 Research Labs," *Pharmalot*, 22 October 2008. Available at www.pharmalot.com/2008/10/merck-to-cut-7200-jobs-close-3-research-labs/. Also see "AstraZeneca Axes Jobs and Plants," *BBC International*, 20 November 2008. Available at www.news.bbc.co.uk/2/hi/business/7739422.stm. D. Ramesh, "GSK to Shut UK Manufacturing Plant by 2013," *ChemicalWeek*, 24

November 2008. Available at www.chemweek.com/sections/pharma_and_fine_chemicals/GSK-to-Shut-U-K-Manufacturing-Plant-by-2013_15537.html. "French Pharmaceutical Company Sanofi-Aventis to Shut Waterford Plant with Loss of 200 Jobs—Irish Job Losses in 24 Hours Rise to 500," Fin-Facts, 14 March 2007. Available at www.finfacts.com/irelandbusinessnews/publish/article_10009429.shtml.

39. N. Taylor, "32,000 French Pharmaceutical Jobs at Risk," Pharma Technologist—Decision News Media, 20 May 2008. Available at www.in-pharmatechnologist.com/Industry-Drivers/32-000-French-pharmaceutical-jobs-at-risk.

Chapter 2

1. Goldman Sachs, *The World and the BRICs Dream* (New York: Goldman Sachs Group, 2006).

2. G. M. Grossman and E. Helpman, *Innovation and Growth in the Global Economy* (Cambridge: MIT Press, 1991). R. E. Lucas, "On the Mechanics of Economic Development," *Journal of Monetary Economics* 22 (1988): 3–42. R. M. Romer, "Human Capital and Growth: Theory and Evidence," *Carnegie–Rochester Conference Series on Public Policy* 32 (Spring 1990): 251–286. See also www.europeplus.org.

3. D. H. C. Chen and C. J. Dahlman, "Knowledge and Development: A Cross-Section Approach," World Bank Policy Research Working Paper 3366, Washington, D.C., 1990.

4. World Bank, *World Development Report: Knowledge for Development* (New York: Oxford University Press for World Bank), 1999.

5. D. De Ferranti, et al., *Closing the Gap in Education and Technology* (Washington, D.C.: World Bank, 2003).

6. W. Cohen and D. Levinthal, "Innovation and Learning: The Two Faces of R&D," *Economic Journal* 99, no. 397 (1989): 569–596.

7. I. Goldberg, et al., "Public Financial Support for Commercial Innovation," World Bank Regional Working Paper, Washington, D.C., 2006. See also www.europeplus.org.

8. *Ibid.*

9. OECD, World Bank, K4D, and UNESCO data in "Global R&D Funding Forecast 2009," *Battelle–R&D Magazine*, December 2009, 4.

10. For detailed description of China's Innovation Policies, see "OECD Reviews of Innovation Policy: China-Synthesis Report," *OECD Observer*, 2007.

11. Klaus Schwab, Ed. "Global Competitiveness Report 2009–2010," World Economic Forum, 2009.

12. "OECD Reviews of Innovation Policy: China-Synthesis Report."

13. *Ibid.*

14. *Ibid.*, 17.

15. *Ibid.*

16. *Ibid.*, 33.

17. T. Jayaraman, "Science, Technology, and Innovation Policy in India under Economic Reform: A Survey," International Development Economic Associates, January 2009. Available at www.networkideas.org/ideasact/jan09/PDF/Jayaraman.pdf.

18. *Ibid.*

19. "Global R&D Funding Forecast 2008."

20. *Ibid.*

21. *Ibid.*, 4.

22. "2009 World's Most Innovative Companies," *Bloomberg Business Week,* April 2009. Available at http://images.businessweek.com/ss/09/04/0409_most_innovative_cos/index.htm.

23. Goldman Sachs, *The World and the BRICs Dream* (New York: Goldman Sachs Group, 2006).

24. Pro-INNO Europe, "Brazil Country Report 2009: Inno-Policy Trend-Chart," European Commission—Enterprise and Industry, 2009. Available at www.proinno-europe.eu/page/innovation-and-innovation-policy-brazil.

25. Glauco Arbix, "Innovation Policy Knowledge Base in Brazil," at "Vision Era Workshop, Helsinki 3031," March 2009.

26. "Brazil to Invest $5 Billion in Biotech Research," Reuters—U.K., 8 February 2007. Available at http://uk.reuters.com/article/2007/02/08/science-brazil-biotech-dc-idUKN0843553820070208.

27. "Global R&D Funding Forecast 2009," *Battelle–R&D Magazine,* December 2009.

28. R. H. K. Vietor and E. J. Thompson, "Singapore Inc.," Harvard Business School Teaching Note, 28 February 2008, 10.

29. D. Senor and S. Singer, *Start-Up Nation, the Story of Israel's Economic Miracle* (New York: Hachette Book Group, 2009).

30. Josh Lerner, *Boulevard of Broken Dreams* (Princeton: Princeton University Press, 2009), 92.

31. "Sustaining Innovation-Driven Growth: Science & Technology 2010 Plan," Singapore Ministry of Trade and Industry, February 2006. Available at app.mti.gov.sg/data/pages/885/doc/S&T%20Plan%202010%20Report%20(Final%20as%20of%2010%20Mar%2006).pdf.

32. C. Enzing, A. Van der Giessen, S. Van der Molen, G. Manicad, T. Reiss, R. Lindner, et al., "Biopolis: Inventory and Analysis of National Public Policies That Stimulate Biotechnology Research, Its Exploitation, and Commercialization by Industry in Europe in the Period 2002–2005," European Union FP6 Contract 514174, Final Report, March 2007.

33. Bio International 2007 Annual Meeting Program, Washington, D.C.

34. "Beyond Borders—Global Biotechnology Report 2008," Ernst & Young Limited, 2008. Available at www.ey.com.

35. *Ibid.*

36. "The Fading Luster of Clusters," *The Economist*, 13 October 2007. Y. Su, D. Deeds, M. Peng, and C. Jung, "Technological and Institutional Transformation: The Biotechnology Industry in Taiwan," paper presented at the Four Decades of International Business Conference, Reading, U.K., 16–17 April 2007. M. Fonseca and J. M. de Silveira, "Building Institutional Competence in Brazilian Biotechnology: Some Theoretical and Empirical Remarks," unpublished manuscript, 2007. H. Gottweis and R. Triendls, "South Korean Policy Failure and the Hwang Debacle," *Nature Biotechnology* 24, no. 2 (2006): 141–144.

37. Josh Lerner.

38. *Ibid.*

39. D. Senor and S. Singer, 87.

40. M. S. Lawlor, "Biotechnology and Government Funding: Economic Motivation and Policy Models," Federal Bank of Dallas Proceedings, Dallas, Texas, September 2003, 131–146.

41. M. Lehrer and K. Asakawa, "Managing Intersecting R&D Social Communities: A Comparative Study of European Knowledge Incubators in Japanese and American Firms," *Organization Studies* 24, no. 5 (2003): 1–792.

42. J. Huang and Q. Wang, "Biotechnology Policy and Regulation in China," IDS Working Paper, 2003.

Chapter 3

1. "Bioeconomy," Wikipedia. Available at www.en.wikipedia.org/wiki/Bioeconomy.

2. Anthony Arundel, Davis Sawaya, and Ioana Valeanu, "Human Health Biotechnologies to 2015," *OECD Journal* (March 2009): 131–207.

3. *Ibid,.* 131–207.

4. *Ibid.,* 148.

5. Eric S. Langer and Eliza Yibing Zhou, "China Today: Defining Chinese Biopharmaceutical Market," *BioPharm International* 20, January 2007.

Available at www.biopharminternational.findpharma.com/biopharm/
Article/China-Today-Defining-the-ChineseBiopharmaceutical/
ArticleStandard/Article/detail/395607.

6. McKinsey & Company, "Thought Starters to Spur U.S.–India Biopharma Collaboration," *Business Monitor International*, June 2008, 12.

7. *Ibid.*

8. RNCOS, "Emerging Pharmaceutical Markets Globally," RNCOS Industry Research Solutions, 1 December 2009. Available at www.rncos.com/Report/IM081.htm.

9. Raymond Hill and Mandy Chui, "The Pharmerging Future," *IMS Health Pharmaceutical Executive* 29, no. 7 (July 2009).

10. G. Steven Burrill, "State of the Industry," Biotech 2010 Life Science: Adapting For Success, BIO International Convention: Chicago (May 4, 2010).

11. *Ibid.*, 17.

12. Raymond Hill and Mandy Chui.

13. *Ibid.*, 2.

14. Burrill.

15. McKinsey Global Institute, "The U.S. Imbalancing Act: Can the Current Account Deficit Continue?" June 2007. Available at www.mckinsey.com/mgi/publications/US_imbalancing_act/executive_summary.asp.

16. "Investing China's Pharmaceutical Industry, 2nd Edition," PricewaterhouseCoopers Report, 2nd ed., March 2009.

17. *Ibid.*

18. Gunjan Sinha, "Singapore's Science Bet," *Science*, 6 March 2009. Available at http://sciencecareers.sciencemag.org/career_magazine/previous_issues/articles/2009_03_06/science.opms.r090006.

19. "INSIGHT: Asia Pacific Pharma & Healthcare," *Business Monitor International* 48, April 2010.

20. *Ibid.*

21. Andrew Corn, "Russia: Big Pharma Seeking Out New Market," *Seeking Alpha*, January 2010. Available at http://seekingalpha.com/article/184340-russia-big-pharma-seeking-out-new-markets.

22. "New Pharmaceutical Market World Order to Rise by 2013," *Pharmaceutical-Technology.com*, 8 June 2009. Available at pharmaceutical-technology.com/news/news56827.html.

23. A. T. Kearney, "Investing in a Rebound—The 2010 Foreign Direct Investment Confidence Index," 2010. Available at www.atkearney.com/index.php/Publications/foreign-direct-investment-confidence-index.html.

24. S. Lahlou, K. Seddik, A. Montaigut, and H. Xia, "Middle Class Income Bands for Urban Population," *MGI Consumer Demand*, 2008.

25. PricewaterhouseCoopers, 4.

26. "China Pharmaceuticals & Healthcare Report—Includes 10-Year Forecasts," *Business Monitor International* Q2 (2010), 13.

27. Raymond Hill and Mandy Chui.

28. Eric S. Langer, *Advances in Biopharmaceutical Technology in China* (Maryland: Bioplan Associates, Inc., 2006), 73.

29. McKinsey & Company, 12.

30. "China Pharmaceuticals & Healthcare Report," 13.

31. Tracy Staton, "China Ripe for Big Pharma Growth," *FiercePharma*, 20 April 2009.

32. Eric S. Langer, 563–596, 627–660.

33. "India's Pharmaceutical Industry on Course for Globalization," Deutsche Bank Research, 9 April 2008.

34. "Healthcare Poised for $77 Billion by 2012," Associated Chambers of Commerce and Industry India, 25 November 2009. Available at www.assocham. org/prels/shownews.php?id=2242.

35. "The Emerging Role of PPP in Indian Healthcare Sector," CII in collaboration with KPMG, 2009. Available at ibef.org/download/PolicyPaper.pdf.

36. J. Dreze and A. Sen, *India: Development and Participation* (New Delhi: Oxford University Press, 2002).

37. "Healthcare in India: Emerging Market Report 2007," Pricewaterhouse-Coopers, 2007, 51.

38. World Health Organization—South East Asia Region, "Country Health Profile—India," World Health Organization, 2001.

39. *Ibid.*

40. *Ibid.*

41. J. Dreze and A. Sen.

42. Deutsche Bank Research.

43. J. Dreze and A. Sen.

44. McKinsey & Company, 11.

45. Deutsche Bank Research.

46. Eric S. Langer.

47. Deutsche Bank Research, 8.

48. Eric S. Langer, 621–660.

49. Deutsche Bank Research, 8.

50. "Indian Biotech Industry to Be $8 Billion by 2015: CII-Yes Bank Knowledge Report," *BioSpectrum*—Asia edition, 30 August 2010. Available at www.biospectrumasia.com/content/300810IND13699.asp.

51. "Indian Industry Overview: Biotechnology," *Directories Today*, 2004. Available at www.directories-today.com/Biotechnology.html.

52. "India BioPharma Product Pipeline Swells," *BioSpectrum*—Asia edition (2011). Available at www.biospectrumasia.com/content/2060118115.asp.

53. "Indian Biotechnology: Innovation and Growth," Biocon report, 2007. Available at www.pharmexcil.com/v1/docs/TechSes-III/22.Biocon-sandeep-Biotechnology.pdf.

54. "BioTechnology in India," Business-in-Asia.com, 2007. Available at www.business-in-asia.com/countries/biotech_in_india.html.

55. Deutsche Bank Research, 9.

56. "Biotech Industry Trends in Korea: May 2007–August 2007," Osong Bio-Technopolis report, 2007.

57. "South Korea Pharmaceuticals & Healthcare Report—10 Year Forecasts," *Business Monitor International*, Q2 2010, 13.

58. *Ibid.*, 5.

59. *Ibid.*

60. L. Kogan, "Harnessing Korean Biotech for the Market: The Importance of IP Protection & Technology Transfer," presented at BIO Korea 2008 OSONG Conference, 8–10 October 2008. Available at www.itssd.org/Harnessing%20Korean%20Biotech%20for%20the%20Markets%20-%20LKogan%20presentation%20-%20Track%208%20-%20Oct%209,%202008.ppt.

61. *Ibid.*

62. *Ibid.*

63. *Ibid.*, 10.

64. "Biotechnology Industry: High-Tech Industry Investment Promotion Team," InvestKorea—KOTRA, December 2006.

65. "Biospectrum Top 20: South Korea," *BioSpectrum* Asia, 2011. Available at www.biospectrumasia.com/content/270808KOR6948.asp.

66. "South Korea Pharmaceuticals & Healthcare Report."

67. "Biotech Policy and Statistics—Country Profile: South Korea," Bio International Convention, 2008.

68. "Biotechnology Overview: Republic of South Korea," BioNet Asia Pacific, prepared by Korea BioVenture Association, 21 July 2008.

69. L. Kogan.

70. "Biotechnology Industry—Invest Korea," Kotra, December 2009. Available at www.mva.org/media(2771,1033)/informationabout_the_Korean_Biotech_industry.pdf.

71. "Emerging Europe Pharma Market to Grow by 125% over 10 Years," *Business Monitor International*, January 2010.

72. *Ibid.*, 4.

73. "RUSANO to Invest for Transdermal Nanodrugs Production," *Nano-technology Now*, 15 November 2010. Available at www.nanotech-now.com/news.cgi?story_id=40785.

74. "Russia's Health Drive to Help Pharma Growth," *InPharm.com*, 22 January 2010. Available at www.inpharm.com/news/russia-s-health-drive-help-pharma-growth.

75. "Turkey Pharmaceuticals and Healthcare Reports," *Business Monitor International* (Q2 2010).

76. "Emerging Europe Pharma Market to Grow by 125% over 10 Years," 4.

77. McKinsey & Company.

78. "Entering the Brazilian Pharmaceutical Market," *Pharmaceutical Commerce*, 22 February 2009. Available at www.pharmaceuticalcommerce.com/frongEnd/main.php?idsection=1091.

79. "By 2012, Legitimate Generics Will Account for 20% of Brazil's Pharmaceuticals and Healthcare Market," *Medical News Today*, 19 July 2008. Available at www.medicalnewstoday.com/articles/115503.php.

80. "Generics to Capture 23% of Pharmaceutical Market in Brazil by 2011," RNCOS, 9 May 2008. Available at www.pr.com/press-release/84294.

81. Developed based on information from "Company Annual Reports," Sanofi-Aventis, 2011. Available at www.sanofi-aventis.us/live/us/en/index.jsp.

82. "The Biotechnology Market in Brazil," STAT-USA, 12 March 2003. Available at win.biominas.org.br/biominas2008/images_up/documentos//Biotech%20Market%20Brazil_Swiss%20Biotech%20Assoc.pdf.

83. "Life Science Industry," *Biominas*, 2009. Available at win.biominas.org.br/biominas2008/File/LIFE%20SCIENCE%20INDUSTRY%20IN%20BRAZIL.pdf.

84. "The Medical Device Market: Brazil," *Espicom* 2 (30 September 2009). Available at www.espicom/Prodcat.nsf/Search/00000535?OpenDocument.

85. "The Medical Device Market: Brazil," *Research and Markets*, September 2009. Available at www.researchandmarkets.com/reportinfo.asp?report_id=58497.

86. "The Pharmaceutical Market: Brazil," *Espicom* (30 September 2009). Available at www.espicom/Prodcat.nsf/Search/00000323?OpenDocument.; See also "Life Science Industry," *Biominas* (2009). Available at win.biominas.org.br/biominas2008/File/LIFE%20SCIENCE%20INDUSTRY%20IN%20BRAZIL.pdf.

87. *Ibid.*

88. "The Medical Device Market: Brazil," *Research and Markets.*

89. "Mexico Pharmaceuticals and Healthcare Reports," *Business Monitor International,* Q2 2010.

90. *Ibid.*

91. *Ibid.*

92. "Reflects Country Competitiveness Data from World Economic Forum," *The Global Competitiveness Report 2009–2010,* 2009

93. Burrill & Company, "Global Pharmaceutical Market Forecast, Biotech 2010 Life Science: Adapting For Success," BIO International Convention, Chicago, 4 May 2010.

94. "Emerging Europe Business Environment Remains Constant," *Business Monitor International* 48 (April 2010): 1–14.

95. Deutsche Bank Research.

96. In 2015, China is projected to have a pharmaceutical market size of $40 billion; South Korea, $15 billion; India, $20 billion; aggregate emerging Central Europe countries, $35 billion; Turkey, $15 billion; Brazil, $20 billion; and Mexico, $19 billion. For more information, see www.pharmaceuticalsinsight.com.

Chapter 4

1. Ernst & Young, "Beyond Borders—Global Biotechnology Report 2010," 2010, 29.

2. *Ibid.*

3. Ben Wildavsky, "The Great Brain Race: The Rise of the Global Education Marketplace," Research Paper, Brookings Institute, Washington D.C., 4 May 2010.

4. "Foreign University Students: Will They Still Come?" *The Economist,* 5 August 2010, 55.

5. *The Kiplinger Letter: Forecasts for Management Decisionmaking* 87 no. 28 (9 July 2010), 1.

6. Lee Billings, "On the Tenth Anniversary of the Sequencing of the Human Genome, What Is That Remarkable Feat's Legacy, and What Does It Mean for the Future?" *SEED,* 25 June 2010. Available at http://seedmagazine.com/content/article/the_once_and_future_genome/.

7. "Biology 2.0—A Special Report on the Human Genome," *The Economist,* 19 June 2010, 10.

8. "The Dragon's DNA: The Next Advances in Genomics May Happen in China," *The Economist*, 19 June 2010, 10.

9. "Biology 2.0—A Special Report on the Human Genome."

10. Ernst & Young, "Beyond Borders—Global Biotechnology Report 2009," 2009, 29, 107.

11. "Biology 2.0."

12. P. Kirk, "Why China Is Now the World Leader in Genome Sequencing Capacity," *Dark Daily*, 28 June 2010.

13. "The Dragon's DNA."

14. "Inhuman Genomes," *The Economist*, 19 June 2010, 11.

15. "Biology 2.0."

16. "Inhuman Genomes."

17. "Chemistry Goes Green," *The Economist*, 3 July 2010, 60.

18. G. Steven Burrill, Burrill & Company, "Biotech 2010 Life Science: Adapting for Success," BIO International Convention, Chicago, 4 May 2010.

19. "The Pharmaceutical Market," Association of Research-Based Pharmaceutical Companies, 2011. Available at www.vfa.de.

20. Bundesministerium für Bildung und Forschung, "Nachrichten," 2011. Available at www.bpi.de.

21. H. G. Grabowski and Y. R. Wan, "The Quantity and Quality of Worldwide New Drug Introduction 1982–2003." *Health Affairs* 25, no. 2 (2006): 452–460.

22. P. Stolk and D. W. Light, "Did the U.S. Eclipse European Research Productivity? An Analysis of Major Reports as Searchlights in the Fog," Report to TI Pharma Escher Project, University of Utrecht, 2008.

23. Vivek Wadhwa, et al., "The Globalization of Innovation: Pharmaceuticals," *Kauffman*, June 2008.

24. "Pharma Summit 2008: India Pharma Inc.—An Emerging Global Pharma Hub," KPMG & CII report, September 2008, 27.

25. "WHO Collaborating Centres Global Database," World Health Organization, 2011. Available at http://apps.who.int/whocc/Reports.aspx.

26. "R&D Personnel," Korean Ministry of Education, Science, and Technology, 2008. Available at http://english.mest.go.kr/web/1752/site/contents/en/en_0241.jsp;jsessionid=VCEkLvqLLeI0elx40zy1DGQUNzbPBkGndgQGakkgik1AQPzwZ11blWLGXdonaYcl.homepageAP1_servlet_engine2.

27. Uri Reichman, Bharat Khurana, and Steven Ferguson, "Biopharmaceutical Research Collaboration Between India and the West: A Guide to Prospective Partnerships," in *Advances in Biopharmaceutical Technology in India*, ed. Eric S. Langer, (Rockville, MD: BioPlan Associates and Society for Industrial Microbiology, 2008), 692–693.

28. *Ibid.*, 661–722.

29. Steven M. Ferguson, Sally H. Hu, and Uri Reichman, "Biophamaceuti-cal Research Collaboration Between Western and Chinese Life Science Organizations: A Guide to Prospective Partnerships," in *Advances in Bio-pharmaceutical Technology in China,* ed. Eric S. Langer (Rockville, MD: BioPlan Associates and Society for Industrial Microbiology, 2006), 978.

30. Reichman, Khurana, and Ferguson, 715–716.

31. Ferguson, Hu, and Reichman, 958.

32. Ferguson, 598.

33. *Ibid.*, 940–956.

34. *Ibid.*, 988.

35. B. Leavy, "Outsourcing Strategy and a Learning Dilemma," *Production and Inventory Journal* 37, no. 4 (1996): 50–52.

36. Ernst & Young (2010), 84–95.

37. *Ibid.*, 9.

38. Ernst & Young (2009), 107.

39. Jack Gardener, *Outsourcing in Drug Discovery,* 2nd ed., A Kolorama Infor-mation Market Intelligence Report, January 2006.

40. Kerry A. Dolan, "The Drug Research War," *Forbes,* May 2004.

41. Alex S. Dai, "The Push for Pharmaceuticals," *Insight,* May 2009.

42. "Novartis Announces USD 1 Billion Investment to Build Largest Pharma-ceutical R&D Institute in China," *FierceBiotech,* 3 November 2009.

Chapter 5

1. James E. McClurg and Todd Johnson, "The Business of Successful Clinical Drug Development," BioPlan Associates, Inc.: *A Quick Guide to Clinical Trials,* 14 May 2008.

2. *Ibid.*

3. *Ibid.*

4. "New Drug Application," U.S. Department of Health & Human Services, 20 August 2010. Available at www.fda.gov/Drugs/DevelopmentApprov-alProcess/HowDrugsareDevelopedandApproved/ApprovalApplications/NewDrugApplicationNDA/default.htm.

5. A. Petryna, *When Experiments Travel* (Princeton: Princeton University Press, 2009), 69.

6. *Ibid.*

7. *Ibid.*, 71.

8. Stephen Berberich, "Biotechs Outsource to Cut Costs," *Gazette.Net*, 28 August 2009. Available at www.gazette.net/stories/08282009/businew175554_32526.shtml.

9. *Ibid*.

10. James E. McClurg and Todd Johnson.

11. Kirsty Barnes, "Bigger Is Better Reveals CRO Survey," *Outsourcing-Pharma.com*, 29 August 2007 Available at www.outsourcing-pharma.com/Clinical-Development/Bigger-is-better-reveals-CRO-survey.

12. *Ibid*.

13. *Ibid*.

14. "Contract Research Organization (CRO) Market in Europe," Frost & Sullivan, August 2006. Silvia Findlaey, "Outsourcing Clinical Trials: Growth Continues," *Pharmaceutical Technology Europe*, May 2009.

15. A. Petryna, 13.

16. Abraham Lustgarden, "Drug Testing Goes Offshore," *Fortune*, 8 August 2005): 57–61.

17. *Ibid*.

18. A. Petryna, 13.

19. *Ibid*.

20. Bio/Pharmaceutical R&D Statistical Sourcebook 2007/2008 (Waltham, MA: Parexel International, 2007), quoted from A. Petryna, *When Experiments Travel* (Princeton: Princeton University Press, 2009), 13.

21. A. Petryna, 13.

22. Rachel Yang, "New Challenges Call for Innovative Approaches," Touch Briefings, 2008. Available at www.touchbriefings.com.

23. *Ibid*.

24. *Ibid*.

25. Minna A. Damani, "Biopharmaceutical Outsourcing: A Comparative Overview of the Landscape Between India and China," *Advances in Biopharmaceutical Technology in India*, BioPlan Associates, Inc., and Society for Industrial Microbiology, January 2008, 643.

26. Umakanta Sahoo and Faiz Kermani, "The Contract Research Industry in India," *Advances in Biopharmaceutical Technology in India*, BioPlan Associates, Inc., and Society for Industrial Microbiology, January 2008, 297.

27. Stephen Berberich.

28. *Ibid*.

29. David Watkins, "What's Wrong with Offshoring R&D?" *ZDNet*, 20 January 2004.

30. Thomas A. Hemphill, "U.S. Offshore Outsourcing of R&D: Accommodating Firm and National Competitiveness Perspectives," *Innovation: Management, Policy & Practice*, October 2005.

31. *Ibid.*

32. Stephanie Overby, "The Hidden Costs of Offshore Outsourcing," *CIO*, 1 September 2003.

33. Thomas A. Hemphill.

34. Mike Ricciuti and Mike Yamanoto, "Companies Determined to Retain 'Secret Sauce.'" *Cnet News*, 5 May 2004.

35. Available at en.wikipedia.org/wiki/The_Constant_Gardener.

36. A. Petryna.

37. Jean-Pierre Garnier, "Rebuilding the R&D Engine in Big Pharma," *Harvard Business Review* 7 (May 2008).

38. World Health Organization data, quoted also at "Outsourcing Clinical Trials: Is It Ethical to Take Drug Studies Abroad?" *Amednews*, 7 September 2009. Available at ama-assn.org/amednews/2009/09/07/prsa0907. htm#relatedcontent.

39. Kevin B. O'Reilly, "Outsourcing Clinical Trials: Is It Ethical to Take Drug Studies Abroad?" *Amednews*, 7 September 2009. Available at ama-assn.org/amednews/2009/09/07/prsa0907.htm#

40. *Ibid.*

41. *Ibid.*

42. *Ibid.*

43. Wynn Bailey, Carol Cruickshank, and Nikhil Sharma, "Make Your Move: Taking Clinical Trials to the Best Location," A.T. Kearney, 2011. Available at www.atkearney.com/index.php/publications/make-your-move.html.

44. Umakanta Sahoo and Faiz Kermani, 289.

45. *Ibid.*, 286.

46. *Ibid.*, 289.

47. *Ibid.*, 294.

48. *Ibid.*, 289.

49. Minna A. Damani, 643.

50. Announcement from AstraZeneca. Available at en.astrazeneca.com.cn/502 867/502748?itemId=8875980&nav=yes.

51. Minna A. Damani, 650.

52. Judyta Watola, "Wybieg Kliniczny," *Gazeta Wybocza*, 23 July 2010, 1–4.

53. "Latin American Clinical Research Brochure," *InTrials*, 2010.

54. Igor Stefanov, "Clinical Trials Come to Russia," Synergy Research Group, Autumn 2007. Available at synrg-pharm.com/article39.htm.

55. *Ibid.*

56. *Ibid.*

57. Burrill & Company, 157.

58. "Latin American Clinical Research Brochure."

Chapter 6

1. M. Porter, "Location, Competition, and Economic Development: Local Clusters in a Global Economy," *Economic Development Quarterly* 14, no. 1 (2000): 16.

2. M. Porter, *The Competitive Advantage of Nations* (New York: Free Press, 1990). D. Lyons, "Agglomeration Economies Among High Technology Firms in Advanced Production Areas: The Case of Denver/Boulder," *Regional Studies* 29, no. 3 (1995): 265–278. J. Saperstein and D. Rouach, *Creating Regional Wealth in the Innovation Economy* (Upper Saddle River, New Jersey: Prentice Hall, 2002).

3. D. B. Audretsch and M. Feldman, "R&D Spillovers and the Geography of Innovation and Production," *American Economic Review* 86, no. 3 (1996): 630–640.

4. M. Fujita, P. Krugman, and A. I. Venables, *The Spatial Economy: Cities, Regions and International Trade* (Cambridge, MA: MIT Press, 1999).

5. D. Lyons.

6. P. Almeida and B. Kogut, "Localization of Knowledge and the Mobility of Engineers in Regional Networks," *Management Science* 45 (1999): 905–917.

7. L. Orsenigo, "Clusters and Clustering: Stylized Facts, Issues and Theories," in P. Braunerhjelm and M. Feldman (eds.), *Cluster Genesis: Technology-based Industrial Development* (Oxford, U.K.: Oxford University Press, 2006), 199.

8. S. Klepper, "The Capabilities of New Firms and the Evolution of the U.S. Automobile Industry," *Industrial and Corporate Change* 11, no. 4 (2002): 645–666.

9. T. F. Bresnahan, A. Gambardella, and A. Saxenian, "'Old Economy' Inputs for 'New Economy' Outcomes: Cluster Formation in the New Silicon Valleys," *Industrial and Corporate Change* 10, no. 4 (2001): 835–860.

10. L. Orsenigo, "The (Failed) Development of a Biotechnology Cluster: The Case of Lombardy," *Small Business Economics* 17, no. 1–2 (2001): 77–92.

11. L. Zucker and M. Darby, "Star Scientists and Institutional Transformation: Patterns of Invention and Innovation in the Formation of the Biotechnology Industry," *Proceedings of the National Academy of Sciences* 93 (1996): 706–717.

12. F. Pammolli and M. Riccaboni, "Geographical Clusters in the Biotechnology Industry," EPRIS Working Paper, University of Siena, 2001.

13. L. Orsenigo, 2006, 213.

14. *Ibid.,* 217.

15. E. Romanelli and M. Feldman, "Anatomy of Cluster Development: Emergence and Convergence in Human Biotherapeutics," in P. Braunerhjelm and M. Feldman (eds.), *Cluster Genesis: Technology-based Industrial Development* (Oxford, U.K.: Oxford University Press, 2006), 64.

16. D. Brown, F. Deneux, E. Halious, and F. Le Verger, "Coming Together— Success Through Clustering," *Prism* 2 (2005): 9–31. J. Albrecht and B. Clarysse, *Biotech Cluster Project: Biopharmaceutical Network Dynamics in Flanders and Sector Competitiveness,* Working Paper, Gent Management School, 2004.

17. L. Orsenigo, 2006, 213.

18. M. Maggioni, "Mors Tua, Vita Mea? The Rise and Fall of Innovative Industrial Clusters," in P. Braunerhjelm and M. Feldman (eds.), *Cluster Genesis: Technology-based Industrial Development* (Oxford, U.K.: Oxford University Press, 2006), 219–243.

19. L. Orsenigo, 2001.

20. L. Orsenigo, 2001.

21. G. Schienstock and P. Tulkki, "The Fourth Pillar? An Assessment of the Situation of the Finnish Biotechnology," *Small Business Economics* 17 (2002): 105.

22. D. Brown, F. Deneux, E. Halious, and F. Le Verger.

23. M. Prevezer and H. Tang, "Policy-Induced Clusters: The Genesis of Biotechnology Clustering on the East Coast of China," in P. Braunerhjelm and M. Feldman (eds.), *Cluster Genesis: Technology-Based Industrial Development* (Oxford, U.K.: Oxford University Press, 2006). China Ministry of Science and Technology, "Joint Office of '863' Plan: The 15-Years' Achievement of the National '863' Plan," *Biotech Volume,* 2001. Available at www.863.org.cu/863-95/biology/bly04-001.htlm. Global bio-clusters, "World of Biotechnology." Presentation at Biotechnology Venture Summit in the Philippines. Washington D.C.: *New Economy Strategies,* 2003. "Biotechnology Statistics," *OECD Observer,* 2006. Available at www.oecd.org/dataoecd/35/56/2101733pdf.

24. Josh Lerner, *Boulevard of Broken Dreams* (Princeton, New Jersey: Princeton University Press, 2009).

25. Dan Senor and Saul Singer, *Start-Up Nation: The Story of Israel's Economic Miracle*, (New York City: Twelve, 2009), 201.

26. "National Biotechnology Development Strategy," Department of Biotechnology Ministry of Science and Technology India, 2008.

27. M. Martino, "India Plots 20 New Biotech Parks," *FierceBiotech*, 8 December2008.Availableatwww.fiercebiotech.com/story/india-plots-20-new-biotech-parks/2008-12-07.

28. An interactive map of bioparks in India, along with the facilities they provide, can be found at the following link: maps.google.com/maps/ms?ie=UTF8&hl=en&msa=0&msid=110835165461481644472.000460cde2bbf13a70 92d&ll=17.757044,80.452881&spn=39.68975,56.601563&z=4.

29. "Bio-Max Institute: Gateway to Bioindustries in Korea," Bio-Max Institute, 2009.

30. "Bio-Max Institute."

31. "Biotech Industry Trends in Korea—May 2007—August 2007," Osong Bio-Technopolis report, 2007, 4–6.

32. Ji-Yoon Lee, "Osong Bio-Technopolis: Korea's First Bio Cluster," *Korea Policy Review*, April 2008, 14.

33. *Ibid.*

34. *Ibid.*

35. "Biotech Industry Trends in Korea," 17.

36. Lara Marks, "Beyond the United States: International Biotechnology Clusters," Silico Research Ltd., April 2007.

37. "Brazil Biotechnology Industry," Massachusetts Office of International Trade & Investment (MOITI), February 2008. Available at www.massbrazil.com.br.

38. *Ibid.*

39. *Ibid.*

40. *Ibid.*

41. *Ibid.*

42. *Ibid.*

43. Scott M. Wheelwright, "Introduction: A China Biopharmaceuticals Strategy," in *Advances in Biopharmaceutical Technology in China*, Eric S. Langer, ed., (Rockville, MD: BioPlan Associates and Society for Industrial Microbiology, 2006).

44. Ernst & Young, "Beyond Borders—Global Biotechnology Report 2010," 2010, 31.

45. Hua Yutao and Fan Ling, "Chinese Bioindustry Parks: Evolution and Growth," in *Advances in Biopharmaceutical Technology in China*, Eric S.

Langer, ed., (Rockville, MD: BioPlan Associates and Society for Industrial Microbiology, 2006), 609.

46. The China map comes from www.muztagh.com/map-of-china/index.html, with annotation for number of parks added using information from Hua Yutao and Fan Ling.

47. *Ibid.*

48. Anna Ohlden, "Pharma and Biotech Companies Plug into Singapore's Integrated Research Network," PRNewswire, 19 May 2009.

49. National University of Singapore, "Biomolecular and Biomedical Sciences," National University of Singapore, 2009. Available at www.chee.nus.edu.sg/research/bbe.html.

50. A. Rowe, "Singapore Shows off Amazing Display of Biotech at 'Biopolis,'" *Wired Magazine,* 13 August 2007.

51. Abdelillah Hamdouch and Feng He, "R&D Offshoring and Clustering Dynamics in Pharmaceuticals and Biotechnology: Key Features and Insights from Chinese Case," *Journal of Innovation Economics* (February 2009): 95–117.

52. Scott M. Wheelwright and Anurag Bagaria, "Biotech Business Parks: Strategies, Incentives, and Niche Markets," BioProcess ASIA-PACIFIC, August–September 2008. Available at www.kemwellpharma.com/PressReleases/1-3%20BPAP-Wheelwright.pdf?SecArch=s&articleid=40829&sectionid=5.

53. Poh-Kam Wong, Yuen-Ping Ho, and Annette Singh, "Industrial Cluster Development and Innovation in Singapore," in Akifumi Kuchiki and Masatsugu Tsuji (eds.), *From Agglomeration to Innovation: Upgrading Industrial Clusters in Emerging Economics* (New York: Palgrave MacMillan, 2009), 69.

54. For more information, see www.zjpark.com.

55. Poh-Kam Wong, Yuen-Ping Ho, and Annette Singh.

56. Bill L. Qin, "China's Century Bet on Biotechnology and a Pharmaceutical Industry—Shanghai Zhangjiang High-Tech Park," *BioscienceWorld,* 2006. Available at www.bioscienceworld.ca/ChinasCenturyBetOnBiotechnologyAndAPharmaceuticalIndustryShanghaiZhangjiangHiTechPark.

57. Yu-Shan Su and Ling-Chun Hung, "A Comparison Study for Biotech Clusters from Different Origins—Do Success Factors Differ?" *Technological Forecasting and Social Change* 76 (June 2009): 608–619.

58. *Ibid.*

59. Yu-Shan Su and Ling-Chun Hung, "Spontaneous vs. Policy-Driven: The Origin and Evolution of the Biotechnology Cluster—The Case of Bay Area in the United States and Zhangjiang High-Tech Park in China," The

Chinese Economic Association (U.K.), 2007. Available at www.ceauk.org.
uk/2008-conference-papers/Full-paper-Yu-Shan-Su.pdf.

60. Singapore Economic Development Board, "Singapore—the Biopolis of
    Asia," EDB-Singapore, 28 April 2010. Available at www.edb.gov.sg/etc/
    medialib/downloads/pdf_documents_for.Par.93513.File.dat/EDB_BMS_
    APR10_FA_web_28042010.pdf

61. Singapore Economic Development Board, "Pharmaceutical and Biotech-
    nology Industry Background," EDB-Singapore, 2009. Available at www.
    edb.gov.sg/edb/sg/en_uk/index/industry_sectors/pharmaceuticals_/indus-
    try_background.html.

62. NewsSummit BioPharma, "Shanghai Zhangjiang," 2010. Available at www.
    newsummitbio.com/cgi/search-en.cgi?f=introduction_en_1_+company_
    en_1_&t=introduction_en_1_&title=Zhangjiang.

63. "Singapore's New Growth Engine: The Biomedical Science (BMS) Indus-
    try," Global Metropolitan Forum of Seoul, March 2010. "Singapore's US$8
    Billion Gamble," *Asia Today* Online, 1 February 2003. Available at www.
    asiatoday.com.au/feature_reports.php?id=21.

64. "Shanghai Zhangjiang Hi-Tech Park," *HKTDC*, 6 August 2010.

65. "Shanghai Zhangjiang Hi-Tech Park," *E-to-China*, 1 February 2009.

66. Singapore Economic Development Board.

67. Available at www.docin.com/p-56743666.html.

68. Singapore Economic Development Board, "Singapore Draws Global Con-
    tract Clinical Research Organisations," 3 March 2010. Available at www.
    edb.gov.sg/edb/sg/en_uk/index/news/articles/singapore_draws_global.html.

69. NewsSummit BioPharma.

70. Singapore Economic Development Board, 28 April 2010.

71. NewsSummit BioPharma.

72. "New Drugs Approved in 2005," Health Sciences Authority, 2006. Avail-
    able at www.hsa.gov.sg/publish/etc/medialib/hsa_library/health_products_
    regulation/safety_information/adr_news_bulletin.Par.67398.File.tmp/
    New_Drugs_2005.pdf.

73. NewsSummit BioPharma.

74. Singapore Economic Development Board, 28 April 2010.

75. Jorge Niosi and Susan E. Reid, "Biotechnology and Nanotechnology: Sci-
    ence-based Enabling Technologies as Windows of Opportunity for LDCs?"
    World Development 35, no. 3 (2007), 426–438.

76. Singapore Economic Development Board, 3 March 2010.

77. Frank Floether, "On the Move: Pharmaceuticals R&D in Asia (Part
    Two)," *Pharma Asia*, 1 October 2009. Available at pharmaasia.com/article-
    8030-onthemovepharmaceuticalsrdinasiaparttwo-Asia.html.

78. Anna Sandström, "Singapore—Aiming to Create the BioPolis of Asia," VINNOVA Analysis VA 2009:13, April 2009. Available at www.vinnova.se/upload/EPiStorePDF/va-09-13.pdf.

79. "The Number of China's Patent Filings Was More Than 10 Times of India's," News Checker, 8 February 2010. Available at newschecker. blogspot.com/2010/02/number-of-chinas-patent-fillings-was.html.

80. Yu-Shan Su and Ling-Chun Hung, "A Comparison Studuy for Biotech Clusters from Different Origins—Do Success Factors Differ?" *Technological Forecasting and Social Change*, 76, June 2009, 608-619.

81. Anthony Faiola, "In Europe, Science Collides with the Bottom Line," *The Washington Post*, 6 September 2010.

82. "South Korea Pharmaceuticals & Healthcare Report—10-Year Forecasts," *Business Monitor International*, Q2 2010, 78.

83. Burrill & Company, "Biotech 2010 Life Science: Adapting for Success." BIO International Convention, 4 May 2010.

Chapter 7

1. "Beyond Borders—Global Biotechnology Report 2010," Ernst & Young, 2010, 23.

2. "GSK Is Changing—Annual Report 2009," GlaxoSmithKline, 2009, 10.

3. "GlaxoSmithKline," Wikipedia, February 2011. Available at www. en.wikipedia.org/wiki/GlaxoSmithKline.

4. "India Pharmaceuticals & Healthcare Report," Business Monitor International, September 2010. "GSK—Flashback," GlaxoSmithKline, June 2010. Available at www.gsk-india.com/about-flashback.html.

5. C. Remondini, "Glaxo to Close Italy R&D Center, Affecting 500 Jobs, Unions Say," Bloomberg, 5 February 2010.

6. "GlaxoSmithKline Q4 2009 Report," GlaxoSmithKline, 4 February 2010, 1.

7. "GlaxoSmithKline Q4 2009 Report," 1.

8. *Ibid.*, 2–3.

9. G. Macdonald, "GSK Selects Parexel and PPD As Strategic CROs," Outsourcing-pharma.com, 21 September 2010.

10. D. Hutton, "Pharmaceutical Licensing Overview," *Datamonitor*, March 2010, 21–22. Adapted from MedTRACK, Deals and Alliances, 4 January 2010.

11. "Drug Research and Collaboration in China," GlaxoSmithKline, 2007. Available at www.gsk-china.com/english/html/research-development/collaborations-in-china.html.

12. R. Pagnamenta, "GSK's Outsourcing Deal Expands Its Indian Presence," *The Times*, 29 March 2007.

13. *Ibid.*

14. Business Monitor International. Also "GSK and Ranbaxy to Collaborate on Drug Discovery and Development," *PR Newswire*, 22 October 2003. Available at www.prnewswire.com/news-releases/gsk-and-ranbaxy-to-collaborate-on-drug-discovery-and-development-72654782.html.

15. Vivek Wadhwa, et al., "The Globalization of Innovation: Pharmaceuticals," *Kauffman*, June 2008, 16.

16. "AstraZeneca—Key Facts," AstraZeneca, 2011. Available at www.astrazeneca.com/About-Us/Key-facts.

17. M. Buttell, "AstraZeneca Looks to Outsourcing," *Next Generation Pharmaceutical*, 2 January 2010. Available at www.ngpharma.eu.com/news/astrazeneca-outsourcing/.

18. *Ibid.*

19. *Ibid.*

20. "Pharma Vitae AstraZeneca," *Datamonitor*, 2010, 15.

21. "AstraZeneca Annual Report and Form 20-F Information 2009: Health in the Real World," AstraZeneca, 2009, 25–27. Available at www.astrazeneca-annualreports.com/2009/downloads/index.html.

22. "AstraZeneca Opens PR&D Unit in Bangalore," *SiliconIndia*, 21 March 2007. Available at www.siliconindia.com/shownews/Astra_Zeneca_opens_PRD_unit_in_Bangalore-nid-35373.html.

23. *Ibid.*

24. "AstraZeneca Public Offer to Purchase remaining shares of AstraZeneca Pharma India, Ltd.," AstraZeneca Global, 4 March 2002. Available at www.astrazeneca.com/Media/Press-releases/Article/20020304--ASTRAZENECA-PUBLIC-OFFER-TO-PURCHASE-REMAINING-SHARES.

25. "AstraZeneca in China," AstraZeneca, 2011. Available at http://en.astrazeneca.com.cn/502867/502748?itemId=8875980&nav=yes.

26. "Jubilant Enters Research Collaboration with AstraZeneca Research Collaboration to Provide AstraZeneca with New Preclinical Drug Candidates," *Jubilant LifeSciences*, 5 May 2009. Available at www.jubl.com/mycgi/jubl-com/mediacenter.pl?id=197.

27. "Research & Development Locations," Novartis, 2011. Available at www.novartis.com/innovation/research-development/rd-locations/index.shtml.

28. A. Drakulich, "Novartis to Invest $1 Billion in China R&D Institute," *PharmTech.com*, 9 November 2009. Available at http://pharmtech.

findpharma.com/pharmtech/Manufacturing/Novartis-To-Invest-Billion-in-China-RampD-Instit/ArticleStandard/Article/detail/638992.

29. "Novartis Pharmaceutical Development Centre, Changshu, China," *Pharmaceutical-Technology.com*, 2011. Available at http://www.pharmaceutical-technology.com/projects/novartis-pharma/.

30. "Research & Development Locations."

31. "Novartis Is Set to Raise Stake in Indian Subsidiary to 90%," *The Hindu Business Line*, 26 March 2009. Available at www.thehindubusinessline.in/2009/03/26/stories/2009032652180100.htm.

32. "Novartis to Acquire 85% Stake in Zhejiang Tiayuan Bio-Pharmaceutical," *Datamonitor*, 6 November 2009.

33. "Novartis to Expand Its Human Vaccines Presence in China Through Proposed Acquisition of a Majority Stake in Zhejian Tianyuan," *Novartis Global*, 4 November 4. Available at www.novartis.com/newsroom/media-releases/en/2009/1352376.shtml.

34. "South Korea Pharmaceuticals & Healthcare Report—Q2 2010," *Business Monitor International*, 2010, 84.

35. *Ibid.*, 84–85.

36. *Ibid.*, 84.

37. *Ibid.*

38. "Roche Corporate Overview for Investors," Hoffmann–La Roche. Ltd., 2010. Available at www.roche.com/inv-corp-prof-e.pdf.

39. "Roche Corporate Overview for Investors."

40. "Roche Annual Report 2009," Hoffmann–La Roche, Ltd., 2010, 1–122. Available at www.roche.com/gb09e.pdf.

41. "Roche from A to Z: Serving Health," Hoffmann–La Roche, 2007, 134. Available at www.roche.com/rochea_z.pdf.

42. *Ibid.*, 134.

43. *Ibid.*

44. *Ibid.*

45. *Ibid.*, 135–136.

46. *Ibid.*, 147.

47. *Ibid.*, 48–149.

48. *Ibid.*

49. "ChemPartner Receives 2009 Most Valuable Partner (MVP) Award from Roche R&D Center China (RRDCC)," *ShangPharma*, 5 February 2010. Available at www.chempartner.cn/index.php?id=410&items=245.

50. Ernst & Young, 22.

51. "PharmaVitae Company Analysis: Eli Lilly & Co," *Datamonitor*, 2010, 11.

52. Ernst & Young, 22.

53. *Ibid.*

54. *Ibid.*

55. *Ibid.*

56. *Ibid.*

57. *Ibid.*, 23.

58. *Ibid.*, 22.

59. *Ibid.*, 23.

60. Linda A. Johnson, "Merck Closing Eight Plants, Eliminating 16k Jobs," *The Reporter*, 9 July 2010.

61. Vivek Wadhwa, et al., 15.

62. *Ibid.*, 13.

63. *Ibid.*, 46–47.

64. Developed based on information from "Annual Company Reports," Merck, 2010. Available at www.merck.com/.

65. "Pfizer," Wikipedia. Available at www.en.wikipedia.org/wiki/Pfizer.

66. Ian Read, "UBS Global Life Sciences Conference," Pfizer, 22 September 2008, 6.

67. "Pfizer Form 10-K," Pfizer, 6. Available at www.pfizer.com/files/annual-report/2009/form10k_2009.pdf. "Pfizer Institutional," Pfizer–Brazil, 2011. Available at www.pfizer.com.br/.

68. "Pfizer Form 10-K," 24.

69. "China Pharmaceuticals & Healthcare Report—Q2 2010," *Business Monitor International*, June 2010, 74.

70. *Ibid.*

71. "Pfizer in China," Pfizer–China, 2009. Available at www.pfizer.com.cn/htmls/edex/edex2.htm.

72. "Pfizer Adds R&D Center in China," *iStockAnalyst*, 28 November 2009. Available at www.istockanalyst.com/article/viewarticle/articleid/3670462.

73. "Pfizer Opens Radiation Biology R&D Center in Wuhan," *ChinaBio Today*, 11 October 2010. Available at www.chinabiotoday.com/articles/20101011.

74. *Ibid.*

75. *Ibid.*

76. *Ibid.*

77. D. Hutton, 16.

78. *Ibid.*, 21.

79. J. Carroll, "Pfizer to Chop Up to $3B from R&D Budget," *Fierce-Biotech*, 4 February 2010. Available at www.fiercebiotech.com/story/pfizer-chop-3b-r-d-budget/2010-02-04.

80. "Biocon Inc. and Pfizer Inc. in Potential $350 Million Insulin Licensing Deal," *BioSpace*, 19 October 2010. Available at www.biospace.com/news_story.aspx?NewsEntityId=198266.

81. D. Hutton.

82. Z. Yan, "Pfizer Grows R&D Work in China," *ChinaDaily*, 10 August 2009. Available at www.chinadaily.com.cn/business/2009-08/10/content_8548101.htm. "Pfizer Announces Expansion of Research and Development Operations in China," Pfizer–China, 25 November 2009. Available at www.pfizer.com.cn/htmls/news/english/20091125134550.htm.

83. "Pfizer Plans More Partnerships in Asia," *Outsourcing-Pharma.com*, 23 September 2010. Available at www.outsourcing-pharma.com/Preclinical-Research/Pfizer-plans-more-partnerships-in-Asia.

84. D. Hutton, 63. "Pfizer Takes Lead Role in Stem Cell Research," *Drug Discovery News*, June 2009. Available at www.drugdiscoverynews.com/index.php?newsarticle=2990.

85. "China Summit: Pfizer March 2009," *Pharma Manufacturing*, 2010. Available at www.opplandcorp.com/pharma/Update%20News.asp.

86. "In China for China: Pfizer Announces Multi-Year Collaboration with Peking University's Health Science Center," Pfizer–China, March 2009. Available at www.pfizer.com.cn/htmls/news/english/200900304.htm.

87. Peter Chang, "Pfizer Will Seek Out More R&D Opportunities in Korea," *BioPharma Today*, 14 April 2010.

88. *Ibid.*

89. *Ibid.*

90. "About Us," Pfizer–Mexico. Available at www.pfizer.com.mx/Acercade Pfizer/Paginas/default.aspx.

91. "Pfizer Launches Global Centers for Therapeutic Innovation, a Network of Research Partnerships, with University of California, San Francisco," *Seeking Alpha*, 16 November 2010.

92. "Pharma-Data, 2009," *Bundesverband der Pharmazeutischen Industrie*, 2009, 20.

93. N. Taylor, "32,000 French Pharmaceutical Jobs at Risk," in *Pharma Technologist*, 20 May 2008. Available at www.in-pharmatechnologist.com/Industry-Drivers/32-000-French-pharmaceutical-jobs-at-risk.

94. "Investors IR Center," Sanofi-Aventis, 8 February 2011. Available at http://en.sanofi-aventis.com/research_innovation/rd_key_figures/rd_key_figures.asp.

95. "Research and Development," Sanofi-Aventis, 8 February 2011. Available at http://en.sanofi-aventis.com/home.asp.

96. C. Elze and M. Thunecke, "The Challenge for Japan's Pharmaceutical Top Twenty: Building on the Lessons of a Broken Model," (Berlin: Catenion, 2008), 2. Available at www.catenion.com.

97. C. R. Albani and Y. Tabata, "Japan—Thinking Global, Acting Local," PRTM, May 2008.

98. "Research and Development Organization," Dainippon Sumitomo Pharma, 2011. Available at www.ds-pharma.com/rd/system/index.html.

99. "Group Companies," Mitsubishi Tanabe Pharma, 2011. Available at www.mt-pharma.co.jp/shared/show.php?url=/e/company/group.html.

100. "Boehringer Ingelheim Company Profile," Boehringer Ingelheim, 2009, 1. Available at www.boehringer-ingelheim.com/content/dam/internet/opu/com_EN/document/01_news/02_Press_and_Informationpacks/Boehringer_Ingelheim_Corporate_Profile_2009.pdf.

101. "Boehringer Ingelheim Financial Highlights," Boehringer Ingelheim, 2011. Available at www.boehringer-ingelheim.com/corporate_profile/financial_highlights.htmldocument/02_Corporate_Profile/Boehringer_Ingelheim_Financial_Highlights_2008.pdf.

102. "Boehringer Ingelheim Company Profile," 1. Available at www.boehringer-ingelheim.com/content/dam/internet/opu/com_EN/document/01_news/02_Press_and_Informationpacks/Boehringer_Ingelheim_Corporate_Profile_2009.pdf.

103. "From Mind to Market," Boehringer Ingelheim, February 2009. Available at www.boehringer-ingelheim.com/content/dam/internet/opu/com_EN/document/07%20industrial%20customer/01%20Biopharmaceuticals/BI_Mind_to_Market.pdf.

104. B. Hirschler, "Boehringer CEO Says Pfizer's M&A Model Doesn't Work," Reuters, 27 March 2007. Available at www.reuters.com/article/idUSL2722075920070327.

105. "Boehringer Ingelheim Inaugurates the Shanghai 'Center of Competence,'" WorldPharmaNews, 27 August 2010. Available at www.worldpharmanews.com/boehringer-ingelheim/1352-boehringer-ingelheim-inaugurates-the-shanghai-qcenter-of-competenceq.

106. Frank Houdard, "Bio-Pharma: China 2010–2020: A Look at the Future: 4th & 5th Global Strategies," *Exolus,* January 2010, 15. Available at www.slideboom.com/presentations/131001/Bio-Pharma%3A--China-2010---2020.

107. "Boehringer Ingelheim Launches R&D Center in Shanghai," *Shanghai Daily,* 31 August 2010. Available at http://en.ce.cn/subject/mncsinchina/mncsinchinamncs/201008/31/t20100831_21777589.shtml.

Chapter 8

1. Steve Hamm, "Big Blue's Global Lab," *Businessweek*, 27 August 2009.

2. M. Dodgson, D. Gann, and A. Salter, *The Management of Technological Innovation* (New York: Oxford University Press, 2008), 27.

3. "The New Zealand Knowledge Economy—At a Glance," New Zealand Department of Labor, 2008. Available at www.dol.govt.nz/publications/lmr/knowledge-economy/index.asp.

4. J. Howells, "Research and Technology Outsourcing," *Technology Analysis and Strategic Management* 11, no. 1 (1999): pp. 19.

5. J. M. Liebenau, "International R&D in Pharmaceutical Firms in the Early Twentieth Century," *Business History* 26 (1984): 329–346.

6. R. Rothwell, "Successful Industrial Innovation: Critical Factors for the 1990s," *R&D Management* 22, no. 3 (1992): 221–239. See also Shantha Liyange, et. al., *Serendipitous and Strategic Innovation–A Systems Approach to Managing Science–Based Innovation* (Westport, CT: Praeger, 2006), 35.

7. R. Rothwell.

8. Shantha Liyange, et al.

9. M. Dodgson, D. Gann, and A. Salter, 64.

10. M. Gibbons, C. Limoges, H. Nowotny, S. Schwartzmann, P. Scott, and M. Trow, *The New Production of Knowledge: The Dynamics of Science and Research in Contemporary Society* (London: Sage Publications Ltd., 1994).

11. M. Dodgson, D. Gann, and A. Salter, 67.

12. Henry W. Chesbrough, "Why Companies Should Have Open Business Models," *MIT: Sloan Management Review* 48, no 2 (Winter 2007): 23.

13. Henry Chesbrough, *Open Innovation: The New Imperative for Creating and Profiting from Technology* (Cambridge, MA: Harvard University Press, 2003).

14. Karim R. Lakhani and Jill A. Panetta, "The Principles of Distributed Innovation," *Innovations* 2, no. 3 (Summer 2007): 97.

15. *Ibid.*

16. *Ibid.*

17. *Ibid.*

18. Henry W. Chesbrough, 2007.

19. Karim R. Lakhani and Jill A. Panetta, 102.

20. Erran Carmel and Paul Tija, *Offshoring Information Technology, Sourcing and Outsourcing to a Global Workforce* (Cambridge: Cambridge University Press, 2005).

21. *Ibid.*

22. *Ibid.*

23. *Ibid.*

24. *Ibid.*

25. "Report: India Leads Growth in Global Engineering R&D," *R&D Daily*, 16 July 2010.

26. *Ibid.*

27. *Ibid.*

28. *Ibid.*

29. B. Piachaud, *Outsourcing R&D in the Pharmaceutical Industry* (New York: Palgrave McMillan, 2004).

30. *Ibid.*, 127.

31. Vivek Wadhwa, et al., "The Globalization of Innovation: Pharmaceutical," *Kauffman* (June 2008): p. 11.

32. Steve Hamm, "Big Blue's Global Lab," *Businessweek*, 27 August 2009.

33. Gary P. Pisano, "Is the U.S. Killing Its Innovation Machine?" *Harvard Business Review Blog Network*, 1 October 2009. Available at blogs.hbr.org.

34. *Ibid.*

35. *Ibid.*

36. B. Adam Rogers and Steven Zhang's "Comments," on "Is the U.S. Killing its Innovation Machine?" *Harvard Business Review Blog Network*, 1 October 2009. Available at blogs.hbr.org 2009.

37. Erran Carmel and Paul Tija.

38. "A Special Report of World Economy—How to Grow," *The Economist*, 9 October 2010, 3.

39. Economic Intelligence Unit, "Innovation: Transforming the Way Business Creates: 2007 Rankings," Economic Intelligence Unit—Cisco Systems White Paper, 2007, 7 and 10.

40. *Ibid.*, 7.

41. *Ibid.*, 7.

42. *Ibid.*

43. "A Special Report of World Economy," 4.

44. Economic Intelligence Unit, 7.

45. Economic Intelligence Unit, 50–52.

46. P. Romer, "Economic Growth," in D. R. Henderson (ed.), *Fortune Encyclopedia of Economics* (New York: Time Warner, 2007). Available at www.stanford.edu/~promer/EconomicGrowth.pdf.

INDEX

A

Academy of Military Medical Sciences (AMMS), 133
access to clinical trials, challenges of, 166-167
advanced economies. *See* Western economies
Advanced Institutes of Convergence Technology (AICT), 211-215
Advinus, partnership with Merck, 254-255
agglomerations. *See* clusters
Agreement on Trade-Related Aspects of Intellectual Property Rights (TRIPS), 12
agriculture, genomic applications in, 119-120
AICT (Advanced Institutes of Convergence Technology), 211-215
AMMS (Academy of Military Medical Sciences), 133
applied science research. *See* R&D
article citations, emerging economies versus Western economies, 26-27
Asian economies. *See* emerging economies
AstraZeneca, 180-181, 239-241

B

basic science research. *See* R&D
Bayh–Dole Act (1980), 157
Beijing Genomics Institute (BGI), 119, 134
Beike Biotechnology Company, 134
big pharma companies, 229
Biocon, 258-260
bioeconomy, future predictions for, 73-75
biologics companies, 229
biopharmaceuticals. *See also* pharmaceutical industry
  future predictions for, 73-75
  global changes in, 229-232
BioPolis, 219-220, 222-225
biotech parks. *See* innovation clusters
biotechnology. *See also* pharmaceutical industry
  applications in industrial biotechnology, 120-121
  in China, 48-49
  development strategies of emerging economies, 10-13
  in India, 54-56
  pharmaceutical industry and, 14-18
  in Singapore, 61-63
BioValley, 205
Boehringer Ingelheim, 264-266
Boeing Dreamliner project, 284-285
Boulevard of Broken Dreams (Lerner), 68

FINANCIAL TIMES

In an increasingly competitive world, it is quality
of thinking that gives an edge—an idea that opens new
doors, a technique that solves a problem, or an insight
that simply helps make sense of it all.

We work with leading authors in the various arenas
of business and finance to bring cutting-edge thinking
and best-learning practices to a global market.

It is our goal to create world-class print publications
and electronic products that give readers
knowledge and understanding that can then be
applied, whether studying or at work.

To find out more about our business
products, you can visit us at www.ftpress.com.